# the
# essentials

**Bill Myers**

**Lin Shaw**

Access to HE

Published in 2004 by:
Nelson Thornes Ltd
Delta Place
27 Bath Road
CHELTENHAM
GL53 7TH
United Kingdom

04  05  06  07 08 /  10  9  8  7  6  5  4  3  2  1

A catalogue record for this book is available from the British Library

ISBN 0 7487 8582 5

Page make-up by Saxon Graphics Ltd, Derby

Printed in Great Britain by Scotprint

# Contents

# Acknowledgements

For our families. Alexandria and Natasha. Louise, Victoria and Richard.

Without the help and encouragement of the Access team at Hastings College of Arts and Technology this book would not have been possible.

# Chapter 1
# The tutorial system and study skills

*National unit specification.*
*These are the topics you will be studying for this unit:*

1   Induction and what to expect at first
2   Tutors, guidance and support
3   The learning process
4   Getting organised

This chapter is designed to do two things:

- to guide you through the early days of the Access course, as you settle into what may be a very different way of life;

- to show you how you can develop skills to make the most of the course and to achieve your ambitions through university and your later career.

# *1* Induction and what to expect at first

You are reading this because you are starting an Access course in the near future, or you may already have been through induction and your first lectures.

Whichever is the case, this opening chapter will be valuable. It aims to explain, in general terms, what to expect in the first weeks as an Access student. It also tries to give advice that – we hope – will be useful throughout the whole course.

On the first morning of the first day you will not be tipped into a classroom and expected to 'get on with it'. All colleges operate an induction programme. Details vary, but there is often an induction week without formal lectures so that you can get to know your fellow students, the lecturers, the facilities and the support provided by the college.

## Organisation and paperwork

Education is expensive. Many colleges receive most of their funding through central and local taxation. The college has a legal responsibility not to waste public money, and the cash it receives is based on formulae that include a headcount of students, the courses they are studying and the hours they attend. The cost of the course varies from one place to another.

You may have enrolled or registered some time before induction, or enrolment/registration may be part of the induction week. During enrolment you will usually be given a student identification card. You should expect to have your picture taken and you may have to pay a small fee for the privilege.

You may have to show your ID card before you can use the library or other facilities. If you lose it – and many students do – you will almost certainly have to pay another modest fee for a replacement.

On registration, you automatically become a member of the students' union. This is run by the students for the students. It organises sports and social events and, along with the college, the union often negotiates discounts with local bookshops and other retailers.

The college has a legal obligation to ensure your safety under the Health and Safety at Work Act 1974. You will probably be given a map of the college and a booklet detailing fire and emergency procedures. Your lectures might be spread across two or more sites, so it is easy to get lost in the first few weeks.

You will not be allowed to smoke on college premises.

Car parking arrangements obviously differ from one place to another. You should make sure you know when and where you can park and whether you need a permit. Once they have got to know each other, many students run car-sharing schemes.

## Facilities

During induction week you will be given a guided tour of the college. You will be shown:

- Classrooms, lecture theatres and other teaching facilities.

- The library, where you will probably be able to borrow videos, audio tapes, CDs, DVDs and books. The library will have private study facilities and a reference section.

- Most colleges now have a specialist IT or computer centre.

- There may be on-site services like hairdressing, a travel agency and gyms or other exercise facilities.

- There is often a choice of several refectories and restaurants. Prices will be reasonable and tailored to student budgets.

- Many colleges centralise student administration into a student services department. The staff are there to handle day-to-day problems with registration, enrolment, finance and organisation. Some might also be able to give advice on accommodation.

- Some colleges have childcare facilities, and help with childcare costs may be available.

## Academic induction

The second part of induction week will focus on the learning programme and pathway-specific information. The overall objective is to let you know precisely what is expected of you, and what you can expect of the college. Some institutions formalise these arrangements into a written learning contract.

Following admission interviews you will already have chosen a pathway to suit your ambitions and chosen career. There will be a final check to make sure that your first choice is still appropriate. Access courses are flexible – you can usually opt for a different pathway or a different combination of study units, but clearly these opportunities reduce as the course progresses.

## Attendance and punctuality

It is impossible to complete your studies without turning up for lectures and tutorials. No amount of private study, talent or basic ability can make up for missing group work and class discussion. For academic reasons, and legal ones, all colleges enforce a minimum attendance requirement – this will be something like 80% or 90% of teaching hours. All colleges have systems for notification of absence.

Genuine absence through illness or inescapable family commitments will be viewed sympathetically, and the staff will do all they can to help you recover lost ground.

The worst thing you can do is simply disappear for a week or two without explanation. The teaching staff cannot help if they do not know you have problems.

You will only be on time for every single lecture if you are exceptionally well organised or incredibly lucky. However, persistent lateness disrupts learning and soon annoys your fellow students. Mature students have to juggle work and family demands; many rely on public transport. Staff will make allowances for occasional lateness, but there are limits.

You should arrange holidays for outside term time.

## Diagnostic tests

During induction week you may be given a series of diagnostic tests. The most common try to assess literacy, numeracy and the ability to handle information.

Your place on the course is secure and does not depend on the test results. They are simply used to identify weaknesses or blind spots as early as possible, before they become barriers to learning.

You will be offered extra help and support if you need it. Undiagnosed dyslexia is not rare and the majority of students have numeracy problems.

## Timetables, schedules and assessment

You will be given a timetable. This is a vital document because it shows:

- The sequence of subjects and units that make up your pathway.

- Lecture timings.

- Teaching staff for each unit.

- Where you need to be. Remember, the college may have several sites and not all lectures take place in classrooms.

- Dates of half-term breaks and holidays.

All units are assessed or examined, but in different ways. Some involve traditional written exams, others ask for essays, presentations or project work. An assessment timetable will be provided – you will know what you need to do and when you have to do it – for each unit.

Assessments, other than formal written exams, have to have deadlines. Typically, you will be given two or three weeks to complete an assignment and there will be a final closing date. There are systems for submitting and 'signing in' completed material for assessment.

## Problems

Nobody sails serenely through any course without some problems and setbacks. Feelings of being overwhelmed by the workload and second thoughts about returning to education hit most mature students from time to time, especially in the first term.

You may have difficulties with a particular subject or groups of subjects, or more often your personal circumstances might make it difficult to keep up generally and to meet all the deadlines and requirements of the course.

The most important piece of advice is also the simplest. If you have a problem, do not keep it to yourself or hide or ignore it. Talk to your tutor.

We now move on to explain how the tutorial system works and the role of the personal tutor.

# *2* Tutors, guidance and support

During induction week you will be introduced to your personal tutor who will support you through the academic year. His or her main role is to identify your needs as an individual learner.

The tutor will keep track of your attendance and achievement and advise you on a confidential one-to-one basis at regular intervals during the course. The tutorial support system ensures continuing review of work and progress. Performance reviews are documents that let you record your learning and make appropriate plans for improvement.

Tutorial support is wide-ranging. You will be encouraged to discuss both general and specific issues. With your permission, some problems may be referred to an appropriately trained counsellor or, if needed, another specialist agency.

## Additional support

If you have a particular problem with any of the core or specialist subjects, extra help is usually provided through the college learning support services. This will be given on a one-to-one basis or in very small group sessions.

Good tutorial support is vital for Access. All of your lecturers will be experts and qualified in a particular field like sociology, physics, anatomy or media studies, but they will also be sensitive to and understand the special needs of mature students. The staff cannot succeed unless you do – they are on your side.

## Looking forward

Access courses are tailored to meet the needs of a range of professions and specifically to prepare students for university entrance. Most students enrol with a particular career goal in mind. However, there will always be some who find their plans and ambitions changing over the course of the year. If this happens to you, it is not necessarily a problem – your personal tutor will be able to offer valuable information and advice.

The demand for university places varies from year to year. If a course is popular and heavily oversubscribed, entry requirements may be altered to include additional or higher qualifications. Pathways may be adapted to meet the requirements of universities.

The final choice of career or further education has to be a personal one, but your tutor is there to help you make appropriate and realistic decisions.

# Lifestyle changes

As an Access student you will inevitably find your lifestyle changing. You will develop new ideas, question previous beliefs and often find yourself unlearning old habits.

By enrolling on and beginning an Access course, you have already taken the first steps in pro-active self-development.

## Action

- What job were you doing?
- How did your life work?

## Thinking about action

- What would you like to be doing?
- How would you like your life to be?

## New idea on action

- Choosing an Access course.

## Change of act

- Enrolling and becoming an Access student.

Self-development empowers. It builds self-confidence and helps you work towards your goals, hopes and ambitions. You will broaden your perspective and begin to feel more comfortable with taking risks and doing things differently. You will develop a different approach to practical and theoretical challenges.

# Strengths and weaknesses

Self-development begins when you start to identify your strengths and weaknesses. You have to be honest and think carefully about the areas you want to develop and improve. Remember: a weakness is not a failing – it is a skill or attitude that needs time and attention.

As a mature student, you have the advantage of accumulated life skills and experience. Learning and study involve thought, analysis and reflective practice – it is these you may need to develop. Constructive criticism is central to marking and assessment. It identifies weaknesses and areas you need to build on. Comments concern your work, not you personally, and you will learn to reflect on and respond positively to this advice and guidance.

Through the course you will be shown different ways of learning and helped to make connections between what you already know and what you need to know.

No two students learn in the same way because life experiences and depths of knowledge vary. New experiences are blended with what you already know, and what you 'are' determines how you learn.

Security and success are essential for growth and learning. Behaviour is controlled by thoughts and emotions. You have more chance of remembering and learning in an environment that encourages feelings and intellect.

See if you can start to identify the learning environment that works best for you.

## What is your learning style?

Who would you nominate as your 'best ever teacher'?

Your nomination can be any person you have learned from, including family, friends or work colleagues.

List three reasons for your nomination, including how that person made you feel.

1.

2.

3.

# Confidence and self-knowledge

Absorbing new facts and information is one of the later stages in learning. It is not an adequate or total description of the overall process. Before we can begin to learn, we have to be willing to change perceptions of the outside world, those around us and – most of all – ourselves.

True confidence and self-esteem are based on self-knowledge. Changing your perceptions can feel threatening and disturbing, but it is essential if you are to make the most of the course. An honest evaluation of personal strengths and weaknesses is the first step towards self-knowledge.

Try the following exercise.

## Self-knowledge

You are planning a new project or group venture. You are the leader or most important person.

Make a list of your strengths and weaknesses.

Ask a member of your family or a close friend to be frank and to help you put together the list.

| Strengths | Weaknesses |
| --- | --- |
| Examples: | Examples: |
| *Good reader* | *Writing an essay* |
| *Able to make visitors feel welcome at work* | *Talking to an audience* |
| *Managing the household budget* | *Arriving on time* |

How could you change your weaknesses into strengths?

# New horizons – new friends

One of the best parts of college life is meeting like-minded people and making new friends. Your fellow students will soon become a support network helping you through the challenges of returning to education.

You will need to share your thoughts and feelings and it is not always easy to find somebody in your personal life who will be as enthusiastic, harassed or as overawed as you may be yourself. Self-development will change the way you think and this may sometimes disturb or confuse the people who are close to you.

Children tend to benefit from their main carer's continued or resumed education. Statistics show that children are more likely to do better in education themselves if their main carer has further or higher academic qualifications.

A close group of like-minded friends provides support and comfort in work and private study. They will appreciate the 'blood, sweat and tears' that you have put into your coursework, assignments and assessments.

# Reflective journal

To help collect evidence of your self-development, you will be asked to keep a journal or diary of events. You need to remember and reflect on experiences and incidents that affect your learning. The reflection process is key. It is learning from experience not the experience itself that is important. You move on from simply articulating or describing an event, to recognising that learning happened and skills were acquired.

To get the most benefit from your diary you should reflect on all significant learning situations and make journal entries on a regular basis. The journal gives a record of changes in your strengths and weaknesses as the course progresses. Include plans and ideas for coursework, and the reasons for your choice of presentations, essay titles and independent study – or anything else that is helping your studies.

The journal may be handwritten or word-processed. Use a ring binder so you can include other relevant paperwork, like draft essays or articles which have shaped your views.

You must be honest about events, thoughts and feelings and write in your own informal style. The time you spend on a journal entry may vary from a few minutes to an hour. Entries ought to be made every week and each new entry must be dated. Comments on the time pressures of your schedule are important. Avoid making entries that are purely day-to-day descriptions.

You will be asked to keep a reflective journal at university; it is useful to develop the habit.

This is how you might set out your journal or diary.

## A reflective diary entry

Think of a recent situation, incident or experience. It may have been enjoyable or distressing.

In the left-hand column, describe what took place. In the right-hand column, describe how you felt, why you had those feelings and what you learnt from the experience. Try to be positive.

| Situation | Reflection |
| --- | --- |
| Describe the incident or experience. | Explain how you felt when it was happening. |
| | Reflect on how you might change your actions if the same thing happened again. |
| | Do not repeat information or details from the 'situation' column. |
| | Try to explain what you have learned. |

With regular journal entries, you will begin to understand how and where you learn well, and also how to cope with learning environments that are not suited to your needs. You will discover why you do not learn in some situations and how to overcome the problems you have identified.

# *3* The learning process

The ability to learn and to transmit our learning to others through language and symbols distinguishes us from most other animals. We are programmed by evolution to be curious. As an adult, you will probably recognise that you have learned more quickly in some situations than others. Educational research has shown that we all have different learning styles.

## Four learning styles

Honey and Mumford (1986) developed a learning styles questionnaire which distinguishes between four preferences or types of learners:

- *Activists* are impulsive – they are happy to have a go at anything new without the need to think it through first. They work well with other people, but like to be at the centre of things.

- *Reflectors* like to think about things carefully before they commit themselves to anything. They play the role of the quiet observer in any group activity.

- *Theorists* analyse and rationalise new situations. They build their own theories about how things work, and take everything rather seriously.

- *Pragmatists* like to try things out to see if they work, experimenting with new ideas and methods. They are down-to-earth people who like to get on with things.

An important thing to remember with this, and other methods that analyse learning styles, is that most people have a dominant but not an exclusive preference.

## Ways of learning

Many theories have been developed to try to explain how people learn. They may be classified according to their different sociological and psychological concepts and frameworks. Theories include:

- Behaviourism – where learning is viewed as a response to a stimulus in a given situation and the formation of habits.

- Neobehaviourism – where learning involves changes in behaviour, conditioning and positive reinforcement.

- Gestalt theory of learning – where learners are seen to organise clues to a problem, see patterns emerge and solutions occur, so learning happens through insight.

- Cognitive theory of learning – cognitive skills involve knowledge rather than feelings, and the learner develops perception and an understanding of principles.

As an adult, your present attitude to learning has been formed by previous experiences and learning situations.

Access students bring with them a wealth of existing knowledge, attitudes, experiences and skills. These influence how and what you learn. Your approach may also be affected by:

- The attitude that family and friends have towards learning.

- The value you place on learning new skills.

- What you believe is expected of you.

Tutors will help you overcome barriers and obstacles to learning. If you have always hated maths, for instance, it will be difficult to see the maths units in a positive light. In an adult environment and with the right kind of teaching, however, most students cope easily with subjects they previously found difficult or impossible.

## Why now?

Inevitably, your early days at college will trigger memories of the last time you sat in a classroom. You have made a major decision, but many students start to question their motives seriously for the first time: 'Why now?', 'Why didn't I continue or complete my education in the traditional way?'.

There is a classical piece of psychological research that will probably help you to understand your motives and timing.

Abraham Maslow (1970) developed a theory called the 'hierarchy of human needs' – it is known more simply as Maslow's pyramid. He believed that human needs could be divided into a series of layers or levels. Personal growth is not possible until the more basic needs have been satisfied.

Physiological needs are the basic survival requirements for food, warmth, clothing and shelter. Once these have been met, we seek physical safety and protection from danger. At the next level, we seek the company and affections of others – first in the family, then in larger groups.

Esteem needs can be broadly translated into our wishes to be competent and to gain approval and recognition. The need to know and understand is often called the cognitive need – we want to understand the world around us.

The aesthetic need concerns art, order, beauty and symmetry. This is not as highbrow as it sounds – many of us meet our aesthetic needs by gardening, redecorating the living room or buying a new pair of shoes.

Maslow's hierarchy of needs

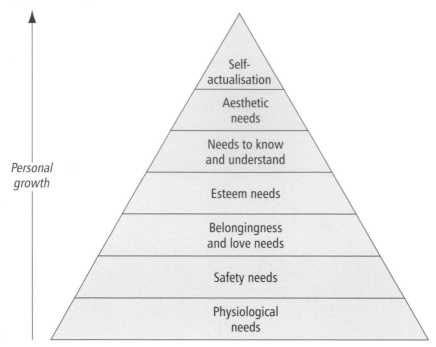

Self-actualisation comes at the top of the pyramid. Once all of the lower needs have been satisfied, we look for self-fulfilment and ways to achieve our full potential.

Later researchers have extended and modified Maslow's work. You may find alternative hierarchies which differ in detail, but the general principle is widely accepted.

Using Maslow may help identify factors which prevent or enhance your learning.

Rogers (1974) described some major barriers to learning:

- Personality – some adults feel unmotivated to learn, or find learning difficult. They refuse to engage in formal education. Anxiety is a common barrier to learning.

- Physical changes – physical difficulties can significantly impede learning.

- Situational causes – preoccupation with things like money, work, job security, family or relationships may severely reduce concentration and the ability to learn.

- Bad relations – negative experiences of school, tutors and teachers lead to learners feeling undervalued and unrecognised.

Rogers further suggested that most barriers to learning can be overcome if people are given appropriate support and respect:

- Motivation – you need motivation and determination to succeed.

- Engagement – you need to become fully involved and committed to continuing education.

- Activity – learning must be an active process which includes problem solving, discussion and taking part in research, investigations, surveys and experiments.

- Evaluation and feedback – you need to know how you are developing and reflect on what you have learnt.

- Reinforcement – encouragement through positive feedback and constructive criticism is essential.

## The past and the future

This exercise will help you to recognise how your experiences have affected your attitude and approach to learning as an adult.

Give examples of the positives or negatives you feel have had an influence.

Think about early memories, opinions of family and friends, and on recent events that might have motivated you to come back to learning.

| Negative factors | Positive factors |
| --- | --- |
| Examples: | Examples: |
| *Hated everything about school.* | *Feel more confident about learning now than when I was young.* |
| *I couldn't wait to get a job.* | |
| *I felt a real dumbo at school when I couldn't understand some things – but was always too shy to ask.* | *I wouldn't let it worry me now if I had to ask questions because I didn't understand something straight away.* |
| *No one in my family ever stayed at school past the age of 15.* | *I really want to become a physio – I can only do it if I get the qualifications.* |

# *4* Getting organised

By enrolling on an Access course, you have shown that you have the motivation and determination necessary to develop and work towards a better, more fulfilling life.

Self-development involves using your abilities to make things happen – a proactive approach. In all professions, personal development is a continuing lifelong process. Study skills make learning possible in the first place; then learning is effective, rewarding and enjoyable.

## Study skills

Almost certainly you will have many conflicting demands on your time and energy. As an adult student, you will get overwhelmed, exhausted and confused unless you organise your life effectively – forward planning is essential.

Private or independent study is an indispensable part of the course. You will need to make time for assignments, background reading and revision. You have probably discovered your preferred learning style, but you also need to think carefully about when, where and how you study best. We are all different. There are no right or wrong answers, but you must identify what works for you and what does not.

By far the most effective way of juggling time commitments is to put together a weekly timetable or schedule. Be honest with yourself – it has to be realistic, not an ideal that you can only meet one week in 10.

Try to keep to the same routine during term time. You will need to record the dates and times of formal assessments and deadlines for essays and other assignments based on private study. Domestic crises are inevitable, but you will cope better if most of the time you keep to a regular pattern of study, work, family commitments, sleep and leisure.

Remember that the minimum attendance requirement is strictly enforced. Most colleges include comments on attendance and punctuality as part of the reference you will need for university admission.

## Personal timetables

It is a good idea to make two copies of your personal timetable. Keep one at home and the other with the books and notes that you bring to lectures. You may be asked for your schedule in tutorials.

Example timetable

|  | 06.00–09.00 | 09.00–12.00 | 12.00–15.00 | 15.00–18.00 | 18.00–21.00 | 21.00–00.00 |
|---|---|---|---|---|---|---|
| Monday |  |  |  |  |  |  |
| Tuesday |  |  |  |  |  |  |
| Wednesday |  |  |  |  |  |  |
| Thursday |  |  |  |  |  |  |
| Friday |  |  |  |  |  |  |
| Saturday |  |  |  |  |  |  |
| Sunday |  |  |  |  |  |  |

- First, fill in the times you are at college, allowing for travelling.

- Then allocate the hours you need to meet family and work commitments.

- Allow time for leisure and relaxation.

- Finally, allocate private study time.

Most students have a very strong preference for a particular part of the day. Do not pretend you are a night owl if you are really an early bird.

Concentration tails off rapidly after about two hours of private study – try to arrange regular breaks of at least 20 minutes during your busiest days.

Some people find that a change is as good as a rest. Experiment with alternating periods of writing and reading or switching between two subjects or assignments.

Alter your hours when necessary. In your reflective journal, note the reasons for change.

It often helps to pin a copy of your timetable at home so that family and friends know when you are available and when you are studying.

# Study aids

You will need a comfortable private space to study at home. Some students need complete quiet; others prefer background noise or music. There are no rules – whatever works for you is right.

It helps to set aside a table or desk to keep your college work away from children, pets and other people. A shelf or small bookcase will be useful for storing books and notes. You will need basic stationery – pens, pencils, A4 paper, folders, a hole punch and plastic folders. A dictionary and thesaurus are essential.

A personal computer or word processor with internet access is an advantage, but it is not essential. Computers and the internet will be provided at college or will be available at public libraries, but remember to adjust your scheduled study time according to their opening hours. If you are not familiar with computers it may be better to wait until you have completed the Information Technology unit before submitting word-processed work.

When you use a computer, always:

- Save your work page by page – to lose a whole essay before you have printed or emailed it is a student's worst nightmare.

- Print out draft copies – just in case your computer decides to crash on the final copy.

- Keep a spare ink or toner cartridge – the ink in printers always seems to run out the night before an essay is due.

- You should label disks with a title and keep a separate list of what you have stored on them. It is a good idea to keep a backup copy. Put your name on any disk that you take to college.

# The obvious question

The most important question is difficult to answer – how much time do you need to put aside for private or home study?

The typical student with typical family commitments will need something like 10 hours a week. Many who are enrolled on the nursing, midwifery and health professions pathways already work in the health sector, often during unsocial hours. If this is your situation try, if you can, to arrange private study for when you are least tired and harassed.

Most of all, do not let private study assignments accumulate. If you need 10 hours a week and you only manage four, then it is clear that after a short time you will have an impossible mountain to climb. Do not fool yourself into thinking you can cram most of your private study into half-term breaks and college holidays – this never works.

# Chapter 2

# Literacy, numeracy and critical thinking

An Access course is divided into many different units. The course is structured this way largely for practical reasons – there is a limit to the number of subjects you can study in any one week or term. The running order of the units is important, as you have to be introduced to the basics before you can move on to the more complicated material.

However, there are two compulsory units that do not fit easily into a neat sequence:

- Communication Skills.

- Research Skills.

Before looking at these units more closely we need to define their scope, how they fit together, their relevance to every other part of the course, and the assessment methods used.

# A good education

Teachers used to talk about reading, writing and arithmetic as the bedrock of a good education. There are fashions in education, but this basic concept has not changed – we just use different labels. The bedrock subjects are now called literacy and numeracy. The Communication Skills unit is about literacy in the widest sense; your numeracy will be developed and improved, if need be, in the Application of Number unit.

For Access students there is a third big idea, normally described as critical thinking. This is the core material for research skills.

Application of Number is a self-contained lecture series leading to a formal written exam. You will be taught how to manage the basic calculations that are needed for most specialist units. No previous qualification or experience in maths is assumed – everything starts from square one.

The Communication and Research units are handled differently. It is a two-stage process:

- The Communication and Research units are timetabled for the early part of the course. These lectures uncover and organise the abilities you already have and show how they will be improved and extended.

- Communication and critical thinking are continuing themes and connecting threads that pull together all parts of the course. Your confidence and skills will grow as a by-product of your learning and private study in every subject.

# Assessing communication and critical thinking

You need to know how these units are taught and assessed. You will find that:

- No lessons will be devoted entirely to topics like spelling, punctuation, grammar, vocabulary, parts of speech, when to use capital letters, sentence construction and so on.

- You will not be given abstract puzzles or problems to develop logic or reasoning ability.

- There will be no spelling tests, grammar exams, vocabulary lists to learn by heart, conundrums or quizzes.

This is what will happen:

- In the communication and research lectures you will be taught the basic concepts that underpin all communication and all critical thinking.

- You will be given tips and hints to help you recognise and overcome the most widespread errors and deficiencies.

- Assessment is indirect. You earn credits for the work you submit in other subjects. For instance, an essay assignment for the Health and Society unit might prove your written communication skills, and a presentation for Introduction to Ethics might show that you have reached the appropriate standard in verbal communication. The research plan for the independent study project, one of the final units of the course, is ample evidence that you have developed the necessary skills in critical thinking.

# A continuing theme

We described communication and research as continuing themes of the whole course and every pathway. You may be awarded credits at level three for both units, but your abilities to communicate and reason will continue to grow and improve. For most of us, this process is lifelong, even if we do not recognise it.

During the book, we return time and again to topics like essays, report writing and verbal presentations. It is impossible to concentrate into one chapter all that is needed to teach and learn communication skills.

# How do we communicate?

It helps to think through what communication really is and how it happens. The different methods and techniques designed to improve your skills ought then to make more sense.

Communication is the reception and transmission of signals. A completely isolated individual could receive signals like the pain of a rotten tooth or a stomach ulcer, but ignoring this special case, signals are received and transmitted to and from the outside world. Living organisms could not exist if they could not also process and store these signals.

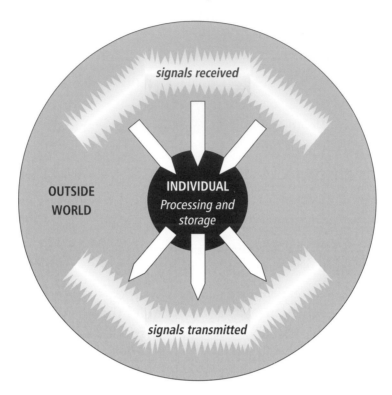

We constantly receive signals from inanimate objects and other living things. Some of us swear at machinery that goes wrong, and others talk to themselves or their pot plants or dogs, but most of our outgoing signals are targeted at other people.

## Two important senses

Learning is characterised by increasing reliance on two of the five senses. This book is likely to have been bought by someone using their sense of sight, or perhaps hearing – if it was recommended by a friend – hopefully not by chewing it or sniffing it, although people will quite often touch or stroke a book before they start reading.

To a physicist, visible light is electromagnetic radiation. This is analysed by the brain, which then processes different combinations of frequencies and intensities to give what we call colour, pattern and shape.

In a very similar way, sound waves are processed by detecting differences in frequency, combinations of frequencies and intensity (or loudness).

# Speaking, reading, writing and calculating

You may be wondering where all of this is heading. What have light frequencies, sound waves, signals and their processing to do with the Communication Skills unit?

These arguments are directly relevant to Access because they explain the usual starting point for most adults returning to education, where they need to be by the end of the course, and how best to make the journey in between.

The diagram is a generalisation – no two students have the same mix of aptitudes, attitudes and experience.

The usual starting point

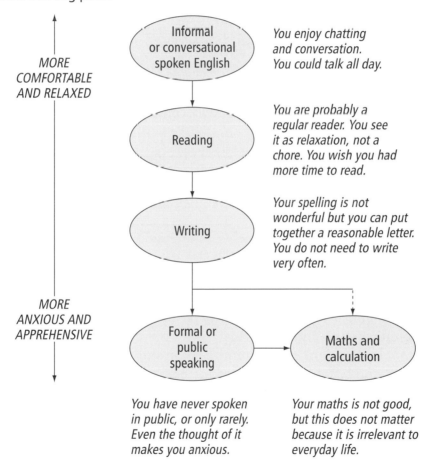

MORE
COMFORTABLE
AND RELAXED

MORE
ANXIOUS AND
APPREHENSIVE

Informal
or conversational
spoken English

*You enjoy chatting and conversation. You could talk all day.*

Reading

*You are probably a regular reader. You see it as relaxation, not a chore. You wish you had more time to read.*

Writing

*Your spelling is not wonderful but you can put together a reasonable letter. You do not need to write very often.*

Formal or
public
speaking

*You have never spoken in public, or only rarely. Even the thought of it makes you anxious.*

Maths and
calculation

*Your maths is not good, but this does not matter because it is irrelevant to everyday life.*

From birth, we are surrounded by noise and speech. The incoming signals only stop when we are asleep or alone. The teaching and learning process is continuous and we are rewarded if we can make our needs and wishes known. You start an Access course with at least 20 years' practice and experience in spoken language. There is no necessary connection between spoken and written language. You might be eloquent and lucid but totally illiterate – as all humans were before written language was developed. As an adult, you make direct connections between conversation, pleasure, leisure and enjoyment – it is good to talk.

For most people, the breakthrough or turning point comes with speciali-sation. If you can read, then you can choose what to read. As an adult you probably have a favourite subject or type of book. You start the course with years of practice and a positive attitude.

If you do not know how to read, then you will not be able to write, but the first skill is usually far more developed than the second. Input is easier than output – you can make sense of a novel or textbook without understanding every word, but you cannot leave gaps and spaces in written work for ideas that you do not have words for. More importantly, from the age of 16 onwards you can live a perfectly normal life without writing more than a few words every month or so – perhaps a birthday card, a shopping list or filling in a form to renew the tax disc on your car. Writing for pleasure is seen as eccentric; reading for enjoyment is normal and natural. You will start the course with mixed feelings about writing.

## Speeches and sums

Public speaking is no more than a one-way conversation with a large group, but it is easy to avoid and most start the course with absolutely no experience whatsoever.

If forced to choose between public speaking and a maths exam, most newly enrolled mature students would agonise over their decision – they are both daunting in the extreme.

## Filling the gaps

The less life experience you have of a particular communication technique, the more time and attention you will need to reach the standards set for Access and university admission. This is why the course focuses heavily on written and verbal presentation communication skills. You will be shown how to fill the gaps and become a good all-round communicator.

## Pictures, images and symbols

Every time someone opens their eyes, the brain is flooded with a constantly changing stream of pictures and images. Of the two dominant human senses, sight is the one used most. The less formal education that a person has, the more likely they are to learn best through images and pictures. This has nothing whatever to do with ability, but merely reflects differing levels of experience and practice.

Complicated ideas and concepts can often be turned into flow diagrams, charts and symbols. If you find that your study diet is becoming too rich in words, try turning some of them into pictures.

# Words and meanings

You will make a slow start with the Research Skills unit unless you understand that some common everyday words mean different things when they are used to describe teaching and learning. We all know what these sentences mean:

> 'That weekend I spent with Archibald, collecting sea shells on the beach, was a critical turning point in our relationship,' said Hermione, sighing with blissful contentment.

> 'I didn't like maths at school. Mr Wilkinson was forever criticising everything I did.'

> 'I am sick to death of your constant criticism. If you do not like the way I cook, then do it yourself.'

> 'Nigel is a research scientist for BP. He spends all day in this huge laboratory, doing spectroscopic analysis of Venezuelan crude oil samples.'

'Critical' can mean important, but in most everyday situations, 'critical' or 'criticism' are words used negatively, to imply anger, dislike, frustration, jealousy or just plain, straightforward bad temper.

Similarly, 'research', as an everyday word, is used specifically to mean the work done by very small numbers of highly qualified scientists in laboratories filled with complicated, expensive equipment.

# Research awareness and critical thinking

In education, the words 'critical' and 'criticism' are used to describe actions that are positive and productive, not negative or spiteful. All of your work, in every unit, will be constructively criticised by tutors, supervisors and lecturers. This is how it works:

- You will prepare a piece of work. A member of staff will read it or listen to it, and perhaps mark it according to a predetermined mark scheme.

- Unless the evidence suggests otherwise, it will be assumed that you did all that you could, bearing in mind your present level of knowledge and experience. Your assignment is unlikely to be perfect in every way.

- Quietly and in confidence, you will be told how you can improve your next assignment or modify the current one. No spite, malice, animosity or display of rank is involved or intended. Constructive criticism, properly delivered and properly taken, builds confidence, ability and dignity – it does not destroy or undermine it.

'Research', as properly and broadly defined, is something we all do every day. You probably do not chew lemons because you remember the results of the one and only lemon-chewing experiment you conducted as a child. Most research does not rely on personal experience. Thankfully, very few of us have been involved in a head-on collision between two cars, but we modify our behaviour because we believe the evidence suggesting that this experiment will have unpleasant results.

Research awareness and critical thinking mean roughly the same thing. In essence, critical thinking is the habit of asking logical questions whenever you are presented with a piece of information. What evidence suggests this information is correct? How was that evidence collected? Who gave me the information? For what reason?

It would, perhaps, be better if critical thinking was called well-informed thinking, soundly-based thinking, selective thinking or – best of all – independent thinking.

A critical thinker occupies the middle ground between innocence and cynicism. The diagram explains this.

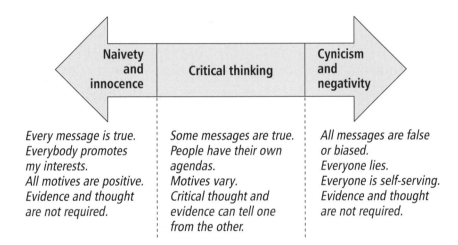

| Naivety and innocence | Critical thinking | Cynicism and negativity |
|---|---|---|
| *Every message is true. Everybody promotes my interests. All motives are positive. Evidence and thought are not required.* | *Some messages are true. People have their own agendas. Motives vary. Critical thought and evidence can tell one from the other.* | *All messages are false or biased. Everyone lies. Everyone is self-serving. Evidence and thought are not required.* |

# Chapter 3
# Communication skills

*National unit specification.*
*These are the topics you will be studying for this unit:*

1  Reading skills
2  Comprehension and critical reading
3  Effective reading
4  Notes and note taking
5  Good written English
6  Written assignments and assessments
7  Referencing
8  Verbal assignments and assessments

Here, we extend the ideas outlined in the last chapter. We take the essential communication skills in a logical order – reading first, then writing and we finish with spoken English. This chapter is practical, not theoretical – it is based around a series of tips, hints and techniques.

# *1* Reading skills

How many times have you started a novel and given up after the first 20 or so pages? Reading for pleasure is just that – when it gets difficult, boring or irrelevant, we stop. Most reading for Access will be rewarding and enjoyable, but you are certain to find some units less interesting than others. You will be able to choose between different authors' explanations of a topic, but you cannot give up on an assignment altogether.

No amount of reading damages normal eyesight, but bad reading habits rapidly bring on pain and exhaustion.

- You must be reasonably warm. Nobody can read for long in a cold or draughty room.

- Concentration lapses even with mild dehydration – make sure you take regular tea or coffee breaks.

- If you are not sitting comfortably, you are certain to get a stiff neck and backache. Try to vary your position, otherwise you will get ankle, elbow and knee pain as well.

- Excessive background noise never helps, but many people find music increases concentration. Conversation from a TV or radio programme is nearly always disruptive at high volume.

- Trying to read in poor artificial light is worse than not reading at all. Eyestrain and headaches are inevitable.

## Reading rates

The best starting point is to estimate your current reading rate, ideally in the first weeks of the course. Find some writing that you have not seen before – not something you have written. It has to be typed or word processed, in a reasonably large font, and avoid a piece with charts, diagrams or tables.

Make sure you are comfortable and see how many words you read in 60 seconds. Repeat the exercise two or three times and work out your average reading rate in words per minute. A cooker timer helps, otherwise get somebody to give you start and stop signals. Read as you normally would – do not accelerate to improve the score.

These figures are no more than very rough guidelines. We are all different and reading rates vary considerably according to what is being read.

| | |
|---|---|
| *Below 200 words per minute* | You have probably picked up some bad reading habits. You need more practice. |
| *200 to 300 words per minute* | This is the average range for most adults. |
| *Over 300 words per minute* | You will need to check comprehension and understanding. |

Note your reading rate in your reflective diary. Do not be alarmed if you seem to be a slow reader, or too impressed if you are hitting 400 words per minute. Old habits that reduce reading rates are easy to unlearn. Rapid readers often need to slow down to improve comprehension. An average of 250 words a minute, with good understanding, is a reasonable target for new non-technical material.

# Eye movement

We read by scanning a line of print in a series of jumps and pauses – called fixations. Some people pause and fixate on every word. With practice, the number of fixations decreases and the pauses between them get shorter. You probably read words in groups of three or four without realising it. People who read for a living fix on whole sentences, whole lines and, sometimes, several lines at a time.

Fixation

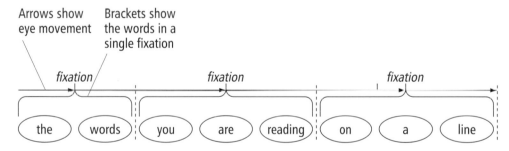

If your initial reading speed is much below 200 words per minute, for non-demanding material, you probably have one or more improvable habits.

# Head movement

A stiff neck after more than about 30 minutes' reading is a sure sign that you are moving your head not your eyes when scanning a line of text. The movements are almost imperceptible but with constant repetition, you will tire rapidly. Bifocals, varifocals and half glasses can make the problem worse, encouraging up/down as well as left/right movements.

This habit often cures itself as soon as it is recognised. If not, experiment with increasing the distance between your eyes and the page to the limit of focus. A bookstand or propping one book in front of another often helps.

# Sub-vocalisation

Quietly speaking or mouthing words as you read, or sub-vocalisation, is much more common than you might imagine. Many of us do it when we read in private. Because we think faster than we talk, sub-vocalisation always reduces reading speed. Again, the problem nearly always corrects itself once it is recognised – it always disappears with increasing reading practice.

# Regression, vocabulary and dictionaries

Regression is the most common poor-reading habit. Everybody does it when they are tired or if they are trying to come to grips with technical jargon.

Regression is going back to a previous word or line to check you have understood its meaning or perhaps to see whether you have missed an important point altogether.

Regression

| the | words | you | are | reading | on | a | line |

Regression leads to these words being read in this order:

| 1st | 2nd | 3rd | 4th | | | | |
| 5th | 6th | 7th | 8th | 9th | 10th | 11th | |
| | | | | 12th | 13th | 14th | 15th |

Sometimes, regression is the only way to cope with bad writing – real meaning does not emerge the first or even the second time around.

Vocabulary is the list of words you understand, although you may not use all of them very often. When you come across a new word, you stop reading immediately. If it is not part of your existing vocabulary, you have three options – ignore it, try to guess its meaning from the other words around it, or look it up. The third choice is the only one that works on an intensive course like Access where you will be meeting new vocabulary every day.

You need to buy a general dictionary – ideally one small enough to carry around most of the time as you would a purse, wallet or house keys. When you come across a new word, look it up. Always go straight to the dictionary, do not put it off. This is tiresome at first, but once you understand a word it will not slow your reading again.

# Glossaries and technical vocabulary

Technical terms are a specialist vocabulary that develops alongside the general one. Lecturers in specialist units should always explain the meaning of a new word. If they do not – ask. Many textbooks include glossaries – brief explanations of technical vocabulary and there may be a recommended specialist dictionary for your pathway.

Technical terms are often used in a very precise way. Make sure you understand how some words can mean different things according to context.

# The daily papers

The ability to communicate always increases as a by-product of specialist reading for the natural and social science units, but you can greatly accelerate the process by getting into the habit of reading a good broadsheet newspaper.

The assumption that broadsheets are stuffy, and only for the elite, is nonsense. You do not have to change your political views and you certainly do not need more than 15 or 20 minutes a day to read the articles that interest you personally.

Buy at least one issue of the *Guardian*, the *Independent*, *The Times* and the *Daily Telegraph*, and decide which one suits you best.

For exactly the same reasons, even 20 minutes a day listening to BBC Radio 4 will help you produce better written work with much less effort. The early morning, lunchtime and early evening news programmes will stimulate your critical thinking, as will the broadsheets.

# 2 Comprehension and critical reading

Rapid reading without understanding is pointless. Everybody has an upper limit to their reading speed, above which comprehension tails off rapidly. However, there are techniques that will help increase both speed and comprehension up to this limit.

An internet search engine works by reading millions of words or phrases in a few seconds. It then selects and lists any article or page containing the key words or phrases you have typed on the keyboard. Search engines reach phenomenal speeds because they are programmed to ignore virtually everything apart from key words. Speed-reading techniques use exactly the same idea.

Skimming or scanning for key words and combinations of key words increases speed and comprehension simultaneously. Techniques are based on reducing the number of fixations and constant accelerations and decelerations in reading speed. Most people skim or scan at something like 600 words a minute, then drop back to around 150 words a minute when they hit key words or phrases.

## Critical reading

If you can read somebody else's writing at about 300 words a minute with full understanding, then the piece is well written. However, style, clarity, value and relevance do not have to go hand in hand. There is a great deal of well-written rubbish and nearly all of the books in a large library will not be relevant to the particular issue you are researching. Critical reading will help identify arguments that are biased, unbalanced or incomplete.

Critical reading leads to critical thinking and then on to original critical writing. All three skills are essential.

A checklist like the one below will help improve your critical reading skills. Make mental or, preferably, written notes whenever you read something new.

- What is the writing trying to achieve? What are its main or central ideas?

- Can you identify its target audience? Is the author presenting a wide-ranging argument or addressing a specific, narrowly defined group of readers?

- How is the information organised? Does the format follow a clear plan or method? There are marked differences between natural and social science textbooks.

- Are arguments supported by evidence? Is this included in the written work or merely mentioned in passing?

- Where did the evidence come from (if it exists)? Is it based on primary research conducted by the author or is it reliant on the work of others, or secondary research?

- If the writing leaves you feeling uneasy or unconvinced, do you know why? Could you point to phrases, sentences or arguments that trigger these doubts and uncertainties?

# Different kinds of statements

It is the author's job to persuade the reader. Provided you have read critically, you have no duty or obligation to accept his or her view just because the writer says so. Statements need not be true.

| Statement | Validity |
|---|---|
| Theorem | A statement that can be proven always to be true. This is only possible in mathematics. |
| Theory | A statement based on experimental evidence. Taken to be true unless or until proved false by further experiment and observation. |
| Assumption | A statement usually based on limited experiment or observation. Assumptions may be true only in some circumstances, places or situations. They can be totally false. |
| Assertion or opinion | A personal statement that is unsupported or poorly supported by evidence. |
| Belief | A statement based on religious faith or moral conviction. Proof is not involved. |

Pythagoras' theorem allows anybody to calculate the length of the third side of a right-angled triangle starting with the length of the other two. Pythagoras' statement has always been true and it always will be.

The statement 'the moon will still exist next Tuesday' is very likely to be true because it is based on many theories developed by physicists and astronomers. However, it is an assumption because there will come a Tuesday when the moon does not exist.

'Men are heavier than women' is another assumption based on evidence. It is often true, but not always.

'Men are safer drivers than women' is an assertion or personal opinion. Motor insurance companies have years of observational evidence to show that this statement is generally false.

'Capital punishment is wrong' or 'there is life after death' are statements of belief. For the individuals making the statements, no proof is looked for and none is needed.

# Associated baggage

English is one of the richest languages in the world because it has grown by borrowing and absorbing words and expressions from many different origins. The two main historical ingredients are Anglo-Saxon and Norman French which, in turn, descended from a group of North European languages and Latin. Along the way we have also taken or stolen from almost every society on Earth.

There are dozens of English words for each idea or concept:

| | | | | |
|---|---|---|---|---|
| anorexic | beefy | big-built | big-boned | buxom |
| chubby | chunky | corpulent | fat | junoesque |
| lean | obese | overweight | paunchy | plump |
| podgy | portly | rangy | rotund | slender |
| slight | slim | solid | stout | sturdy |
| svelte | sylphlike | thick-set | thin | trim |
| tubby | underweight | well-covered | willowy | wiry |

A reader can be coaxed or persuaded towards a conclusion just by placing the right words in the right order – without supporting evidence. At its extreme, this technique becomes vicious propaganda.

# *3* Effective reading

To use your valuable time effectively, you will have to assess other people's written work quickly and efficiently. Some sources will be relevant, others will not. You need to know what to read and where to find it.

It is important to keep track of your reading. When you use external information, you will, at some stage, have to quote the origin or source in detail.

Keep a notebook to record author, title, page number, publisher or website every time you use an information source. Later, it can take hours to find the appropriate reference if you do not work methodically.

## How to begin

Start with the college library. On health-related pathways you may also be able to use the more specialist libraries of local hospitals. Do not buy a book unless it is well written and will be useful regularly and frequently. Then, decide what you need. Do you want background, a particular aspect of a topic or a specific piece of well-defined information? You might be looking for a single statistic or 30 pages of description and explanation.

## Survey and evaluation

Next, you need to survey and evaluate the literature before you begin to read. Ask the following questions.

### Title

- Does the title clearly indicate its subject?
- Is the book recommended by your lecturers or by professional practitioners?

### Book cover

- Is there a summary of chapters, issues or topics included in the book?
- Is there evidence of the author's approach?

### Author

- Is the author an acknowledged expert on the subject?
- Has the writer's style been recommended for clarity and accessibility?
- Is the author known for a particular point of view?

## Publication date

- If you have a book more than ten years old, is it a 'classic' or is it outdated?

- Is the book the most recent update? Always try to get hold of the latest edition of a textbook or published statistics.

## Country of publication

- Was the source written and published in the UK? If not, the material may not be relevant, accurate or appropriate.

## Bibliography

- Does the author quote other sources? The bibliography may guide you towards further material. Be wary of books without bibliographies.

## Websites

- Is the website linked to, or provided by, an academic institution?

- Is the material suitable for serious research? Websites are useful references, but take care – unlike books, their content does not undergo rigorous scrutiny. If you include information from the internet you must submit a printout of the article and enough information to allow tracking and validation of the source.

## Contents and indexes

- Can you immediately tell how the book is laid out?

- Does the index give specific or detailed information?

- Are there sub-headings for each chapter?

## Skimming

A book or other source may look promising but still not be useful, relevant or easy to read. Skimming can save hours of wasted time. This is how it is done.

First, turn to the preface and introduction:

- Is the book still relevant?

- What impression does the preface give you about the book as a whole?

- Are the author's intentions clearly stated?

Then to the first page:

- Is the writer's style and layout clear or obscure?

- Is the wording, jargon and terminology user friendly?

Finally, look at the first and last paragraph of what seems to be the relevant chapter or chapters:

- Are the introductions and conclusions clear?

- Is the writing easy to follow?

Only spend your precious time on detailed reading if the source passes all of these tests.

# Reading journals and articles

Academic journals and articles are vital information sources. Their language will assume some prior knowledge. You will need practice and it is best, at first, not to rush through an article. Most journal articles are research reports.

As always, it helps to make notes.

## The introduction

- This will give the reasoning behind the research. Try to pinpoint the theories applied and the questions asked.

- Has the author stated the hypothesis or research question clearly and concisely?

## The main body of the article

- What research techniques have been used to test the question?

- Do you think the design and method chosen is the best approach?

- Could you interpret the author's results differently?

## The conclusion

- Are the author's conclusions relevant, acceptable and well supported?

- Do you think the article has set out a convincing argument?

## The recommendations

- Research often suggests the need for a change in practice or procedures. Do you think the article justifies the recommendations made?

# Paste pot and scissors

You might consider completing an assignment by simply cutting articles from books and journals.

This way of working is not acceptable and will be rejected by tutors and lecturers.

An assignment needs to show that you have understood and processed source material, not just made copies of it. Your criticism and comments are essential, valuable and reasonable, provided you support the arguments you make.

Different sources often reach different conclusions – do not be afraid to compare and contrast.

# *4* Notes and note taking

Concentration levels vary when you are reading or listening to new information. Taking notes will pin down key points and help you process information. They give a permanent record to be used later, and good note taking dramatically improves memory.

You will soon learn to pick out the information that makes the main argument. With practice you will be able to identify key issues and produce a condensed version of a lecture or written work, ending with a short summary or conclusion.

Include translations or explanations, in your own words, of technical terms or vocabulary that you have not met before. Make sure you have an accurate record of important diagrams, tables, charts or numbers.

Use key words, bullet points and sequences. Numbering helps, so do abbreviations provided you stick to a system that will still make sense weeks or months after the event.

Class discussions and questions are often the most valuable part of a lecture. Make sure you note good questions and helpful answers.

You may not understand some material when it is first presented. Highlight areas for clarification.

Try to finish with a brief summary of what you think you have been taught and the interconnections between sequential arguments.

## Memory, recall and revision

The most successful students are those who read through their notes for the day – before they go to bed. This need not take more than 15 or 20 minutes and it is the only way of improving memory that has been proved to work for everybody in all situations and subjects.

It sometimes helps to tidy up notes that are not completely legible or clear, but do not be tempted into a complete rewrite. This is tedious, time consuming and does not improve recall for most students.

Notes are personal and idiosyncratic – everybody has a different system. Somebody else's notes will probably not make sense, especially a few weeks or more after the event.

Revision is always difficult and sometimes impossible without a full set of notes from the unit concerned.

# Organisation

In any one week you will be collecting notes from something like eight or nine different units or subjects. Chaos, confusion and pre-exam panic are likely unless you get organised. Use a black or dark-coloured pen. Pencil fades and is difficult to read.

Scroll-top reporters' note pads are too small; lined A4 paper is best. Double-space the notes so that you can correct and amend legibly if need be.

Number each page and head the first one with the date, time, subject and lecturer concerned.

Keep notes for each unit in a separate folder, wallet or binder. If you can afford it, use colour-coded paper to distinguish one subject from another.

Notes are valuable and often irreplaceable. Make space at home for the collection of folders and binders that will accumulate as the course progresses.

Do not throw notes away at the end of a unit or when you have finished the course. Study is a continuing process. What you learn in Access will be relevant when you move on to university.

Even with the best intentions, and regardless of ability, some students cannot get the hang of note taking. If this is your problem, do not hide it – tell your personal tutor.

# *5* Good written English

The credit schemes for all assignments give marks for the use of good English.

In most groups of mature students, there are a few with dyslexia. The condition can sometimes remain undiagnosed well into adulthood, causing sufferers to believe they have a general all-round lack of ability. Diagnostic testing during induction week picks up most problems, but dyslexia is sometimes not evident until the first essay assignments are marked.

If you find spelling, grammar, punctuation and sentence construction difficult, do not immediately assume you are dyslexic. The cause is much more likely to be lack of practice. If you are genuinely dyslexic, you will be offered special help.

If English is not your first language, you may need special one-to-one help and support. Extra sessions are more easily arranged in the early weeks of the course. If you think you have problems, do not struggle on – see your personal tutor straight away.

## Where to begin

It is vital to begin with a proper understanding of the differences between good and bad (and correct and incorrect) writing. Correct English is written work that obeys the rules of spelling, punctuation and grammar. Good English is a series of words that transmits a message clearly, bearing in mind the needs of the audience.

## What is expected?

You will not be expected to produce eloquent, lucid written English from day one. However, your tutors and lecturers will want to see sustained and gradual improvement over the course. The ability to write correct English and good English develops in parallel, not separately.

Constructive criticism of style, spelling, punctuation and grammar is often hard to take. Nobody is 'getting at you' or trying to make you feel foolish if your first efforts are returned covered in corrections and suggestions for improvement.

Most of the rest of this topic talks about correct English, and we finish with some guidelines on sentence and paragraph construction – the starting point for good English.

# Spelling

You will not learn to spell if you do not read widely or write on a regular basis. However, persistent problems with some words and some types of words are incredibly common. No book is ever published without editing and proof-reading. An author's manuscript is usually checked three or four times before it goes to print. Mathematicians, natural scientists and those who prefer logic and order often have problems.

# Phonetics

Languages like Spanish and Italian tend to obey a relatively rigid set of simple rules. Most of all, their spelling is phonetic – words are spelt as they are spoken. The Spanish for 'football' is 'futbol'.

English spelling is not phonetic. The classic examples are words ending in 'ough':

| | | | | | | |
|---|---|---|---|---|---|---|
| bough | cough | although | enough | borough | through | hiccough |
| plough | trough | dough | rough | thorough | | |
| Slough | | though | tough | | | |

First you have to learn how to say a word, and then how to spell it – there is no other choice.

# Spellcheckers and dictionaries

As part of the Information Technology unit you will be shown how to put together word-processed documents. The computer package you use will include a spellchecker – as long as your spelling is something close to the right sequence of letters, the programme will automatically suggest a correction. This facility alone is a massive incentive to get on with the Information Technology unit.

You will not always be sitting in front of a computer screen when you are writing. You must have a dictionary to hand, at all times, to extend vocabulary and to check spellings. There is no point in buying a dictionary and not using it every time you want to confirm meaning or spelling. Small, portable electronic spellcheckers are available at reasonable prices.

# Capital letters

Using capital or upper-case letters wrongly is a common error. Remember that the first letter of the first word in a sentence has to be a capital, but that elsewhere only I, names and titles begin with uppercase letters. Printing or typing a word entirely in capitals to add emphasis, as in 'correct English need NOT be good English', is always wrong.

'English' here begins with a capital letter because it is the name of a language. It is sometimes difficult to decide if a word is being used as a name. In this book we often write Access with a capital because it is the name of a course, but we use lower case in sentences like 'students need access to a good library'.

Headings and sub-headings often look best as a string of capital letters, but there are no rigid rules apart from consistency. For instance:

| | | | | | |
|---|---|---|---|---|---|
| Chapter one | or | Chapter One | or | CHAPTER ONE |
| Chapter two | | Chapter Two | | CHAPTER TWO |

## Abbreviations and contractions

Do not use abbreviations or acronyms without explaining their meaning at least once. For example, coronary heart disease – commonly abbreviated to CHD – should be written like this:

… coronary heart disease (CHD) …

Once you have done this, the abbreviation is acceptable.

Some abbreviations have two meanings – AA stands for Alcoholics Anonymous and the Automobile Association. The use and ownership of the abbreviation WWF had to be settled in court. It had been claimed both by the World Wildlife Fund and the World Wrestling Federation. This is yet another reason for defining your abbreviation at the start.

Contractions are shortened versions of two words with an apostrophe showing what has been left out. For example:

A — Do not miss lectures otherwise you will not make good progress.

becomes

B — Don't miss lectures otherwise you won't make good progress.

or even

C — Dont miss lectures otherwise you wont make good progress.

A — is the full version. This is what you should nearly always use in written work.

There is only one exception:

**B** shows the contraction of 'do not' to 'don't' and 'will not' to 'won't'. Contractions of this sort can be used in written work if you are quoting the exact content of a conversation. If you are showing reported speech, you must use inverted commas – quotation or speech marks – like this:

Belinda said, 'Don't worry about the odd misspelling. Your essay structure couldn't have been better.'

**C** is a contraction without an apostrophe. It is incorrect in every circumstance.

# Slang

Slang should always be avoided in written work unless it is part of a direct and relevant quotation. It often confuses and may even offend. During the early 1960s, John F. Kennedy, the US president, and Harold Macmillan, the British prime minister, became friends. Kennedy was startled when Macmillan began private conversations with words like 'And how are you today, old fruit?'. To an Englishman educated before the First World War, 'old fruit' meant chum, friend or pal. To the American president, an 'old fruit' was an elderly gay man.

Even the mildest expletives like 'bloody' and 'damn' must not be used in written work and verbal presentations. The same holds for potentially racist, sexist or other politically incorrect terms. Wrong versus right is not the issue – the central point is that conventions vary enormously and if even one person in your target audience is offended or hurt by an ill-chosen word, then you have failed to communicate. Written work is a permanent record. Its eventual audience is unknown and unknowable.

Never use a string of asterisks or exclamation marks in place of a generally unacceptable word or phrase. This is a big mistake – it will offend and confuse.

# Idioms

We say 'soaked to the skin'. The equivalent in Spanish is 'soaked to the bone'. Idioms are language-specific and often peculiar to smaller groups or regions.

Do not use idioms in written work unless there is no other way of getting your message across. They do not transmit full, complete or clear information. Compare these two sentences:

In the late stages of pregnancy, most women feel under the weather.

Backache, swollen ankles and mild anxiety are common in the late stages of pregnancy.

# Clichés

A cliché is a series of words that have become victims of their own success. They must not be overused because, at the end of the day, taking one thing with another, you must not throw the baby out with the bathwater. There are no golden rules, but this is the best advice available at this moment in time.

One cliché often helps, but there should never be more than one in any piece of writing. We could just have written one sentence:

It is best not to overuse clichés.

'At this moment in time' just means 'now'. If you do use a cliché, make sure it is appropriate. Do not write 'a three-year university course is a game of two halves' – because it is not.

Proverbs are ancient clichés – the same rules apply.

# Punctuation

There are some unbreakable rules of English punctuation, but detail and precise use is often a matter of style and preference.

## Full stops and commas

A sentence cannot be one word, but it might just be two. No matter how long, or how short, it must start with a capital letter and end with a full stop, unless this is replaced by a question mark or exclamation mark.

England triumphed! What next?

Commas are used to break sentences into more manageable chunks, but also to separate ideas and make them easier to understand. Two or more shorter sentences usually have more impact than one long one.

Commas are also used to separate items in a list:

Anorexics suffer from anaemia, low blood pressure, slow heart rate, swollen ankles and osteoporosis.

## Questions, exclamations and accents

A question should always end with a question mark; never use more than one. Question marks are used for questions posed by the writer and for those asked by others but quoted by the author. A question mark takes the place of a full stop.

Do not use exclamation marks in serious or academic writing.

## Apostrophes

There are fixed rules for using apostrophes and these must not be ignored:

- To show possession or ownership.

  Before the s if it refers to one person or thing

  I marked Martin's work.

  After the s if it refers to more than one person or thing

  Milly, Molly and Mandy had handed in their assignments, so I decided to mark the students' work that evening.

- The word 'it' is an exception. Confusion between its and it's is probably the most common punctuation error. An apostrophe is only used with 'it' to show a contraction; 'its', without an apostrophe, shows ownership:

  It's always wrong to leave a baby crying in its pushchair.

  It's is short for it is. Its means the pushchair belongs to the child.

- Apostrophes show that a letter has been left out in a contraction:

  don't     can't     mustn't     '000 tonnes     10 o'clock

- Never use an apostrophe to make a plural:

  apples and pears     *not*     apple's and pear's

## Quotation marks, inverted commas

Quotation marks or inverted commas (sometimes called speech marks) have two main uses.

They are used to show that the writer is quoting another person's precise words.

  'It's really cold in here,' said John to the client. 'I don't know how you can stand it.'

  'The client seemed totally unaffected by the cold,' wrote John in his report of their meeting.

Single inverted commas can also be used to draw attention to terminology or a more common word which is being defined or discussed:

  As commonly used, the word 'interview' describes a process with a certain level of inbuilt stress and tension.

## Colons and semicolons

Confusion between colons – : – and semicolons – ; – is very common.

The colon is used to show that you are about to present some information to illustrate a point. For example:

  Manchester United's popularity can be seen most clearly at Old Trafford: over 60,000 people attend every match there.

A colon is also often used to introduce a list:

> An overnight frost can be expected in the following areas: Kent, East Sussex, West Sussex, Surrey and Hampshire.

The semicolon is different. It is used to separate one idea from another, usually to compare and contrast, as in these examples:

> In the past, natural science was concerned with the world about us; the supernatural sciences were the study of religion, philosophy and theology.

> Commercial organisations start life as one or two people with a money-making idea. Most fail; a few grow into huge companies.

Semicolons can also be used to separate lists. For example:

> The following speakers will be contributing to the conference: Professor Richard Rose, the leading Scottish expert on flowering perennials; Dr Iris Holland, a spring bulbs specialist; Mrs Theresa Green, the eminent arboricul-turalist; and Mr Cuts, the UK's topiary champion.

## Hyphens, dashes and brackets

Most hyphenated words are part way along the evolutionary road to becoming single longer ones. There are endless arguments and very few clear-cut rules. Take your dictionary's advice and be consistent. Do not, for example, mix co-operation and cooperation in the same piece.

Dashes can be used instead of colons:

> First-year university students often do not know how to punctuate – especially mathematicians and engineers.

Brackets are best kept for referencing. Constant or frequent use soon becomes disruptive and irritating.

# Sentence and paragraph construction

These are guidelines, not instructions:

- A sentence with more than five or six punctuation marks is often too long – unless you are using commas or semicolons to indicate a list.

- Vary the length of sentences as often as possible. Do not be afraid to mix the longest with the shortest. Impact decreases as length increases.

- Do not get preoccupied with spelling. This is the most common reason why schoolchildren give up writing, and then reading. If you have a spare hour, read a book – do not set yourself endless spelling tests.

- Never use a long word if you can find a shorter one. Words of three, four or more syllables reduce reading rates as well as comprehensibility.

- Written work must be divided into paragraphs. A new paragraph should be used to introduce a new big idea.

- A single hand-written or word-processed page has to contain at least two paragraphs, or parts of two paragraphs. You can ignore this advice if you interrupt text with visual images or tables of numbers. A single-paragraph page is very tiring to read.

- Only write in paragraphs longer than around 15 printed lines if you are trying to explain a complicated sequential argument where each step or stage is essential and cannot be left out. This will not happen very often.

- Write short paragraphs, of two or three lines, if you are presenting a simple but pivotal point. In this case, the shorter the better, but again it should not be routine.

- Many consecutive short paragraphs read like machine-gun fire. A string of long ones is like a sedative. You should not alarm the audience, or send them to sleep.

## Lightbulb events

A lightbulb moment or event is the sudden realisation that a previously baffling idea makes sense.

Access courses ought to be about switching on as many lightbulbs as possible – in the right order. Your particular lightbulb moments will come from conversations with fellow students and lecturers, lectures themselves and background reading.

If a particular book, article or lecture handout does it for you, then you are responding to written style as well as content. This is vital information. Make a copy of the relevant page or pages and see how it is put together. Pay attention to the way sentences and paragraphs of different lengths are mixed and matched. This is the best possible guide to your individual or natural written style. Copy it first, amend it, develop it, and then make it your own.

# *6* Written assignments and assessments

Quality control or quality assurance are the general terms used to describe the procedures that ensure goods and services are up to standard, consistent, safe and reliable. Education is a service – the Access certificate is one of its end products.

Examination and assessment are part of education quality assurance. A qualification that was unreliable or inconsistent would soon become devalued and eventually worthless.

Assessment methods vary from one unit to another. They include:

- The minimum attendance requirement.

- Observation by lecturers and tutors.

- Essay assignments.

- Traditional time-limited written exams.

- Oral presentations.

- Seminars and debates.

- Group or cooperative projects.

- Practical investigations and experiments.

Several methods are used to assess students' performance in each unit. The minimum attendance requirement is compulsory for all.

To ensure fairness and consistency, your work will be judged according to predetermined marking schemes or marking criteria. Subject lecturers mark assessments in the first instance. A sample of all work is then cross-checked with other lecturers and then again by experts not employed by the college. These extra safeguards are called internal and external verification.

## Some general rules

You will be given guidelines and instructions for all assessments; make sure you have read and understood these before you plan or write. If in doubt – ask. You may be asked to submit a plan, draft or outline before the final version.

All written work must carry the assignment title on the front page, your full name, your student group or pathway, and a date. Pages should be numbered and clipped or bound together so that nothing gets lost.

Keep a paper or floppy-disk copy of everything you submit for assessment. When the work is returned, make sure you file it in a safe place. In the last weeks of the course you will have to put together a folder of all your assessed material for external verification.

Assignments and assessments have deadlines or final submission dates. Extensions can be negotiated in exceptional circumstances, but the habit is not encouraged. Universities take deadlines very seriously – late work is usually rejected.

# Writing reports

A report is written in a formal style, to give information or to record the findings of an investigation. It has to show its purpose, evidence and a conclusion.

The report must be set out in a logical order. Here is a basic template.

## A report

*Title*

The name or title of your report.

*Introduction*

Explain the purpose or point of the report and the steps you will take to reach a conclusion.

*Sub-sections*

Use sub-sections to divide the work into easily digested units in a logical sequence. Each should be headed and numbered.

*Conclusion*

A clear statement of the conclusions supported by your investigations.

*Recommendations*

It may be appropriate to include a recommendation or series of recommendations based on your investigations and conclusions.

*Appendix*

An appendix is used to show supplementary or detailed material, which, if included in the main body of text, would disrupt the flow of the report. Appendices (plural, pronounced 'a-pen-diss-ees') often contain graphs, diagrams, statistics or detailed experimental results.

*References and bibliography*

You need to list details of all the information sources used.

Avoid emotionally loaded, vague or inappropriate language. Sentences should be short and concise; vary the length of sentences and paragraphs to add interest.

## Essays as assignments

If you have been away from formal education for many years, the prospect of writing an essay will seem daunting, and an instruction to write 1,000 words feels, at first, as if it will take forever. You will be taught how to write a reasonable essay starting from square one – lack of previous experience is not a handicap. You will soon find that trying to keep your essays within a word limit is a bigger problem than finding enough words to complete the assignment.

Essays are very widely used as an assessment method because they:

- Show your ability to think clearly and logically.

- Demonstrate that you have understood factual material.

- Test your independent study and research skills.

- Allow you to make connections between your life experiences and the course material.

- Prove that you can construct an argument that will inform, interest and hold the attention of the reader.

## Guidelines and instructions

Assessments have to be structured so that your work can be marked fairly – so they must all include instructions and guidelines clearly defining what needs to be done.

For an essay assignment, you will start with several different kinds of information.

A title or subject for the essay will be provided by your lecturer. It will include key words – these are the most important guidelines of all. For instance:

'Discuss the factors which, during the 20th century, led to the foundation of the National Health Service.'

Discuss means that some kind of comment is required; a simple list will not do. You will have to decide which were the most important issues and which were trivial and incidental.

Factors is in the plural, therefore if you suggest that the NHS came about for just one reason, you will not meet the assessment guidelines.

The NHS was founded in 1948 and the 20th century began in 1901. These instructions limit the scope of the essay and incidentally reduce the workload. You should probably talk about what happened in 1906 before the major events of 1918 and then 1945. The title key words will tell you where to start looking for additional and background information.

Finally, you should be able to see that the title could trigger a great deal of work. You will need to be selective in what you include and what you leave out.

# Word counts

A target word count will always be provided. It might be a guideline or a firm instruction.

- Not more than 1,000 words is a firm instruction.

- Write 1,000 words is a guideline. You should aim to complete within ± 10% of the total given – in this case not less than 900 or more than 1,100 words.

Most lecturers will exclude quotations, appendices, bibliographies and reference lists from the word count and also disregard charts and tables – check with the teaching staff before you start. Include a final word count on the front page of the completed assignment.

# Essay planning

Before you begin you need to define and identify your readers or audience. Remember that the main purpose of an essay is to inform its readers and to hold their attention.

The content should clearly show that you are making connections between your own experiences, the Access course and private study. Your views and opinions need to be balanced with other evidence. Unsupported statements of opinion, pure description or personal anecdotes are not acceptable.

Planning and preparation is essential. Without a plan you will struggle for hours on end, only to produce a disappointing essay.

To organise material, you may find it helps to write a list of headings and then sub-headings or notes to link the main points. A better alternative method is a spider diagram.

## Spider diagrams

Take the essay used in the previous illustration:

> 'Discuss the factors which, during the 20th century, led to the foundation of the National Health Service.'

Your spider diagram might look like this. Use a piece of A4 paper turned sideways.

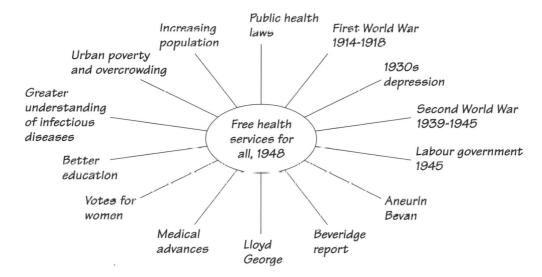

You will immediately see useful links and connections, you will be able to pinpoint the main issues and you will not miss important ideas or concepts.

## Essay structure

There are some simple rules. An essay has three parts:

- Introduction.

- Main body.

- Conclusion.

Introduction:

- Outlines the areas your essay will cover.

- Allows readers to see you have interpreted the guidelines correctly.

Main body:

- Will show your knowledge of the subject and ample evidence of supporting research.

- An appropriate and logical sequence will demonstrate the relevance and accuracy of your essay.

- A balanced argument, for and against, will prove that you have understood that most issues are complex and difficult.

Conclusion:

- No new information should be included in the conclusion.

- You may, however, include ideas for further research that emerge from your work.

## Collusion and plagiarism

Collusion and plagiarism will mean that essays are rejected. Collusion is pretending that a cooperative effort is the independent work of one student – your lecturer will always notice if there are close similarities between two people's work. Plagiarism is presenting someone else's work as your own.

Collusion and plagiarism are the most serious breaches of academic discipline. You will fail a unit or even the whole course if you ignore the rules.

# 7 Referencing

Here we explain why work needs to be referenced, when it should be done, and how it should be done. Referencing is compulsory, not an optional extra that you can choose to include if you have time.

Your written assignments and assessments will be partly or largely based on the thinking, research, investigations and experiments of published experts in a particular field. Referencing acknowledges that your work would not have been possible without their help.

## Intellectual property and plagiarism

Referencing is more than just good manners. The law in the UK recognises two kinds of property or possessions. Real property is all the goods and objects that you own. Intellectual property describes the things you have produced as a result of thought or intellect. Patent and copyright laws give intellectual property rights. Plagiarism – pretending that somebody else's intellectual property is your original effort – is theft, just as stealing a car is theft.

By publishing their work in a book, journal or on the internet, most authors are giving automatic permission for you to use it as a source of information – provided it is properly referenced and acknowledged.

## Referencing and assessment

Appropriate referencing proves to an assessor that you have understood and then met the assessment guidelines.

- It shows that you have combined the course material with private study and independent research.

- It demonstrates an ability to select relevant, appropriate and accurate background and support.

- Referencing clearly distinguishes your views and opinions from those of others, or of experts in the field concerned.

## Referencing and the social sciences

Work that involves the social sciences, at any level, has to be referenced. We explain why with a simple illustration.

You are asked to consider why some parents are refusing immunisations for their children. You might put together a questionnaire for your classmates or carry out a random survey of local residents.

This research is simple and cheap but it is also new and unique. It has never happened before – with these participants answering your particular set of questions – the same sample questioned again a few days later may have changed their views and opinions. Referencing is vital because different methods can lead to different conclusions and you will have to choose amongst competing behavioural theories or previous research to develop and support your argument.

## Numbers and brackets

The numerical system uses small superscript numbers in the text. The Harvard system works with brackets.

The following examples are fictitious.

*The numerical system*

> Alfred Adams found that the traditional English blackbird pie contained between 15 and 28 blackbirds, not always the four and twenty as suggested in the nursery rhyme.[12]

*The Harvard system*

> Alfred Adams (1997) found that the traditional English blackbird pie contained between 15 and 28 blackbirds, not always the four and twenty as suggested in the nursery rhyme.

The subscript number [12] or the name and a date for an author directs the reader to a full reference at the back of the book or end of the chapter concerned.

Imagine the book made a total of 150 references. Alfred Adams' work would be reference number 12 of 150 in numerical order, or probably one of the first in the Harvard system list, which would arrange the 150 references in alphabetical order by author's surname.

## The full reference

Both systems set out the full references in the same way. Sequence and detail are important. This may seem tedious and pedantic, but remember, the object of the exercise is complete clarity. This is how it works:

| Item | Example |
| --- | --- |
| Author's surname followed by initials | Adams, A |
| The year of publication, in brackets | (1997) |
| The title of the book, in italics | *Pies of Northern Europe* |
| Edition of the book | 2nd edition |
| Volume number, if appropriate | 3 |
| Chapter or page number | Page 147 |
| Place of publication | Oxford |
| Publisher's name | Dainty Dish Press |

The full reference must then be shown in this way:

> Adams, A (1997). *Pies of Northern Europe*, 2nd edition, Vol. 3, p. 147. Oxford, Dainty Dish Press.

A book with two authors is referenced within the main text and in full by quoting both names. The sequence is that shown in the book – this may not be alphabetical. If there are more than two authors, you can use the first author's name followed by et al., meaning et alia, the Latin for 'and others', but this is not compulsory.

The abbreviation Ed. after a name means that he or she edited or compiled a book with contributions from many authors.

So, for example:

| | | |
|---|---|---|
| Adams, A, and Eve, B | – | two authors |
| Adams, A, Eve, B & Serpent, S | – | three authors |
| Adams, A et al. | – | three or more authors |
| Adams, A Ed. | – | Adams is the editor |

You will sometimes find the word ibid in a reference list. This is an abbreviation of the Latin ibidem, meaning 'in the same place'. In the numerical system, this is equivalent to ditto – the source was the same as the previous one listed. All Harvard system references to the same book or source must be shown in full.

## Journal referencing

In the Harvard system, the abbreviated main text reference is the same as that for a book. For example, Alfred Adams (2001) but the end-page full reference is slightly different. It needs to contain this information:

| Item | Example |
|---|---|
| Author's name | Adams, A |
| Year of publication, in brackets | (2001) |
| Title of article | The new EU apple pie regulations – too little, too late? |
| Title of journal, in italics | *The Pie Lover's Gazette* |
| Issue number, in bold | **194** |
| First and last page number of the article | 14–22 |

The full reference would be shown as:

> Adams, A (2001). The new EU apple pie regulations – too little, too late? *The Pie Lover's Gazette*. **194**. 14–22.

## Website referencing

It is worth repeating our previous warning. Material from websites is not regulated or subject to any kind of quality control. What might seem at first to be a valuable information source can turn out to be worse than useless.

If the home page does not say that the site is provided or sponsored by a familiar or reputable organisation, treat it with extreme caution. Government, university, BBC and professional association sites are as reliable as any book or journal, but others may deliver biased, incomplete or incorrect information.

The internet is a marketplace as well as an information provider. Commercial organisations and non-commercial pressure groups set up websites because they are a cheap way of reaching large audiences. Their messages are designed to promote a particular opinion or point of view – balance, validity and thorough research are not their main concerns.

Some flexibility is allowed in website referencing, provided the information source is described clearly and fully. If somebody reading your work cannot find the site and the pages you have used quickly and without confusion, then your reference is inadequate. As a minimum, an internet reference must include:

- A full website address.
- An author.
- A page or section reference.
- The month and year you visited the site.
- The site's home country.
- The sponsoring organisation.

If you cannot find all of this detail, in particular an author or authors, then it is best to look elsewhere.

Research often ends up as a paper chase through a series of books and other information sources. If possible, you should try to trace the original source. Keep a copy of the web pages you have used.

Your lecturers may give firm instructions for the sequence and content of website references.

## Newspapers, TV, radio and fictional material

Although some newspaper articles or TV and radio programmes have serious well-researched content, these do not usually make reliable information sources. Broadcast material is fleeting and temporary – exactly what good research should not be.

If you do use material from newspapers, TV or radio, then the principles of referencing still apply – the reader must be able to track your original source quickly and without confusion or ambiguity.

For references to newspaper articles you must show:

- Author or editor. Some articles are written by teams of journalists – give as much information as possible.

- The headline or title of the piece.

- The name of the newspaper in full and in italics.

- The date of publication.

- The page number, or numbers, where the article can be found.

Keep a clipping and the paper's title or masthead pasted together on a piece of A4 paper.

For broadcast material, the rules are similar. You should show:

- Author, editor or presenter.

- The title of the programme or part of the programme you have used.

- Channel or station identification.

- Date and broadcast time – remember, many programmes are repeats.

If you have advance warning of a broadcast that looks interesting, try to make a video or audio recording of it.

# Bibliographies

'Bibliography' just means a list of books. This is normally the last page of an essay or a piece of written work following the full reference list. You should give details of the books you have used to complete your work but not included as direct references. A bibliography is arranged in alphabetical order by author's surname.

# How many references?

There are no strict rules but there are guidelines:

- Any assignment with an element of social science but without references or a bibliography will be rejected.

- Do not introduce an important fact, statistic or new idea without at least one reference.

- The more extreme your arguments or conclusions, the more background you will need. You cannot disagree with the majority view if you do not understand what the majority view is.

- If you are comparing or contrasting several views or opinions, you must demonstrate an understanding of all the alternatives.

- The more complex the subject, the more background you will need and therefore the longer the reference list and bibliography ought to be.

## Organisation again

When you write your first essays, you may work on until you are happy with the final result and think that the last job is tidying up and adding the references and bibliography. If you have not kept a reading list, this last 'tidy up' takes more time than the whole of the rest of the exercise put together.

# *8* Verbal assignments and assessments

Access students are often alarmed when they discover that some assessments involve speaking in public. This alarm approaches horror or terror in about half of most groups of mature students. Public speaking is just another one of the skills you will be taught. There are well-established techniques that can turn even the most anxious and inexperienced student into a good speaker.

Different practical techniques apply, but – in every case – the more you plan ahead, the more comfortable you will be. Making it up as you go along, or hoping it will be all right on the night, is certain to increase your fears, doubts and anxieties.

Fears and phobias are not the same thing. Loss of sleep before a 'performance', sweaty palms, shaky knees and a dry mouth do not prove you have a public-speaking phobia. They are normal, natural and universal reactions to stress. You will be taught how to control these side effects just as you will be taught how to write an essay or calculate the area of a circle.

## Seminar presentations

Seminars are relatively informal events with significant audience participation. Lecturers often arrange for students to take part in seminars as a relatively painless stress-free introduction to public speaking.

Typically, a seminar involves one or two teachers plus a class or group of students studying the same unit or pathway. The topic or subject may be preset or you might be asked to choose one of your own. A fixed period of time is allocated and usually four or five students are asked to prepare a joint presentation. This will involve research, data collection and the preparation of handouts, flipcharts or other visual aids.

The presenting group should encourage audience participation – questionnaires, quizzes and practical demonstrations are effective techniques.

## Debates

A debate is a series of formal presentations controlled by pre-agreed rules. It finishes with a vote of its participants and audience, and a definitive result. Debates underpin all democracies – in the UK we make and alter laws by debates in Parliament during which all elected MPs have the right to speak and vote.

Debates are the best way of discussing highly charged issues. The subject for debate – called the motion – is usually written in controversial language, for instance:

'No woman over the age of 40 should be entitled to fertility treatment on the NHS.'

'Euthanasia – mercy killing – should be permitted in the UK.'

'Tobacco tax should be increased so that a packet of 20 cigarettes in the UK costs at least £15.'

Generally, the more controversial the statement, the more lively the debate.

## The chair, the proposers and the opposers

Debates are strictly time-limited. They are controlled by one person, elected or selected as the chair or chairperson. The chair manages proceedings and nobody is allowed to speak without his or her permission. The chair does not contribute to the arguments.

The case for the debate is presented by two people – the proposer and a seconder. The case against is made by the opposer, who also has a seconder.

Debates are won or lost by a combination of reasoned argument, statistical evidence and appeals to emotion. If you are asked to speak, your presentation should take all of these factors into account.

It is the job of the chair to keep order, and the responsibility of all participants not to descend into lack of courtesy or personal abuse. Most debates are fascinating and rewarding. Many find that their public-speaking nerves evaporate when they are moved to speak on an issue which interests them personally and emotionally.

Evidence of a debate will be needed for assessment and internal and external verification. Be prepared to write summaries of the case for and against and the result of the debate.

## Rules for a debate

These are guidelines. Your group may decide to alter the detail:

- *The Chair* opens the debate by stating the motion and introducing the speakers, making it clear which are the proposers and which the opposers.

- *The Proposer* – speaking for the motion – talks first, usually within a set time limit.

- *The Opposer* – speaking against the motion – contributes next, within the same time limit as the proposer.

- *The Seconder* – speaking for the motion – speaks third, and will usually try to answer some of the points made by the opposer.

- *The Seconder* – speaking against the motion – talks last, and will also try to answer some of the issues raised by the proposer.

- *The Chair* then asks the audience if they want to add to the debate. This is often called 'taking contributions from the floor'. Everyone must have a chance to speak.

- *The Proposer* – speaking for the motion – then sums up, trying to answer points raised from the floor.

- *The Opposer* – speaking against the motion – finally sums up, again trying to answer points raised by the audience.

- *The Chair* calls a vote – normally everyone present is eligible to vote – and then declares the result. You may ask an independent third party to count or confirm the votes cast.

# Planning a verbal presentation

Planning for verbal presentations is similar in many ways to planning written work. A spider diagram is particularly helpful.

Introduction:

- This should outline the areas and issues you will be covering in your presentation.

- The first 30 seconds are important – try to grab the audience's attention immediately. Many excellent verbal presentations begin with a question, an anecdote or a quotation.

Main body:

- Key points need to be set out in a logical order.

- You should distinguish between central and supporting arguments.

- Deliver manageable chunks of easily digestible information, rather than a continuous stream of words and numbers.

Conclusion:

- As a conclusion, summarise the main arguments.

- Repeat the central message of the presentation.

- Do not add new information in your closing remarks.

# Scripts and prompts

The ultimate verbal presentations are the major roles played by actors in live stage plays. Every word, tone of voice and action has to be learned. Live debates in Parliament are equally challenging, but almost every other kind of verbal presentation uses some kind of script or prompt. Films and most television performances are repeated, cut and edited again and again to give a flawless end product. A live 30-minute TV news programme rarely goes wrong because it has been rehearsed through the day and the presenter is reading from an autocue. This is a machine that shows a full script, word by word, in large easy-to-read letters scrolling forward slowly on a video screen.

Actors and politicians give superb verbal presentations because that is their job. They are specialists who spend a lifetime perfecting their techniques. You must not judge your presentational abilities against these world-class professionals.

You might want to write a word-for-word script for your presentation, but do not use this on the day. There is a much better way – especially if you are inexperienced and, therefore, inevitably anxious and nervous.

## Cue cards

This is how it is done.

Buy some cards. You will need two at least, plus a card for each minute of your presentation. For a five-minute presentation you will need seven cards and for 10 minutes, prepare 12, and so on. The stiffer the card, the better. If you use ordinary paper and your hands are shaking you will pass anxiety signals to the audience and exaggerate your own nerves.

Cue cards are part of planning. The first prompts your opening remarks and the last summarises the conclusions. In between, write one card for each big idea or issue.

Each card should include key words and phrases, on one side only, not a full script. At the bottom of each card, in a different colour, include the words you will use to link one card with the next.

Number each card at the top right-hand corner and punch a hole in the top left-hand corner. Sort the cards into the right sequence and thread a piece of string or wool through the holes. Knot the string or wool. When you are nervous, you get clumsy – if you drop the cue cards all you have to do is pick them up again – they will not get scrambled or lost.

A cue card

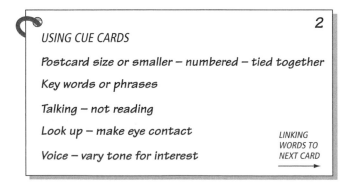

Make time to rehearse your first presentations with friends or fellow students.

# The delivery itself

Remember four things:

- You do not have to be a superstar. The presentation is designed to transmit information, not as an entertainment or amusement.

- The lecturers are on your side. They know how you feel and they want you to do well.

- The audience – your fellow students – will not give you a hard time because they know it is their turn next.

- The relief and elation that follows an adequate let alone a successful presentation is more than enough reward for pre-presentation nerves. This is why actors want to be actors and politicians want to be politicians.

Unless your group or class is quite small, presentation assignments will spread across two or three lecture sessions. You will know which day you have to make your speech but perhaps not the precise time slot. Some lecturers ask for volunteers to go first, others decide the running order themselves. If you are anxious, try to make your presentation one of the first – you will not be able to concentrate on the other presentations if you are worrying about yours.

As the presenter, you have automatic status and authority as an expert. The audience does not know what you know – they want to hear what you have to say.

Your major task is to involve the audience and hold their attention. Here are some hints.

Organise yourself before you start:

- Set up the room as you want it.

- Place visual aids, in order, on a desk or table.

- Check that equipment is working.

- You will need half a glass of cold water in case your mouth dries. Do not fill the glass in case you spill it, do not risk a hot drink, and avoid paper cups.

Face the audience and show enthusiasm:

- Vary the tone and volume of your voice.

- Make sure the people at the back of the room can hear.

- Keep your head up, do not speak to the floor.

- Above all, smile.

Try to transmit confidence:

- Be properly prepared.

- Dress comfortably, in clothes that give you confidence.

- Sit or stand in a relaxed position.

- Rest your hands, clasp them in front of you or hold onto your cue cards.

- Head up, shoulders back and remember always to smile.

You may feel dreadful on the inside, but this hardly ever shows on the outside.

Try not to:

- Move around too much – in particular, do not pace around the room.

- Jangle keys or fiddle with rings, clothes or hair.

- Stare out of the window.

- Focus on just one person or one part of the audience.

- Leave visual aids on view for longer than necessary.

If you ask questions, remember to allow time for answers. Tell the audience when they will be able to ask questions – either during or after the presentation. After is usually best.

## Distractions

Some distractions can be safely ignored – like a mobile phone ringing or a coughing fit from someone in the audience – others need immediate action. A fire alarm is the most obvious. Be prepared to ask somebody to close doors and windows if you are interrupted by pneumatic drills, police sirens or any other kind of noisy distraction.

Whispering or talking amongst the audience is impolite – you should not do it to others and they should not do it to you.

## Visual aids

Visual aids help an audience understand and remember. They increase impact and highlight or emphasise key points.

Visual aids add variety and interest because they:

- Give the audience a rest from focusing entirely on the speaker.

- Give the presenter support.

- Send a message that is stronger than words alone.

- Inform visually.

Everything should be simple, clear and easily seen from all parts of the room. Do not try to present too much information at one time.

## Flipcharts

Flipcharts can be prepared in advance, or you can write them during the presentation. They are good for showing diagrams and graphs, or for information you might want to 'revisit'.

They are only suitable for small groups. Write legibly in two or three colours, using marker pens for bold print – check that they can be read from the back of the room.

If you are preparing flipcharts beforehand, write only on every second or third sheet. The page underneath might show through the one on view. This breaks concentration and spoils impact.

## Overhead projectors, videos and audio tapes

An overhead projector (OHP) displays information printed or written onto acetate film sheets. The image is large and easy to see – useful for large audiences.

You can prepare the sheets in advance, or you can write them during the presentation – you can create, amend, or add information as you go.

OHPs are a good technique for showing diagrams and charts and for material you want to display more than once.

Practise with the machine. On the day, always check that it works, and focus the image before you begin. It is a good idea to have a spare bulb handy or even a back-up projector.

Turn the projector off between slides. The noise of the fan, the bright light and the blank screen is distracting.

Pre-recorded materials are powerful tools in moderation. Only use them for short clips and abstracts. You are the presenter, not just the machine operator.

## PowerPoint®

PowerPoint® is a Microsoft® word-processing application package designed to produce slides or handouts in a range of formats. The final product can be exceedingly polished and professional but is rarely suitable for absolute beginners – consider it for the presentations that you make later in the course.

Sophisticated support material can reduce, rather than enhance, the authority of your presentation if it is wrongly used. As with pre-recorded material, the presenter should not be seen merely as a button pusher or machine minder.

## Interactive boards

Electronic interactive boards are increasingly popular. Systems vary, but typically you will be able to display material that you have pre-prepared and saved to a disk or CD.

Interactive boards can help in putting together a superb presentation, but only with practice and familiarity.

## Handouts

Handouts are a very effective way of reinforcing and supporting spoken words. Do not prepare cluttered pieces of paper crammed with information – concentrate on key words and phrases. A handout of a diagram can save you the time and trouble of drawing it during your talk.

You should have no more than about four or five A4 sheets to support a 10-minute presentation. Each page must be headed and numbered.

The biggest problems with handouts are timing and distraction. If you distribute a full set of papers before you begin, some of the audience will switch off, or read rather than listen. Handing out single sheets as you go causes chaos and is best avoided. Unless you need a diagram or chart during the presentation, saving handouts until the end of the session is the safest option.

## Equipment, models and demonstrations

A demonstration is sometimes valuable or even essential. It is difficult, for example, to talk about body temperature without showing a thermometer.

Equipment and models must be simple, and demonstrations should be reliable.

If you are going to pass equipment or a model around the audience, obviously it must not be heavy, dangerous or fragile. You may need several examples – say, three or four thermometers for an audience of 30.

Audience participation makes for a memorable presentation, but think about timing. People find it difficult to settle back and refocus after a 'hands on' activity. This sort of thing is best left for later in the presentation.

# Chapter 4
# *Research skills*

## *National unit specification.*
## *These are the topics you will be studying for this unit:*

1   Take nothing for granted

2   Quantitative and qualitative research

3   Interviews

4   Questionnaires

5   Observational research

6   Results analysis and presentation

Research skills are taught and assessed as part of every unit and every pathway. You will find more background and extended coverage spread across a number of chapters:

| *More information on* | *Chapters* |
| --- | --- |
| Research as critical thinking | Literacy, numeracy and critical thinking |
| Literature research | Communication skills |
| Research design | The independent study project |
| Results and presentation | Application of number |

Depending on pathway, you may also be taking Scientific Communication and Method and/or Methods in Psychology as specialist units. Scientific Communication and Method looks at natural science research in considerable detail; Methods in Psychology does the same job for the social sciences.

# *1* Take nothing for granted

This chapter introduces a way of thinking that will be new to many. Its aim is to make you research aware. Like communication, research skills are a continuing theme of every unit from the beginning through to the end of the course.

All day, every day, we are bombarded by messages or information coming from other people and the world around us. We tend to take most of these for granted. Advertising, for instance, is all around us.

> 'This shampoo will make your hair four times smoother.'

> 'This disinfectant kills 99% of all household germs.'

Somebody who is research aware might ask the following questions:

- About the shampoo: Four times smoother than what? By implication, the advertisers are saying four times smoother than it was before, but the statement is not clear. How is smoothness compared? Who did the comparison?

- Turning to the disinfectant: What are household germs? Are they different from hospital, garden, office, factory or school germs? Where did the figure of 99% come from? Who did the measurements? What happened to the other 1%? Did they go on to become dangerous? How could we kill these resistant survivors?

## Innocents, cynics and sceptics

A total innocent believes everything and a complete cynic believes nothing. A sceptic is a person capable of independent, logical and critical thought. A sceptic is a critical thinker who rejects innocence and cynicism and comes to his or her own conclusions, based on the available evidence.

When presented with a new piece of information, a critical thinker will ask:

- Where did this information come from?

- Who produced it, and for what reason?

- Does the information include definitions of the terms and vocabulary it uses?

- Is the information based on assumptions or assertions?

- And – most important of all – what evidence is given to support the claims or statements made?

As part of the Access course, you will be encouraged to test your previous assumptions and beliefs. Some will stand up to critical thought and analysis, many will not. It is often difficult to exclude personal bias.

Innocents and cynics reach rapid and certain conclusions. An essential element of research awareness is to realise that life is usually not this simple. More often than not, critical thinkers will need more information and evidence before reaching a decision – they are not swayed by first impressions.

# Self confidence and self esteem

Research is a creative activity. It demands imagination and constant questioning. An inevitable bonus of becoming research aware is a major boost to self confidence and self esteem. You will soon learn that your views and conclusions are valuable – you should not rely on other people's opinions 'just because they say so'.

# What is research for?

Put at its simplest, research goes to the heart of human progress and development. It increases our knowledge and understanding of the world around us and the people that live in it. At a more practical level, we can distinguish between pure research and applied research.

Pure research is fuelled by curiosity. In the beginning, it may have no obvious or specific purpose.

Applied research is more familiar – it is aimed at solving a predetermined problem or giving answers to a closely defined question.

Research can also be sub-divided into description and explanation. Descriptive research is the collection of information; explanatory research looks for cause and effect. It asks questions like 'why does this happen?' and 'why do people behave like this?'.

## The scientific method

Research is based on the scientific method. The point of the method is to eliminate subjective judgements, personal opinion, guesswork and narrowly based intuition.

Medical research has shown that much of the folklore relating to health is erroneous. It has also found that some customs and traditions are beneficial and should be encouraged. Without the scientific method, it would be impossible to tell one from the other.

## Hypothesis

Meaningful research is not a haphazard affair. Prior thought and planning is always involved. Generally, experiments follow the same pattern.

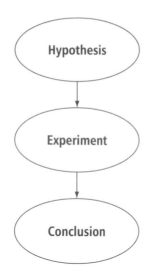

**Hypothesis** — A hypothesis is an idea or proposition to be tested.
It may be based on previous research.

**Experiment** — An experiment is designed to test the hypothesis.
It must be capable of proving the hypothesis false or of suggesting it may be correct.

**Conclusion** — The experiment reaches a conclusion concerning the hypothesis.
Conclusions nearly always indicate the need for further experimentation.

## Methods and process

The scientific method underpins all research, not just the traditional experimental sciences of chemistry and physics. Modern healthcare is based on the biopsychosocial model. Translated into plain English, this means that we now believe that health and well-being are a complicated interaction of biology, psychology and sociology. Health is not just the absence of diseases and disorders that can be detected by physical examinations and laboratory tests; it also depends on personal attitudes and beliefs, and on a society that encourages health and health-promoting behaviour. It follows that research in the health sector has to rely on many different methods, not just simple laboratory experiments.

## Research methods

We may further distinguish between the different methods used to describe, explain or predict how the world works and why things happen. The diagram (opposite) gives the detail.

## Data collection

The simple collection of descriptive data is the foundation of healthcare research. In the UK, there are legally enforced systems for data collection.

For instance, total UK population is measured by 10-yearly censuses. These also show population by region, county, city, town and district. Births, deaths and marriages have to be registered. Place, date and cause of death must be recorded. This gives data on life expectancy, infant mortality, birth rates, trends in diseases and disorders and so on.

The NHS and private health providers are legally obliged to collect, record and process a huge mass of health-related information. This includes admissions, procedures undertaken, length of stay, drugs administered and so on.

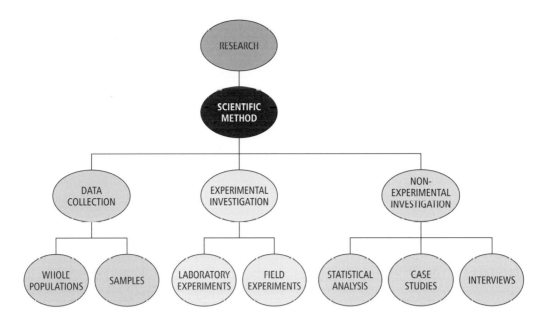

Data can be gathered from whole populations or from representative samples.

## Experimental investigations

The essence of experimental investigation is close control. Typically, two variables are the subject of the experiment and everything else is held constant and unchanging. Social science laboratory investigations are difficult and perhaps impossible. A chemist could determine the difference in melting points between two pure substances, but a sociologist could not precisely control all of the external factors that caused two groups of people to behave differently.

A field experiment is conducted under real, not laboratory, conditions. To investigate the behaviour of a crowd of football supporters, the investigator has to buy a ticket and go to a real football match.

## Non-experimental investigations

Some of the most valuable medical research takes place away from laboratories and without direct patient or client contact. The NHS employs many medical statisticians. Their work is to compare sets of descriptive data in an attempt to find correlations or associations between two or more variables.

Most of our knowledge concerning the influence of lifestyle on health started with statistical analysis. We know, for example, that lack of exercise and an unbalanced diet increases the risk of many diseases and disorders.

## Case studies

Case studies are widely used as teaching aids in medicine and healthcare. Usually, the progress of a particular client or group of clients is closely monitored through a course of treatment and then on to some final conclusion. Particular note is made of turning points observed or important decisions made by the practitioners involved. The case study is then documented or 'written up' in considerable detail and used as a model or simulation to train practitioners who are likely to face similar challenges in the future.

## Interviews, questionnaires and surveys

People are complicated. Behaviour and its motivation cannot be understood unless questions are asked and answers are analysed. Interviews, questionnaires and surveys are the basis of research in social science. These methods are considered in detail later in this chapter.

## Reliability and validity

All research ought to be reliable. This means that measurements must be accurate and consistent. Reliability is not often a problem in natural science research because we have invented instruments to measure things like temperature, length, weight and pressure. Reliability is always a problem in social science, because characteristics like aggression, depression and self esteem cannot be measured – they can only be judged or ranked.

Validity is a different idea. An experiment may be reliable but not valid. To take a simple example, a psychologist might ask an elderly patient: 'Who were the British prime ministers in 1946, 1956 and 1966?'. This investigation is completely reliable because there are only four possible scores – no right answers, or one, two or three correct replies. The question, however, may not be a valid test of long-term memory – it might only prove that the client was interested in politics, or, conversely, was not interested at all.

## Ethics

Social science research investigates people and their behaviour. Just because something can be done, it does not mean that it should be done. Ethics is about drawing lines and boundaries that must not be crossed. There are some fundamental principles:

- Ethical considerations must be built into the planning and design of every investigation.

- The researcher alone should not be free to make all ethical judgements. Professional bodies have ethical codes of conduct. Ethics committees of independent experts may allow or prohibit research. The final decision is theirs.

- Social science research must preserve human dignity, health and wellbeing. Health is defined in physical and psychological terms.

- Research without the informed consent of the participants or with deception is prohibited in all but the most extreme and exceptional circumstances.

- Consent may be withdrawn at any stage in an investigation or experiment. No reasons or justifications are required.

- Children or vulnerable adults, who may not be able to give informed consent, do not have second-class or inferior rights. Everything must be done to preserve their dignity, health and well-being. Reluctance to continue taking part in an investigation must be regarded as withdrawal.

- Confidentiality must be respected. It must be impossible to identify an individual from the published results of investigations.

- There should be no benefit of doubt. If ethical issues cannot be resolved, or if opinions are divided, the investigation must not proceed.

# 2 Quantitative and qualitative research

People have two kinds of characteristics – those that can be measured directly using tools and instruments, and those that cannot be measured but can be judged, ranked or assessed.

Quantitative research produces results which can be shown as quantities or numbers. For example, about 700,000 babies were born in the UK in the year 2000. Each of them was weighed at birth and their weights recorded. An average UK birth weight could be calculated.

There is also, for example, considerable qualitative research investigating women's views of the service provided by the NHS during pregnancy and childbirth. The results of these studies cannot be summarised by a single number – nevertheless, it is essential and genuine research.

Qualitative investigation in healthcare is concerned with thoughts, feelings and emotions. It has to be based on social interaction – through question and answer – because there is no instrument that can measure things like anxiety, confidence, optimism or depression.

## Measurement

There are four kinds of measurement:

- By category.

- By order or rank.

- By interval.

- By ratio.

### Category

Category measurement is straightforward and familiar. You might find that a patient or client was female, pregnant, AB blood group and a resident of Northamptonshire. For gender there are only two possibilities; likewise for pregnancy – you are either pregnant or not. There are four categories in the ABO blood group system, and you can only be one of these.

The fourth category – in this case, residence – can be manipulated by the investigator. An experiment might divide participants into two categories: those resident in Northamptonshire and all those that live elsewhere. The number of residence categories could be extended significantly if this was relevant to the investigation.

No hierarchy is presumed in category information. For example, being female and blood group AB is not better than being male and blood group O.

## Order, rank or sequence

Many measurements are expressed as a sequence or rank.

Ranking is a popular technique in consumer and market research. You might be asked to arrange 10 TV programmes or eight brands of soft drink into an order of preference. The word 'preference' is important. Market research tries to identify the most popular product – not the one that is best in any absolute sense.

In healthcare investigations, rank measurements usually try to establish some genuine hierarchy rather than just preferences. Patients can be asked to rank pain on a scale of 0 to 10, where 0 is freedom from pain and 10 is unbearable or excruciating. This technique is valuable but far from foolproof.

For any particular respondent we can be practically certain that a rating of 8 would be far worse than a rating of 2 given on a previous occasion, but this does not mean that 8 is four times worse than 2.

Interviews and questionnaires often use words instead of numbers to produce orders or ranks. The principles are identical.

### Example

Question:  *The accident and emergency service at Hospital X has improved over the last three years. Tick the box that most closely corresponds to your view.*

Answer:

| Strongly agree | Slightly agree | Do not agree or disagree | Slightly disagree | Strongly disagree |
|---|---|---|---|---|
|  |  |  |  |  |

## Interval and ratio measurements

Measurements by category or rank are difficult to analyse. Statistics like average, maximum or minimum values cannot always be calculated and comparisons between different sets of categories or ranks may have little meaning.

'Real' numbers and quantities do not present these problems because all of the common units of measurement work with fixed intervals. This may seem like a pointless glimpse of the obvious, but it is the foundation of all quantitative measurement and all science.

The difference between 101 g and 100 g is the same as the difference between 4 g and 3 g. This means that weight calculations always give precise and definitive answers. So 400 g is exactly twice as much as 200 g; 1 kg minus 300 g is precisely 700 g, and so on.

You cannot add, subtract, divide or multiply the results of experiments whose measurements involve categories or rankings.

## Objectivity, subjectivity and bias

It is important to remember that measurements in healthcare do not always produce true or real values. The characteristic being measured may be highly variable, so that a quantity recorded at any particular time may not be representative or typical of the client's true condition. Instrument accuracy varies, as does the skill and experience of the person doing the measuring.

Some measures are more objective than others and less likely to be influenced by human error and expectation. The most objective measurements are those involving simple or purpose-designed instruments like weighing machines or automated blood analysers.

Interviews and questionnaires work with subjective measures, so human bias is always a factor. Both the investigator and the participant can show bias. The investigator may expect a certain set of responses based on the client's appearance or manner. Unexpected responses can be seen as errors or of lesser significance.

Social desirability bias is common. Participants typically under-report behaviour like smoking, excessive alcohol consumption and unsafe sexual habits but over-report desirable characteristics like exercise and good diet.

A third kind of bias involves recall. Asking a participant to remember or describe past behaviour gives less reliable results than investigation of what the client did today or yesterday, for example.

## Populations and samples

Research begins with a hypothesis. For example:

'Regular exercise increases cardiovascular efficiency.'

'Wheelchair users have limited access to the NHS.'

'General practitioners working in the London borough of Newham are more highly stressed than GPs working in the London borough of Bromley.'

The target population for the first hypothesis could be everybody in the UK or even the entire population of the world.

The population for the second hypothesis is a smaller group with two shared characteristics – they are wheelchair users and potential clients of the NHS. It may, however, be difficult to define wheelchair user – does this include infre-quent or temporary use?

The third hypothesis is different. It defines precisely two groups and a total population of a few hundred.

All research has to operate within limited resources. There is never enough money, equipment or trained people to support all of the experiments and trials that might give valuable results. Most research works with samples selected from target populations. The word 'population' has a special meaning in statistical theory – it describes the entire group from which a sample is chosen. A population need not be a collection of people. A mechanical engineer might select a sample of bolts from a population of bolts for strength and safety testing.

It is not usually possible to test a whole population regardless of its size. In our third hypothesis, many of the London GPs would be too busy to spare time for a non-essential research project.

## Sampling methods

Statistical analysis is used to reach conclusions about populations based on sample measurements. Statistical theory breaks down if the sample is not representative of the population. A biased sample is the opposite of a repre-sentative one.

It is sometimes difficult to select a representative sample and even more difficult to confirm that the sample is representative. Returning to the GP stress hypothesis, those that volunteered to take part in a survey are likely to be less stressed than the population overall. Special methods would be needed to select representative samples from both groups of GPs.

Random sampling is the most statistically reliable method. A sample is truly random if every member of a population has an equal chance of selection and if the choice of one member does not influence the chances of another member being chosen.

Many populations have some kind of identifying number – typically a patient number or a National Insurance number. Special computer software has been designed to select random samples from these large groups.

## Primary and secondary sources

Information gathered via your own research, or by others conducting an experiment that you have designed, is called a primary source. Everything else is a secondary source.

Because research is a continuing process, secondary sources are always used in the development of new hypotheses and new original research projects.

# *3* Interviews

The word 'interview' usually describes a process with inbuilt stress and tension. The police interview suspects; job candidates are usually outnumbered by their interviewers; TV commentators interview or 'grill' politicians in front of audiences of millions.

In social science, interview techniques are designed to minimise stress. They are private in all but the most exceptional circumstances and only rarely include more than two people – the interviewer or researcher, and the interviewee or participant.

Interviews are used to investigate behaviour that cannot be observed, or at least not ethically observed. The technique can also be used to research reasons for particular behaviour patterns or to reconstruct significant past events.

There are three kinds of interview:

- Unstructured.
- Semi-structured.
- Structured.

## Unstructured interviews

An unstructured interview has no formal agenda and, within reasonable limits, no fixed time frame. They allow a great deal of freedom for both parties and opportunities to develop any relevant issue. Participants are likely to feel relaxed and to talk with few inhibitions.

## Semi-structured interviews

In a semi-structured interview, the investigator starts with a list of general headings or topics for discussion – the interview has a predetermined goal or objective. Some freedom is allowed but the interviewer does not depart for long from a defined schedule. Semi-structured interviews are less demanding for the researcher than unstructured techniques.

One disadvantage is that valuable information may be lost if it does not fit readily into the chosen framework. Bias is also a risk, because the extent to which questions may be reworded or re-sequenced is difficult to decide as you go along.

## Structured interviews

Aside from privacy, there is very little difference between a fully structured interview and a questionnaire that is delivered through face-to-face meeting. A number of questions are devised and usually printed in full on a pre-prepared form. The investigator asks the questions precisely as written and in a sequence that should not be altered. Only a limited number of responses are catered for – often the researcher will tick one of several boxes that best matches the participant's response. Structured interviews are usually time-limited and shorter than the semi-structured or unstructured alternatives.

The results of structured interviews are easy to analyse. Cross comparisons amongst groups of participants can be straightforward because all have been asked the same questions in the same way. The investigator need not be highly skilled.

Structured interviews are not useful, and usually not ethical, as tools to investigate sensitive or complex issues. The interviewer may also misinterpret replies and the participant may not understand some questions. There are no opportunities to correct these misunderstandings.

## Interview techniques

You think interview techniques might give useful information for the independent study project. Ask yourself these questions:

- How and where will you find the people you need to interview?

- How many respondents should you contact?

- How long will the whole exercise take?

- How will you record the interview results?

- Will you be asking sensitive or delicate questions?

- Do you have enough background and experience to approach this issue with empathy and tact?

# Closed and open questions

Two kinds of questions can be included in interviews and questionnaires.

Closed questions demand definitive answers or a restricted choice of replies. These are used mainly in quantitative research like structured interviews and most questionnaires.

Closed questions may compel respondents into inappropriate or inaccurate choices – with an inevitable loss of valuable information. One advantage is that closed questions are time efficient and easy to document and analyse. For example:

'How long did you stay in hospital following your hip operation?'

Open questions are commonly part of qualitative research – answers are not pre-specified in any way. They give freedom of response, allowing a much wider range of replies. For example:

'Do you feel you were discharged from hospital too soon after your hip operation?'

Open questions are more difficult for both the investigator and the participant. They have to be devised with care and replies usually require much thought and effort.

## Closed and open questions

Think of a topic that interests you. Devise two sets of questions to investigate this topic – five closed questions and five open questions.

Interview a friend or classmate and make detailed notes on his or her replies for each set of five questions.

- Were the responses as you expected?

- Did you have to prompt the interviewee or give more information?

- Was anything unclear or ambiguous?

- How long did the interview last?

- Would you delete or change any of the questions if you repeated the exercise?

# *4* Questionnaires

A questionnaire is a list of questions designed to collect information from a relatively large group. There are overlaps and similarities between some interview and some questionnaire techniques. Interviews and questionnaires may be combined and targeted at large audiences – this research is one kind of survey.

## Survey methods

A survey need not involve face-to-face contact between an interviewer and a series of participants. Questionnaires can be delivered by post, by electronic means like email, or they may be circulated among defined groups like the employees of an organisation, students at a school or college, or members of a particular occupation or profession. Some market research is conducted via telephone surveys.

The physical separation of investigator and respondent has benefits. Postal surveys can be much cheaper than transporting teams of people around the country, and they eliminate the possibility of investigator bias. However, postal and circulated surveys have many disadvantages:

- You cannot be sure that the addressee – the carefully selected participant – actually completed the survey. It might have been answered by a friend, partner or relative.

- It is impossible to judge the truthfulness of any response. This is a general problem for all social science research but some interview techniques and some interviewers can spot and eliminate lies, half-truths and fantasy.

- The participant can read all of the questions before choosing replies. Sequenced or structured questioning to investigate an issue in greater depth is impossible.

Low or unpredictable response rates are the greatest disadvantage. There are two problems:

- A survey becomes very costly if only a small percentage of questionnaires are returned. Market research companies offer incentives, but even so, typical response rates can be less than 1%.

- More importantly, low response rates produce biased samples. People that always return surveys are not usually representative of most target populations.

# Designing a survey

As part of the assessment for this unit you may be asked to design and conduct a survey. This will be a rewarding exercise, provided you tackle the project in a logical sequence.

- You need to start with a formally written hypothesis. What proposition are you testing? What information are you looking for?

- The hypothesis defines the target population. How will you contact them? How will you confirm the validity of the survey sample?

- At the outset, you need to decide how the survey results will be processed and analysed.

- You next need to devise a set of draft questions. It is nearly always a good idea to run a preliminary trial of these with fellow students or colleagues. This will identify problem areas.

- All questionnaires have to be supported by a checklist, a form or a document of some kind. Once questions have been finalised, the form can be designed.

We can now look at each of these stages in detail.

## Hypothesis and target population

The hypothesis may be general, specific or comparative. In the first case, no special precautions are needed to identify the respondents for a survey – almost anybody will do. The more general the survey, the less valuable its results are likely to be – usually this kind of research is only descriptive.

Most hypotheses are specific and are aimed at slices or sub-sets of the overall population, for example mothers with young children, retired men, car mechanics, etc.

Sometimes your survey will want to compare two different groups, such as smokers and non-smokers or men and women.

From the beginning you need to have a firm idea of sample size – too small and its results will be unreliable, too large and you will not have time to complete the exercise. There are no hard and fast rules, but 50 respondents is the minimum sample size for most hypotheses. Similarly, you ought to have a target interview time allocation for each interview. This translates into the number of questions you are going to ask. Most surveys have between 15 and 30 questions. The fewer the better, provided the questions are well designed.

## Processing and analysis

This aspect of survey design must be considered before the work begins, never once you are faced with a pile of completed questionnaires. The replies to closed questions are relatively easy to handle. Usually these are coded or ranked to produce percentages or some measure of average and range. Open questions are more difficult. Often these can only be summarised using a qualitative commentary.

## Question design

Again, you must start with the hypothesis. What information is essential and what secondary information might be useful? If your hypothesis is selective or comparative, the first one or two questions need to be identifiers or quota questions. For instance, a survey on car preference ought to start with 'Do you own or have use of a car?'.

Comparative surveys need to establish quotas. A survey comparing male and female behaviour would obviously be unreliable if you interviewed 48 women and six men. Gender is usually self-evident but some quotas may not be as easy to define.

The framing, phrasing or wording of the questions themselves is never easy. There are many traps and pitfalls for the unwary and the inexperienced. The key ideas are clarity and brevity.

## Questions not to ask

Vague questions are pointless. For example, 'Do you eat fruit regularly?' leaves the respondent to decide what regularly means – is it once a day, once a week, once a month or every Christmas? Better alternatives would be 'Do you eat at least one portion of fruit a day?' or 'On an average day, how many portions of fruit do you eat?'.

Double questions should be avoided because accurate replies might be impossible. For instance, 'Do you like watching football and cricket on television?'. Participants might like one or the other, both or neither.

Some single questions can have double answers. These should also be avoided. A respondent might be asked if he or she is an employee, self-employed, part-time, full-time or unemployed. Most of us could tick two boxes in answer to this question.

Leading questions are the commonest fault in questionnaires. By accident, a question can be worded so that one type of answer is more likely than another, regardless of the participant's real views. 'What is it that you like about your Access course?' is a leading question. An alternative might be 'What part of your Access course do you most enjoy?'.

Hypothetical questions usually give meaningless answers. For instance, 'If you were a surgeon, what would you regard as an acceptable salary?'.

Questions including jargon, technical terms or those that require calculations should only be included if the target population is certain to have the appropriate skills or background. Surveys aimed at nurses can safely use words like 'hypertension' and 'spontaneous abortion'. For a more general audience, 'high blood pressure' and 'miscarriage' would be better words.

Social desirability bias is a big problem in question design and one that cannot always be overcome. The more sensitive the question, the more neutral and unbiased the wording must be. Any hint of judgement or criticism should be eliminated.

## Unethical questions

Even as a student, your research survey must conform to the codes of the appropriate or local ethics committee.

Offensive questions are not permitted under any circumstances. More importantly, the person designing the research might be a poor judge of what is likely to cause offence. Some areas are obviously inappropriate for public survey research, but other issues can cause unexpected problems. Age and income are the best examples. Questions concerning income should not be included if at all possible and many respondents will refuse to divulge their age, even within five- or ten-year brackets.

You should always discuss potential ethical problems with teaching staff and supervisors. Sensitive questions give biased results, especially if sample size is reduced by many refusals.

## Question sequence

The ordering of questions is important. There are some general rules:

- The simplest closed questions, including the identifiers and quota questions, should come first.

- Sequence is vital for linked questions, and the more complex issues and open questions should be saved for the end of the list.

- If you are asking participants to choose one of a number of options, these should not be placed in what you think is the likely order of popularity.

- Many surveys are designed so that not all respondents are required to answer all the questions. Make sure that instructions like 'If the answer to question 4 is no, please go to question 10' are clear and accurate.

## Designing the forms

A traditional survey involves an interviewer asking questions of a participant with the interviewer completing a form or document. Two people are present and interacting, but only the interviewer needs to be able to understand and navigate his or her way around the form.

In postal surveys, no interviewer is present, so it follows that the form – the questionnaire itself – must be clear, precise and user-friendly.

Other variants are possible. The participant might fill out the questionnaire with the interviewer offering help and assistance as needed.

Therefore, first you have to decide if the interviewer or the participant will be filling in the form.

The document has to be prepared and presented to a high standard. Grammar, punctuation and spelling must be perfect and questions have to be clearly numbered with enough space allocated for any reasonable reply. The questionnaire should be word-processed. Remember, many people have trouble reading font sizes smaller than 11 point – 12 point is better. It is false economy to cram 20 questions onto two A4 pages when three or four pages would give a cleaner, clearer layout.

Be creative in the use of lines, borders, tick boxes and different font sizes. Sometimes arrows can help to indicate sequence, but the end result should not look fussy or cramped.

At the beginning of the survey, explain its purpose clearly and briefly. Where possible, guarantees of confidentiality and privacy should be given. A postal survey should show a completion or closing date for last returns.

At the end of the questionnaire, you should thank participants for their time and trouble.

The questionnaire itself is not the only piece of paper you will need to design. You will also need a control document of some kind. For traditional interview and questionnaire surveys, this should show:

- Date, time and place where participants were interviewed. Often a time period is sufficient rather than precise details for each interview.

- Quota tallies if needed – for example, running totals of male and female respondents.

- A record of the number of refusals and the numbers, if any, who refused to complete the survey or parts of the survey after initial agreement.

- A note of any exceptional conditions.

## Questionnaires

Questionnaires are a very popular general technique for collecting information. You will find examples in most newspapers and magazines. Cut and copy three or four. Try to find a mix of topics and issues – serious as well as trivial.

Look at each questionnaire in detail:

- What mix of open and closed questions is used?
- How is the questionnaire laid out and sequenced?
- Are the instructions clear and user friendly?
- How long did it take to complete?
- Did the questionnaire hold your interest?
- Were there questions which you could not or would not answer?
- If you are told how to analyse the results, do you think this is a fair or reasonable way to do it?

# 5 Observational research

In one way or another, all research is observational because it is an essential part of the experimental design sequence. That is:

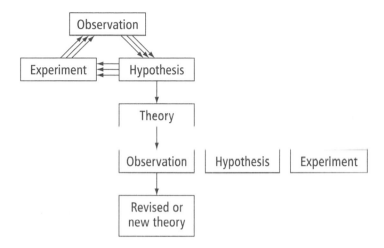

In the social sciences, observational research has a narrower meaning. There are two categories – non-participant and participant observation.

## Non-participant observation

Here, the observer takes no part in the behaviour being observed. Ideally, the observation should not be detectable by the subjects of the research. The investigator merely watches, listens and takes notes.

These experiments can give valuable insights into normal or natural behaviour.

Non-participant observation can be used to study behaviour in circumstances that would be difficult or unethical to simulate. In a large general hospital, for example, simply sitting in an outpatient waiting room or in an accident and emergency centre might reveal a great deal about individuals in stressful or irritating situations.

Non-participant observational techniques do, however, have many drawbacks:

- It is often impossible to avoid detection for more than brief periods. Abnormal or unrepresentative behaviour is virtually guaranteed if people think they are being watched.

- This research is qualitative, difficult to analyse and difficult to duplicate or confirm. Two different observers often reach different conclusions.

- There is major scope for misinterpretation and error. It is, for instance, impossible to prove cause and effect. You could observe or hear raised voices, but this might be usual behaviour for the subjects concerned, not a response to a three-hour wait in casualty.

## Non-participant observation

To collect information about food choices and eating habits, you decide to observe the behaviour of students and staff in the college restaurant or canteen.

- How will you do this?
- What are the advantages and disadvantages of this technique?

# Participant observation

With this technique, the observer becomes part of the group or situation under study. Deception need not be involved – a lecturer might ask to 'sit in' on a discussion or debate between two groups of students, for example.

Deception or pretence must, however, be used if a research project is not to be influenced by the presence of an 'outsider'. A researcher wanting to understand how a building site works might get a job as a bricklayer's labourer and observe from the inside, not revealing his or her true profession.

The degree of involvement in participant observation can vary. Ideally, the observer should have the smallest possible influence on the group under study, consistent with an ability to make and record meaningful observations.

A health researcher might decide to join a smoking cessation self-help group posing as a non-expert. Clearly, this researcher should avoid being elected chairman or secretary of the group.

All of the problems of analysis, reliability and misinterpretation apply more or less equally to participant and non-participant observation. Participant research can be conducted in greater depth, but its results are inevitably biased, unless the researcher is exceedingly competent and experienced.

# Observational research ethics

Many research supervisors and ethics committees take strong positions against observational research, especially participant experimental designs. It is difficult to deny the argument that the more valuable the results become, the more unethical the investigation is likely to be.

There can be little objection to simple anonymous observation in public spaces or situations, but anything more needs careful consideration. As a generalisation, an alternative technique should be chosen if at all possible. The dividing lines between observation, snooping and spying are very narrow and difficult to draw.

## Participant observation

You want to investigate weight loss, so you decide to join a slimming club as part of your research design.

- How do you gain access to the group?

- Will your observations be open or secret – that is, overt or covert?

- How will you record what you see and hear?

- Will you alter the natural behaviour of the group?

- Are you behaving ethically?

- If you have chosen to be a covert observer, should you become friends with one or more of the group?

- What will happen if or when the group discovers your real motives?

- Will your research be biased if you do not lose weight, or if you reach your target weight rapidly and easily?

# 6 Results analysis and presentation

Results can be presented as numbers or pictures.

The pictorial presentations you need to understand are:

- Tables
- Graphs
- Pie charts
- Bar charts and histograms.

The numerical presentations you need to understand are:

- Average or arithmetic mean
- Median
- Mode
- Range.

## Tables

Tables are familiar but often badly used and presented. There are some basic rules:

- A table must have a title so that it can be extracted from your report and used by another researcher.
- Every row and column should be headed.
- You should show totals for each row and column and a grand total at the bottom right-hand corner if appropriate. Consider giving totals and subtotals in bold print.
- Figures in columns should be right-aligned, for example:

| WRONG | WRONG | RIGHT |
|---|---|---|
| *Left-aligned* | *Centred* | *Right-aligned* |
| 1,042 | 1,042 | 1,042 |
| 131 | 131 | 131 |
| 24 | 24 | 24 |

- Very large tables with many rows and columns are difficult to read. Split or divide into several smaller ones if possible.

- Often tables make more sense if values are given as percentages rather than absolute numbers. Sometimes it helps to show both.

- Always check additions and subtotals. Rounding may be needed with percentages.

### Example

An investigation of attitudes towards smoking, by age

Question – 'Smoking should be banned in all public places.'
Location – Exeter, May 2002

|  | 15 to 24 | 25 to 34 | 35 to 44 | 45 to 54 | 55 to 64 | 65+ | Total |
|---|---|---|---|---|---|---|---|
| Strongly agree | 10 | 21 | 12 | 7 | 12 | 8 | 70 |
| Slightly agree | 8 | 9 | 8 | 9 | 20 | 17 | 71 |
| No strong view | 5 | 3 | 8 | 7 | 5 | 2 | 30 |
| Slightly disagree | 12 | 10 | 4 | 4 | 6 | 11 | 47 |
| Strongly disagree | 6 | 6 | 2 | 4 | 7 | 12 | 37 |
| Total respondents | 41 | 49 | 34 | 31 | 50 | 50 | 255 |

These numbers are much easier to understand if they are further summarised and turned into percentages.

'Smoking should be banned in all public places.'

| Age bracket | Strongly or slightly agree (%) | No strong views (%) | Strongly or slightly disagree (%) | Total (%) |
|---|---|---|---|---|
| 15 to 24 | 44 | 12 | 44 | 100 |
| 25 to 34 | 61 | 6 | 33 | 100 |
| 35 to 44 | 59 | 23 | 18 | 100 |
| 45 to 54 | 52 | 22 | 26 | 100 |
| 55 to 64 | 64 | 10 | 26 | 100 |
| 65 plus | 50 | 4 | 46 | 100 |
| Total | 55 | 12 | 33 | 100 |

# Graphs

A graph is a picture or pictorial representation of information. It is an excellent way of summarising a complex set of results.

The raw material or starting point for the simplest graphs is a two-column table showing the observed relationship between two things or variables.

## Example

Average ambulance response times to emergency calls in region X during 2003, by month

| Month, 2003 | Average response* time in minutes |
|---|---|
| January | 16 |
| February | 16 |
| March | 10 |
| April | 11 |
| May | 8 |
| June | 7 |
| July | 6 |
| August | 9 |
| September | 9 |
| October | 11 |
| November | 12 |
| December | 14 |

*Response time is defined as the time elapsed between receiving an emergency call and the arrival of the first ambulance at the accident or emergency scene.*

You should note that we are already working with summarised or condensed information. A response time of, for example, 15 minutes in January would be an average of many call-outs.

A pattern is detectable from the table but a graph gives a clearer and more immediate idea of what really happened.

## Axes, origins and scales

You can draw a graph by hand or by using a computer package. In both cases, the rules are the same:

- The horizontal line or axis is called the *x* axis – remember 'x is across'.

- The vertical line or axis is called the *y* axis – remember 'wise up'.

- The point at the bottom left-hand corner of the graph where the two axes meet is called the origin.

- By convention, time is always shown on the horizontal or *x* axis because most of us imagine time as flowing forward or from left to right. In other graphs there are no strict rules governing which variable should be shown on which axis. Choose the clearer or more logical layout.

- Each axis has to be labelled and divided into equal intervals. For instance, in our example (opposite), one unit equals one month or one minute of response time.

- Each point on the graph is called a plot or a plot point. These are usually marked with a small cross, dot or circle.

- In most presentations, the plot points are joined together. This is the plot line.

The graph shows the results of the ambulance investigation. Abbreviated labelling is perfectly acceptable, provided the labels are clear – in this case Jan for January, and so on. You will also notice that this particular graph has a false origin. In other words, the vertical scale starts at five minutes not zero minutes. Using false origins usually gives better presentation.

Drawing graphs takes time and patience. Always check the final version against the original tabulated results.

You will often see two or three sets of information or plot lines on a single graph. In our example, you could also show ambulance response times by month for the previous year using a dotted plot line for 2002. In multiple presentations, accurate labelling is essential.

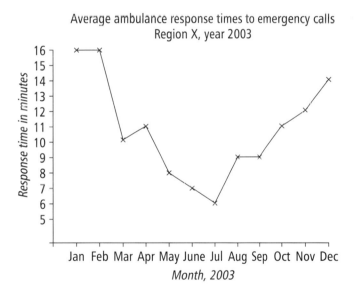

Average ambulance response times to emergency calls
Region X, year 2003

# Pie charts

Pie charts are the best way of presenting most category information. They are frequently used in newspapers and magazines because they are so easy to understand. You need to know how to put together a pie chart. Again, the start point is tabulated information, for example:

**Family size in region A, December 1991**

| Women who have given birth to: | Number of women |
|---|---|
| no children | 180 |
| one child | 213 |
| two children | 593 |
| three children | 298 |
| four children | 92 |
| five or more children | 51 |
| Total respondents | 1,427 |

Incidentally, the heading for this table shows the importance of precise wording. Family size could be judged in other ways, for example to include stepchildren or adopted children, or by research involving couples or fathers. Each experimental design would produce a different set of numbers. An appropriately worded questionnaire would avoid sensitive issues like marital status and stillbirths.

## Percentages and angles

A pie chart is a circle divided into a number of segments or slices. A full circle has 360 degrees, so we have to calculate the angle for each slice.

### Example

| Category | Number | % of total | % of 360° 'slice angle' |
|---|---|---|---|
| no children | 180 | 13 | 47 |
| 1 child | 213 | 15 | 54 |
| 2 children | 593 | 42 | 151 |
| 3 children | 298 | 21 | 76 |
| 4 children | 92 | 6 | 22 |
| 5+ children | 51 | 3 | 10 |
| Total | 1,427 | 100 | 360 |

The calculations only need to be accurate to the nearest degree and percentage point.

A pie chart can be drawn by hand using a protractor and compasses or with a specialist computer software package. By convention, the first slice usually starts at the 12 o'clock position and you work clockwise around the circle.

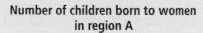

**Number of children born to women
in region A**

Research conducted December 1991

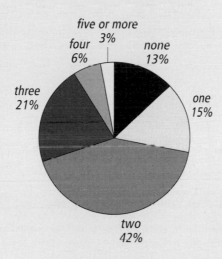

The segments can be shaded or coloured. Pie charts should not be used to show sub-divisions into more than about 10 categories – the chart then becomes very difficult to read. It is good practice to show a pie chart alongside the table of original results. Others can then choose between detailed or summary information.

You cannot tell from this chart or table how many women have five, six or more children because these large families are grouped together under one heading. Summary presentations always sacrifice some detail for the sake of clarity and easy understanding.

# Bar charts and histograms

Graphs and pie charts are not suitable for presenting the results of large investigations. Bar charts and histograms are better, in particular for continuous variables – things that are measured rather than counted.

## Example

An outpatient clinic treats people suffering from anorexia nervosa. Clients are weighed regularly and it is thought that weight after six months from first attendance at the clinic is a good indicator of progress. Over a period of years, the clinic has collected 4,216 six-month weight recordings. Clients are weighed very accurately so nearly all the recordings are different. It would be difficult to draw a graph or pie chart to show this much information.

# Classified information

Bar charts and histograms work with classified data. In our example, each of the 4,216 measurements would be allocated to a class or category.

The data is first examined to find a maximum and minimum value and then the range or difference between the two.

*Example*

| | |
|---|---|
| Heaviest patient | 59.3 kg |
| Lightest patient | 32.1 kg |
| Range | 27.2 kg |

This range of 27.2 kg can be accommodated within 10 weight bands, each of 3 kg. It is important that each weight band is the same size. The clearest bar charts have between eight and about 15 classes – there are no strict rules. The table shows the 4,216 measurements grouped into 10 classes.

| Eating disorders clinic, Hospital B 1996 to 2003 | | |
|---|---|---|
| Class | Six-month weight (kg) | Number of patients in each weight class |
| 1 | 32–34.9 | 48 |
| 2 | 35–37.9 | 107 |
| 3 | 38–40.9 | 499 |
| 4 | 41–43.9 | 692 |
| 5 | 44–46.9 | 1,042 |
| 6 | 47–49.9 | 989 |
| 7 | 50–52.9 | 570 |
| 8 | 53–55.9 | 201 |
| 9 | 56–58.9 | 56 |
| 10 | 59–61.9 | 12 |
| | | 4,216 |

Finally, the table of classified information is used to draw the bar chart or histogram – the two presentations are very similar. A bar chart uses simple vertical lines; a histogram shows the same information as adjoining blocks. Most people find histograms easier to understand.

Often the class information can be shown in full detail on the horizontal scale* – if not, an explanatory key must be given.

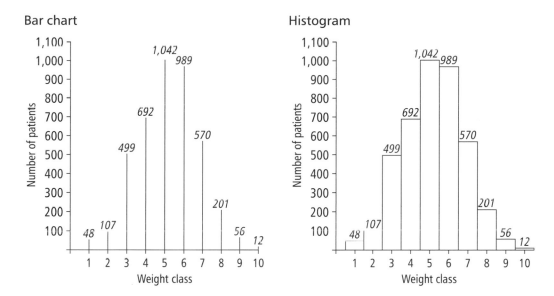

Bar chart

Histogram

## Averages or arithmetic means

The average, properly called the arithmetic mean, is the most commonly used statistic. It can, however, be misleading.

### Example

Three groups of five-year-old boys had their heights measured to the nearest centimetre. The results were as follows:

| Boy number | Set A (cm) | Set B (cm) | Set C (cm) |
|---|---|---|---|
| 1 | 107 | 104 | 96 |
| 2 | 108 | 105 | 96 |
| 3 | 108 | 106 | 98 |
| 4 | 108 | 107 | 99 |
| 5 | 108 | 107 | 105 |
| 6 | 108 | 110 | 119 |
| 7 | 108 | 110 | 119 |
| 8 | 108 | 111 | 119 |
| 9 | 109 | 112 | 121 |
| Total | 972 cm | 972 cm | 972 cm |
| Average | **108 cm** | **108 cm** | **108 cm** |

The three groups have the same average height.

If these were the results of an investigation into the influence of diet on growth, then the average height, used in isolation, would miss some important differences between the groups – it does not take account of variation or spread.

You can tell just by looking that Set C is much more varied than Set B, which in turn varies more than Set A. A five-year-old boy of 121 cm is exceptionally tall for his age; one of 96 cm is unusually short.

# Median

The median is perhaps best described as another kind of average that makes some allowances for variation. It is simply the middle number of a set once it has been arranged into ascending or descending order. In this example, the median height is that of boy number five – therefore:

Four boys are taller than the median boy and four are shorter. It does not matter that, in Set A and Set B, more than one boy is the median height.

|        | Median height (cm) |
| ------ | ------------------ |
| Set A  | 108                |
| Set B  | 107                |
| Set C  | 105                |

The median is calculated slightly differently if the group has an even rather than an odd number of members. Say we removed boy 9 from Set C:

There are now two middle boys, number 4 and number 5. The median is the average of their two heights:

| Boy number | Set C minus boy 9 (cm) |
| ---------- | ---------------------- |
| 1          | 96                     |
| 2          | 96                     |
| 3          | 98                     |
| 4          | 99                     |
| 5          | 105                    |
| 6          | 119                    |
| 7          | 119                    |
| 8          | 119                    |

|               | Height (cm) |
| ------------- | ----------- |
| Boy 4         | 99          |
| Boy 5         | 105         |
| Median height | 102         |

# Mode

The mode of a set of numbers is simply the most common or the one there is most of. All groups of numbers must have an average and a median, but they need not have a mode, or there might be two or more modes or modal values.

|  | Mode or modal height (cm) |
|---|---|
| Set A | 108 |
| Set B | 107 and 110 |
| Set C | 119 |

The mode looks like an odd statistic at first glance, but it is sometimes used in healthcare to describe the usual value of a characteristic in a population. Remember that 'usual' need not mean desirable. The modal body weight in developed countries, for example, is higher than the ideal weight for nearly all age groups apart from infants and the very elderly.

Modes are widely used in economic research. The strength of a local economy can be judged by the difference between the modal pay rate and the national minimum wage. The greater the gap, the stronger the local economy.

# Range

Range is calculated very easily if a set of numbers is placed in order. It is the difference between the maximum and minimum values.

**Example**

|  | Maximum height (cm) | Minimum height (cm) | Range |
|---|---|---|---|
| Set A | 109 | 107 | 2 |
| Set B | 112 | 104 | 8 |
| Set C | 121 | 96 | 25 |

Range is a useful measure of variation for small groups of numbers that are very differently spread – like our example.

# Chapter 5

# The independent study project

## National unit specification.
## These are the topics you will be studying for this unit:

1. What is the independent study project?
2. Choosing a topic
3. Proposals and timetables
4. Structure
5. The written report
6. Abstracts
7. The verbal presentation

An independent study project is one of the compulsory units for all Access pathways, but unlike the other skills and disciplines that we have called the essentials, it is timetabled for the end of the course, not the beginning.

We suggest you will need to read or consult this chapter at least twice – once in outline during the first term and again in detail when you come to planning and preparing your individual project.

# *1* What is the independent study project?

The title of this unit almost describes itself.

You will be helped and supported every step of the way but the work itself is an individual, independent effort. The final report carries your name alone and you will be making all of the important decisions concerning its subject, scope, structure, methods, sequence and presentation.

## Negotiation

Subject choice is negotiated between each student and a tutor, who will be assigned to supervise the project from start to finish. The supervisor may be a specialist lecturer or your personal tutor. Most colleges will ask you to write a brief proposal to support the choice you have made – before you start the work itself.

It does no harm to start thinking through the issues that interest you most once you have settled into the first term. Your ideas will almost certainly change and develop – keep notes in your reflective diary of how you are thinking and feeling.

## Bringing it all together

The project allows you to bring together all of the skills and techniques learned during the course, together with knowledge acquired from some specialist units. It demonstrates an ability to find and use appropriate information sources, organise research and write a reasoned, well-constructed report.

You will also be asked to present your report, in brief, to a small group – most often your classmates and a project supervisor.

## More work, more credit

The target word count for the independent study is not the same for all issues and topics, but plan on a total of between 3,000 and 6,000 words.

The project obviously involves more work than other units. This is recognised in two ways. The time allocation is generous and you will be given several months' notice of final submission dates. The project earns more credits towards the final certificate. Typically, it is worth three credits at level three compared with one credit at level three for each of the natural or social science units.

# 2 Choosing a topic

It probably helps to start with the reasons for not choosing a topic. The object of the exercise is to give students as much freedom and opportunity for creativity as possible – there are not many exclusions.

## What not to choose

Original proposals are often too ambitious in terms of time, cost or effort. In conversation with your supervisor, a feasible project sometimes emerges by limiting or editing an initial good idea. Any project needing significant travel is unlikely to be workable.

You will be strongly discouraged from choosing a topic in which you, or one of your close family, are personally involved. This restriction seems odd at first, but with a little more thought it makes good sense. If your child is autistic, for example, and you are unhappy with the care he or she is getting, then a project on this topic is likely to become an emotional crusade. You will find it difficult or impossible to present a balanced case.

For the same reasons, do not choose a morally or religiously contentious issue if your faith or beliefs make it impossible for you to support one side of the argument.

Personal involvement can be difficult to define – there are always grey areas. These problems are easily resolved through open and honest conversations with your project supervisor.

You should not choose a topic that relies exclusively or very heavily on one specialist unit. Above all, the supervisor will want to see a mix of the social and natural sciences in your proposal – for example, it must not be all biochemistry or all sociology.

## How to choose

Most students are spoilt for choice. Their problem is deciding amongst several equally attractive alternatives. You may start the course without a special interest but quickly discover which areas best suit your personality, aptitudes and background. Your supervisor will help. He or she will suggest brief preparatory or comparative research – a final decision is then much easier to make.

If you have no ideas and the starting deadline is approaching, there are a number of alternatives:

- Discuss the problem with classmates who have already chosen a topic. Their ideas may trigger an idea, approach or issue you had not considered before.

- Talk to the person who teaches your favourite subject. They will often suggest a topic based on the material you most enjoy and find easiest to understand.

- Current issues are fertile ground for the independent study project. Get hold of the most recent copies of the more serious Sunday papers and a selection of specialist journals. Even a headline can spark a good idea.

# The research question

Hypothesis (plural: hypotheses) is just another name for the question whose investigation is the point of your project. Titles that are not framed as questions are hardly ever acceptable – the project is research based, not just a descriptive or historical essay.

Here are some examples of how it should and should not be done:

| Likely to be accepted | Likely to be rejected |
|---|---|
| Does childhood health benefit from a rural environment? | Some aspects of child health in rural North Wales |
| Why are some women frightened of 'the pill'? | A brief history of female contraception |
| Have we finally conquered infectious disease in the UK? | How mankind defeated smallpox |
| Should primary care be the first priority for scarce NHS cash and manpower? | The funding of the NHS |
| How will the role of the GP change over the next 10 years? | The best GP I have ever met |
| Why do teenage girls start smoking? | The relationship between smoking and social class |
| Should the treatment of sports injuries be free on the NHS? | My knee operation |
| Why do some parents refuse immunisation for their children? | The biochemical basis of immunisation |

# 3 Proposals and timetables

Your college may have its own rules, but the study topic choice is usually finalised in two stages. The first of these is a series of informal conversations with your supervisor, followed by a structured written proposal. During the first stage, you need to think about:

- The scope and workload. Have you taken on too much? Or is the issue too narrowly defined? 'Biting off more than you can chew' is a common problem – you may need to add words, qualifications or limits to the hypothesis.

- How will you collect the information you need to answer or investigate the research question? The more techniques you choose, the better the project is likely to be.

- What are the ethical issues? Will your project only work if strangers are prepared to disclose personal or sensitive information in interviews, surveys or questionnaires? How will you safeguard their privacy and confidentiality?

- How will you process or analyse the information collected?

## The proposal

The written proposal form will look something like this.

| Proposal for Independent Study | |
|---|---|
| **Name:** | |
| **Title:** | Your objective, question or hypothesis. |
| **Introduction:** | What is your study about, and why have you chosen the subject? |
| **Aim:** | What do you hope to achieve? |
| **Research method:** | What research methods will you use? Will you use existing data or collect new information by observation, interview or survey? Why? Ethical issues – how will you ensure privacy and confidentiality? |
| **Resources required:** | Computer access, library material, financial considerations, for instance: paper, postage, telephone calls, photocopying, and transport. |
| **Tutor's comments:** | |
| **Date:** | |

Important aspects of the proposal may change as evidence accumulates and your investigation moves forward. This is good news, not bad, provided you keep your supervisor fully in touch and up to date. Be ready to submit modified proposals as work progresses.

# Timetables

You may be asked to submit a timetable to show how your work will progress week by week. During the last weeks of the course, you will be giving most of your time to the independent project. You may have one or two smaller assignments to complete, but the formal lecture programmes will have finished. It is vital that you use this 'free' time efficiently. The bigger the task, the more you need to plan ahead.

A timetable is the best way of keeping track – this is the agenda for regular meetings with your project supervisor and personal tutor.

---

## Independent Study

**Name:**

**Tutorial:**                                         Date

List work completed to date and any unexpected difficulties or problems.

**Activities scheduled for week beginning** (date):

Include:

        data collection,

        IT work,

        drafts,

        tables,

        graphs

        and so on.

**Signed by tutor:**

**Date:**

---

# *4* Structure

There is no universal structure that suits all independent study projects. Your supervisor will talk you through the format that will work best for your chosen topic. Previously, we have shown how to write reports and essays. The same principles apply to structuring the independent study.

As a guideline, the layout ought normally to include eight sections. Sequence is important:

- Abstract.

- Introduction.

- Literature review.

- Research design and methods.

- The investigation.

- The results.

- Conclusions.

- References and bibliography.

An abstract is a brief summary of the whole project. We show how this is produced in topic six of this chapter.

## Introduction

The introduction needs to be brief and concise. A stranger reading your final report may not have time to look at more than the abstract, the introduction and the conclusions.

State the focus for your study, its relevance and the question or questions you are trying to answer. If possible, close with two or three sentences that link the introduction to the next section. Are you, for example, researching a crowded area where many have gone before? Is there an acknowledged expert in the field? Is this a new issue or one that has been questioned or considered for hundreds of years?

## Literature review

Here the word 'literature' is used in the widest sense to include books, journals, websites or any other information source that you have found relevant and useful.

The literature review establishes your credibility as someone whose views should be taken seriously. You are allowed, even encouraged, to disagree with Doctor Smith and Professor Jones, for example, but only if you can show a clear understanding of their work in the first place. Comparing and contrasting previously published work is the most valuable technique of all.

Make sure you show balance and selectivity. Search for opposing views and do not include irrelevant material as 'deep background'.

The sequence of the review should give the reader an outline of how your thinking has grown and developed as you were planning the project.

If this does not end up as one of the largest sections in the report then you probably have not done enough research.

# Research design

This can also be called research methods, experimental design, research methodology or any combination of these and similar words. There are no strict rules.

Replication is one of the founding principles of research. Based just on your written report, a complete stranger working in another place and at another time should be able to copy your methods and produce identical or very similar results. If this stranger needs to contact you personally for clarification or advice, then your report needs more work.

You should include:

- How samples were chosen and from what groups. Dates, times, places and numbers are essential.

- The methods used, their purpose, how they were designed and any details of trial runs, rehearsals or pilot studies.

- How you collected, organised and processed your data and results.

- How you handled ethical issues and, in particular, how this may have limited the scope of the research.

As a general rule, include as much information as possible. If in doubt, do not leave it out.

A diagram or flow chart is the best way of summarising and presenting research design. It does not have to be complicated. A simple series of words in boxes joined by arrows can tell the whole story.

Include blanks of questionnaires and interview forms. These are best shown in the appendix.

# The investigation

This section describes what you did, rather than why you did it, but it can often be combined with research design.

However, you will definitely need to separate the two if your investigation hits unexpected problems or if you altered the research design significantly as it progressed. You may, for example, have to scrap part of a questionnaire if many respondents are reluctant to give the information you need.

An investigation that gives unexpected results or even the reverse of what was expected is not a failure. More often, it is a resounding success – you have discovered something new and different.

# The results

An investigation produces two kinds of results. These are usually called raw data and processed or analysed information. To illustrate the difference, suppose you were interested in the opinions of a sample of about 100 women. Views alter over time, so one of your questions might ask for the respondents' ages or, more usually, an age bracket. The raw information might be 100 numbers. You could show these as an appendix but include a summary in the results section.

> ### *Example*
>
> Of the 112 respondents questioned, 51, equivalent to 46% of the sample, gave their age as between 35 and 40. There were smaller numbers of younger and older respondents. 19 of those questioned, 17% of the sample, preferred not to reveal their age.

Wherever you show results, they must be organised into properly headed tables, charts or graphs.

You should briefly discuss the precautions you have taken to eliminate errors and list those that may be inevitable or unavoidable. In our simple illustration, might some women have not given their true age? Would the data collected be an overestimate or an underestimate of the real average?

# Conclusions

Do not add any new information in your conclusion.

Your project started with a question; the conclusion ought to give an answer. Equally validly, you might find that the question cannot be answered at all, or cannot be answered completely. It helps to refer back to the introduction, the literature survey and your research design. Do not overclaim. A conclusion not supported by research and evidence is worthless.

You should finish with a brief consideration of all, or most of, the following points:

- What new questions or issues have been raised or highlighted?

- Do your conclusions point to the need for changes in professional practice or procedures?

- What are the overall strengths and weaknesses of your work? If you did it again, what would you alter or improve?

- And – last of all – do you have recommendations for further work?

## References and bibliography

A reference list and a bibliography are essential. Use the Harvard or the numerical system, not a mixture of both. You have volunteered for about five or six days' extra work if you have not kept detailed notes of all your information sources as you go along.

# 5 The written report

Elsewhere we have shown how to put together most kinds of written reports. In this topic, we discuss the extras needed for the write-up of the independent study project.

## Scientific language

Reports are meant to deliver information clearly and efficiently – they are not novels, plays or TV scripts. Avoid emotional, vague or value-loaded language. For instance:

The results of the first questionnaire of 3 May were confusing and probably unreliable. Its design was changed and the exercise was repeated on 10 May.

Not

I was really upset when the first tests went wrong. Unfortunately I had to go back and start again, which took nearly a week.

Avoid the first person singular – 'I'. To translate, this means:

The research design is based on the structure first suggested in Practical Social Science Techniques – Scott (1974).

Not

My original idea for the independent study came after reading a book that really impressed me. I thought it was easily the best place to start.

The media image of the natural or social scientist is an untidy man in a white coat or a tweed jacket. He always wears glasses and has a beard. We are also led to believe that social scientists have bigger, bushier beards than chemists or physicists, and that the length of the beard shows seniority. Most of all, scientists use impenetrable, complicated and baffling language.

All of this is, of course, utter nonsense. Your report should be written in plain, everyday English. Use technical terms only where they are needed – not for the sake of it.

| This is good, clear scientific language | This is confusing, pompous rubbish |
| --- | --- |
| Jack and Jill went up the hill to fetch a pail of water. | Jack and his sibling Jill made an ascent of the escarpment to replenish their supply of aqueous fluid, using a one gallon open-topped behandled stainless steel container. |
| Jack fell down and broke his crown | Jack sustained a fall, as a consequence of which he suffered a cranial fracture. |
| and Jill came tumbling after. | Being thus destabilised, the same fate befell Jill within a similar time frame. |
| *Total number of words: 25* <br> *Words of one syllable: 22* <br> *Words of two syllables: 3* <br> *Words of more syllables: 0* | *Total number of words: 55* <br> *Words of one syllable: 32* <br> *Words of two syllables: 14* <br> *Words of three syllables: 8* <br> *Words of four syllables: 1* |

# Drafts and rewrites

The independent study project is the bridge between the Access course and the standards you will be asked to meet in your first university year. It is therefore rigorously assessed.

To help you make the most of the unit – and to maximise your mark – you will be asked to present drafts of the project before you complete the final version. Some students find this tedious and even irritating, particularly if the process is repeated five or six times in a few weeks. Always remember, constructive criticism is in your interests – it is not a lecturer being pedantic or small-minded.

# The document itself

The look of the finished report is important. It has, above all, to be user-friendly. Your supervisor will give format guidelines and instructions. These vary, but this is the kind of checklist you will be working to:

- Do not exceed the word count. The total usually excludes titles, tables, footnotes, references, the bibliography and appendices, but check to make sure exactly what is counted in and out. Show the word count on the front or final page of the main text.

- You may have to have the report printed or bound. You will be shown how and where this is done.

- Keep a back-up copy on disk and another paper copy.

- Use A4 paper throughout. Print on one side only.

- Your work might have to be presented in double-line spacing. There will be firm instructions concerning margins, but a 4 cm left-hand margin means that you will not lose words or detail after binding.

- Unless you are told otherwise, the final version should be in black print on white paper. Fonts and font size may be specified – if not, use a 12 point sans serif font for the main text.

- All pages have to be numbered, including appendices. Page numbers in the top or bottom right-hand corner work best.

- Do not overdo the appendices. Three, at most, is the usual guideline. Their content has to be indicated and cross-referenced from the main text.

- Try to space and position tables, charts and diagrams so that they break up pages of text, to add relief and interest. Tables are usually numbered and nearly always titled.

- Unless you are very sure of your ground, do not include fold-out tables, inserts, or anything else that makes the end product difficult to assemble.

## The front cover, running order and sub-divisions

Many supervisors insist on a standardised front cover and a precise running order for the contents. It helps if the front cover is thin card, rather than paper. Consider using card dividers to separate the main sections.

<u>TITLE</u>
<u>IN UPPER CASE</u>
<u>AND</u>
<u>UNDERLINED</u>

Access to Higher Education

Independent Study

<u>Name of college</u>

<u>FORENAME SURNAME</u>
<u>Date of submission</u>

A typical running order would be:

1  Blank page.

2  Title page – repeat the cover page.

3  Abstract, on page 2.

4  Acknowledgements, if required, on page 3.

5  List of contents, with page numbers.

6  List of diagrams, charts and tables, with page numbers.

7  The report itself.

8  References page.

9  Bibliography page.

10  Appendices.

## Assessment criteria

Your supervisor will have marking criteria or a mark scheme for the independent study. This may contain the following.

Presentation:

- Is the work presented clearly with good use of English?

- Is the pictorial material – graphs, charts, tables – appropriate and produced with care, showing information clearly and accurately?

Clarity:

- What standard of clarity, logic and coherence has been demonstrated?

Knowledge:

- Is the content relevant?

- Does the work show a good understanding of facts and theories, and have they been used correctly to support arguments?

- Have these facts been used imaginatively and creatively?

Supporting literature:

- Is there evidence of constructive use of research and literature?

- Does the work provide evidence of broad reading?

- Has the student made connections between existing research and the new material presented, incorporating relevant information to support and develop his or her own ideas?

Analysis:

- Can the student defend and justify an opinion?
- Is the analysis reasonable and logical?

Referencing:

- Is referencing used effectively throughout the written work?
- Does the report contain a reference page and bibliography set out according to the guidelines given?

Your independent study will prove you are skilled in the following:

- Time management.
- Effective study habits.
- Understanding the ethical, financial, and health and safety aspects of academic work.
- Written communication.
- Word processing and IT.

# 6 Abstracts

An extract is a chunk or piece taken from a written document without any further editing or amendment. An abstract is different   it is a specially written, highly condensed summary of the whole work. An abstract can also be called a précis.

As a general rule, it should be around 5% of the word count of the original; this means between 200 and 300 words for an abstract of the independent study project.

As a class exercise or assignment you may be asked to make an abstract of a report that you have not seen before. Putting together an abstract of your own work is easier and there are some tips that give good results whatever the origin of the document.

## How to do it

Do not even think of starting the abstract until your main report is finished or very nearly finished. If you are abstracting somebody else's work do not start until you have read it through carefully at least once – skim reading is not good enough. In the beginning forget about the 200 or 300 word limit.

- Ignore the appendices, references and bibliography.

- Make a copy of the original and get hold of a highlighter or marker pen.

- Start with the introduction. Highlight the hypothesis or research question plus, at most, two more of what seem to be the most important ideas. Highlight whole sentences not individual words.

- Go to the conclusions and do the same thing again. At most, select four sentences. Include important numbers if these are an essential part of a conclusion. If the conclusions are listed or numbered, choose the most important and ignore the rest.

- You now have a beginning and an end. In between there will be a literature review, a research design, a description of the investigation and a results section. Keep to this sequence in the abstract.

- Highlight the most important sentences in the literature review, the research design and the investigation.

- Results are handled differently – you are usually looking for numbers. Find the main tables, charts or diagrams and highlight their headings and their totals or subtotals – ignore the detail.

# The target word count

- Now assemble all of your highlighted sentences, in the right order, on a separate piece of paper. Count the words. You will probably have something between 10% and 25% more than you need.

- Put the original document to one side and edit the draft abstract. You may find whole sentences that are not critical. It often helps to split longer sentences into shorter ones. Try replacing commas or semicolons with full stops. Remove adjectives and adverbs unless these are essential. Count the words again, and repeat the process until you are about 30 words below the maximum allowed.

- Use these 'spare words' to write links and connections, if needed, between the edited sentences taken from the original. Put the final version aside for at least an hour, then read it again to make sure it flows logically and smoothly.

- Obscure abbreviations, without explanation, are not acceptable, even in an abstract.

There is no such thing as the perfect, unique or ideal abstract. Any set of words which retains the meaning is acceptable.

The word count guideline will usually be given as a maximum – you do not have to write exactly 200 or 300 words, for example.

You can produce an excellent abstract of your own work, or anything else stored on a disk or CD, using the copy, cut, paste and edit functions of a word-processing package.

# 7 The verbal presentation

The final part of the independent study project is an oral or verbal presentation. Typically, a day is set aside and each member of the group makes a short presentation to his or her classmates. This is the last assessment for the independent study project and usually the last of the whole course.

You may want to read or re-read the suggestions for preparing and planning verbal presentations, in particular the techniques that help to reduce anxiety and keep nerves under control.

This last presentation is usually the easiest. Your confidence will have grown with practice, you will know a great deal about your subject – and most of all, you will be looking forward to a well-earned break.

## And finally

If you have been reading this chapter during the first weeks of the course or even before your first lectures, then these closing words are written specially for you.

In planning this book, a great deal of thought went into how to describe the independent study project and, more importantly, where it should come in the chapter running order. There are two problems.

For new students, the project may look like a totally daunting and almost impossible obstacle to climb. It is hard to believe at the outset that in six or seven months' time you will have developed the skills and confidence needed to cope and cope easily.

On the other hand, the book would be incomplete without a full description of the project and how best to plan and organise the work needed to complete the assignments.

## A compromise

The final decision was a compromise. The independent study chapter is, we hope, a complete and comprehensive guide to subject choice, planning, research, report writing, presentation and assessment. We do not pretend that the project is a few days' work, but we also try to show how to tackle it sensibly and methodically.

If you are still not convinced, we have a suggestion. Do not dwell or concentrate on this chapter until it is time to begin planning the project. On second reading you will find it far less intimidating.

Feedback from past students suggests that many found the independent study project the most rewarding and interesting part of the course.

# Chapter 6
# University admission

Access courses are designed to prepare mature students for university admission. From day one of the course, you should be aware that:

- Universities welcome older students. On average they tend to be more reliable, more committed, more organised and obviously more experienced than many students in their late teens and early twenties.

- The Access certificate is a valuable commodity. You will not be admitted to make up numbers, or on any kind of preferred terms. Your certificate is the equivalent of the usual A levels, the International Baccalaureate or their Scottish equivalents.

- In the UK, university admission procedure is centralised. Direct application to a particular university only happens in exceptional circumstances.

- All universities employ admission officers and admission departments. They are obliged to select on academic merit and suitability alone, but thereafter the admission office is free to make its own choices.

- Universities differ enormously in history, size and specialisation. Not all of them offer all courses and all subjects.

- Admission requirements vary from one university to another, and from one year to the next. Popular courses are usually oversubscribed. No qualification, Access or traditional, can guarantee entrance.

- Admission involves an application form and sometimes an interview.

## UCAS and NMAS

University application is made via the University Central Admission Service, abbreviated to UCAS (pronounced 'you-kass'). Entrance to diploma courses in nursing or midwifery is handled differently. The central body is the Nursing and Midwifery Admission Service, NMAS (pronounced 'enn-mass').

The two bodies have different procedures and different deadlines.

## Essential advice

It is impossible to give advice that is completely accurate and appropriate for all students, courses and universities. Requirements and procedures have altered in the past and will do so again in the future. Always check that you have the latest information before you start filling forms and making choices.

## UCAS

Most colleges keep supplies of UCAS forms and they are available from Careers Advice Centres. You can also apply for a form online or by post directly from UCAS. If you have problems tracking down the paperwork, talk to your personal tutor.

You may apply for a degree course before you finish Access. The final application date is usually in late December for admission in September of the following year.

Applications for more than one university are permitted and this is usual for younger students. However, personal and family commitments often limit the choices for those applying from Access. The only sound advice is to discuss your options with college staff and the university admission departments. Many universities run open days for potential students. These are useful and informative.

The UCAS form obviously has to be completed correctly. A small fee is payable to cover UCAS's administration costs. You cannot submit more than one UCAS form in each academic year. The form will need to be accompanied by an academic reference from your tutor.

You may be invited for an interview. This is usual for mature students and those without traditional qualifications.

# NMAS

There are two routes to becoming a qualified nurse or midwife – via a degree or through a diploma. Applications for degrees are handled by UCAS. Nursing degrees are science based and may involve preparation for a specialist branch of nursing such as paediatrics or mental health.

Diploma courses in Nursing and Midwifery are funded to encourage entry into the profession. Students are university based but also seconded to a local hospital. In return for a monthly payment, you will be working with a mentor within a hospital environment. You have to be available during nights and weekends, and you have to meet a schedule devised around the hospital's needs not individual preferences. Unlike universities, hospitals do not close for weekends or long summer holidays.

During diploma training you will be paid for your services – you will not have a grant or student loan that has to be repaid.

The diploma arrangements often suit mature students with families or other dependents, but they are not an easy option for all. Always take advice before you decide.

## NMAS timetables

Unlike UCAS, NMAS will not accept applications until you have completed the Access course. Most diplomas have two entry dates, one in September and the other in March. You need to plan ahead and plan carefully – again talk to your tutors before you decide.

## The NMAS form

It is best to assume that your chances of admission to a diploma course will be damaged if your application form is not neatly and carefully completed. In many areas there is fierce competition for places, so it is good sense to ensure that your form shows a conscientious and professional approach, and that you can follow instructions.

- The form itself is only available directly from NMAS.

- Before you fill in the form, make several photocopies of it and use these for practice runs until you are entirely happy with what you are going to write on the real thing.

- Proof-read all entries before you complete the final version. Spelling mistakes, grammatical errors and poor punctuation all give a bad impression. Your tutors will help.

- Use black ink and do not use correcting fluid. Take care not to crease or crumple the paper.

- Do not forget to enclose the administration fee – without this, your application will be rejected.

## The NMAS personal statement

The NMAS form includes space for a personal statement, which must be included. In the statement you are asked to say why you are a suitable candidate to become a diploma student. Bearing in mind the competition for places, you must ensure that this statement makes as strong a case as possible.

You should draft the statement carefully. It is a good idea to write the first draft, leave it for a time and then read it again. You will probably write several drafts and make many corrections before you have a final, word-perfect version.

The statement can be typed or handwritten. It should neatly but completely fill the space provided – this will show that you can organise your thinking and writing effectively.

Try to show that:

- You have researched the university and course you want to study.

- You are committed, hard working and looking forward to the challenges of the diploma.

- You have a particular specialist academic interest.

- You are a good communicator and good with people.
  Avoid clichés such as 'I have always loved little children' and 'I am a very kind person'. Be imaginative.

- You have a life outside work and study.

- You are focused. It is not a good idea, for instance, to apply for both the nursing and midwifery courses. They suit different kinds of people. If you show indecision, both applications might fail.

- You are organised and effective in your domestic life.

## Tell the truth

You will be asked to leave your degree or diploma course if it is found that your UCAS or NMAS form included untruths or significant exaggerations. This can happen at any stage of the course.

Rejection is immediate and unavoidable if you have failed to disclose a criminal conviction. A police check is a condition of entry for courses involving contact with children or vulnerable adults. Health checks may also be required.

## Diploma interviews

Universities are not obliged to see applicants, but all diploma candidates are interviewed before a place is offered. Preparation is essential and many colleges run classes in interview technique.

Use a copy of your application form as a 'revision guide'. Remember, the interviewers will have the original in front of them. For example, you might be asked about the Wimbledon championships if you have said you are keen on tennis.

Make sure you are up to date with recent, headline or contentious events in the health sector.

Be prepared to answer the questions 'Why this course?' and 'Why this university?'.

Make sure you have a mental list of three or four personal strengths and at least one weakness that you are 'working on'. This is a favourite question for interviewers.

Before the day of the interview, make sure you know exactly where it is being held. Most university sites are large, with dozens of different buildings and departments. Plan to arrive at least 30 minutes early.

On the day, you are certain to be anxious, but remember that anticipation is far more nerve-racking than the event itself. Dress suitably but in a way which will boost your self-esteem, turn off your mobile phone and – above all – remember to smile.

# Chapter 7

# Information technology

*National unit specification.*
*These are the topics you will be studying for this unit:*

1 Hardware, software and systems
2 Application packages
3 Security, health and safety
4 The internet and email

IT stands for information technology; ICT is short for information and communications technology. These expressions have come to mean the same thing – the use of computer systems in the handling, processing and distribution of information.

There are three main kinds of information: words, numbers and pictures.

# *1* Hardware, software and systems

A computer, or a computer system, is just a tool or a machine. All machines work in the same way:

A can opener is a machine – the input is a sealed can, the processor is some kind of clamping and cutting device, and the output is the opened can and the can lid. In the same way, an oven is a machine. The input is raw food, the output is cooked food, and the processor is a collection of devices like a heater, thermostat, timer, fan, and so on.

The diagram shows the essential features of a computer system. It is still a machine – more accurately a group of interlinked machines.

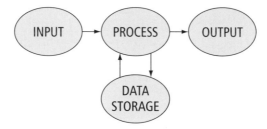

The boxes linked together to make the system are called hardware. Input, output and data storage devices are usually called computer peripherals or peripheral hardware, because they are connected around the periphery or outside of the processor.

The earliest computers took up whole rooms or sometimes several rooms. Technological advance has made computer systems smaller, more reliable and much cheaper. Desktop systems are the most familiar, but portable and compact machines like laptops, notebooks and personal organisers are becoming increasingly popular.

## The central processing unit

The box that sits at the middle of the system, the computer itself, is the central processing unit or CPU. CPUs have three main components:

1   A control unit that manages the sequence and timing of operations and the transfer of information between the CPU and the peripherals.

2   An arithmetic and logic unit, ALU – effectively the brain of the computer.

3   An immediate access data store – this is the built-in memory of the CPU.

## Input devices

A keyboard, similar in design and layout to an older manual or electronic typewriter, is by far the commonest input peripheral.

The standard keyboard is highly flexible, but other kinds are designed for particular applications. Most retailers use specialist keyboards – you will have seen these in fast-food restaurants, filling stations, bars and cinemas.

Most personal computer systems are sold as integrated packages – they all include a keyboard and also a mouse.

A mouse is a second kind of input peripheral. The movement of a mouse over a flat surface generates electrical signals. These are fed into the CPU to control the movement of a cursor across a screen.

There are other input devices. Some computer game packages use joysticks. A scanner turns a picture into electronic input, so does the memory card from a digital camera. Other peripherals convert sound into an input that can be recognised by the CPU. The retailing, finance and banking sectors rely on input devices like bar-code readers and peripherals that recognise the information held on credit cards, cheques and paying-in slips, for example.

## Data storage

The diagram (overleaf) shows the main devices used to store data.

A central processing unit cannot work without some built-in memory. This is called internal or main data storage.

The read-only memory, or ROM, holds all the instructions that control the basic functions of the CPU. ROM is built in when the CPU is manufactured and it cannot be accessed or altered by the user. Data in the ROM is permanent – it is not lost when power is switched off or interrupted accidentally.

RAM, random access memory, is also built into the CPU during manufacture. It stores instructions, programs and data temporarily during processing. Data in the RAM is lost when power is switched off.

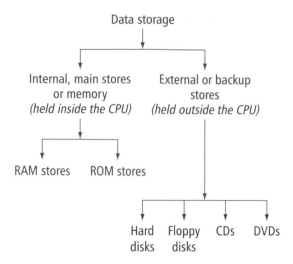

Hard disks are made of metal covered with a thin film of magnetic material. They store large amounts of data and are contained inside a sealed unit called the hard disk drive. The drive unit itself is housed in the same box as the CPU. Hard disks store mostly programs, completed work and documents awaiting printing.

Floppy disks are made of plastic coated with magnetic material. The commonest have a diameter of 3½ inches. The disk is protected by a plastic or cardboard case. Information can be written, or recorded, onto a blank floppy disk, or read, or taken from a disk prepared previously. Floppy disks are used mainly to store documents that are also saved on the hard disk. All important information needs to be backed up. Floppy disks are light, small, easily transported and easily stored.

Floppy disks are cheap and convenient but their storage capacity is limited. Hard drives and floppy disks process information magnetically.

# Optical disks

Optical disks work with a different system. A low-intensity light or laser beam reads information from an optical disk; a higher-intensity laser beam writes information onto a disk. Compact discs (CDs) and DVDs are optical disks.

Optical disks can store enormous amounts of information.

Optical disks are ideal for storing complex programs, very large documents or graphics and pictures. Even a simple graphic takes up much more storage space than a page of text. Most computer systems include a CD drive. This usually feeds information directly to the CPU, bypassing the hard disk.

Four kinds of optical disk are available. The newer kinds need more complicated drive units.

- A CD-ROM is recorded or written once by its supplier. It can be read over and over again, but it cannot be overwritten by the end user.

- A CD-R (a CD-read) is sold as a blank disk. It can be written onto once by the user and then read many times in the same way as a CD-ROM.

- A CD-RW (CD-read write) can be written, read, deleted, rewritten and reread over and over again by the user.

- A DVD (a digital versatile disk) works in the same way as a CD, but can store typically five to ten times more information than a conventional CD.

# Output devices

Output peripherals convert processed information into a form we can recognise and use. There are two main kinds.

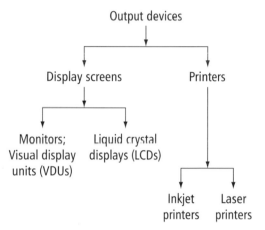

Monitors, or visual display units (VDUs), are identical in principle to TV screens. Almost all now give colour as well as black-and-white pictures. Desktop computer packages often include a VDU. As with televisions, screen size is a diagonal measurement, not the width or height of the display.

TV technology is too heavy and too fragile for smaller screens. Mobile phones, calculators, digital watches and portable PCs like laptops and notebooks use liquid crystal displays (LCDs). LCDs are often more difficult to read than monitors because reflections and the viewing angle distort the display.

The quality and reliability of VDUs has increased dramatically over the last 20 years. However, flickering screens cause eye strain, as do displays that are not sharply focused.

A monitor composes pictures by altering the colours displayed by a grid of tiny squares called picture elements or pixels. For a given screen size, a high resolution monitor has more pixels and smaller pixels than a low resolution monitor. A high resolution screen gives a sharper, clearer picture.

Display screens are versatile and easy to use, but they cannot provide permanent records or hard copy. Printers give output that can be stored and distributed. Most hard copy is print on paper, but standard printers are also used to prepare film sheets for overhead projectors.

Inkjet printers, sometimes called bubblejet printers, work by spraying microscopic ink droplets onto plain paper. The droplets merge and coalesce to form letters, numbers and the components of pictures and graphics. The inkjet process gives high-quality results, and is especially suitable for colour printing. Inkjet printers are almost silent.

Laser printers use the same technology as photocopiers. They are expensive to buy but relatively cheap to use based on cost per printed page. Monochrome and colour laser printers give a high-quality end product.

## Hardware in summary

The diagram shows in more detail the kind of computer system you will use. The arrows show the flow of information through the hardware.

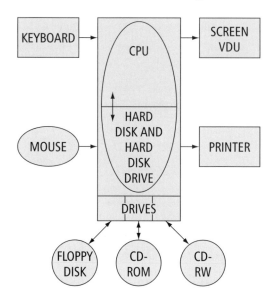

## Software

A computer program is a set of instructions that tell the computer system what to do. Software is the general term used to describe any kind of computer program or more usually a group of related programs. The flow diagram (opposite) shows the three main kinds of software.

Most of the people who now use computers are not highly trained mathematicians, software specialists or engineers. Software designers have developed programs to make human interaction with computer systems as easy and straightforward as possible. Interface programs allow anybody to tell a computer what to do without having to read and understand a large instruction manual. Similarly, systems software is built into the hardware by the manufacturers and you could use a computer every day for years without knowing this kind of software exists.

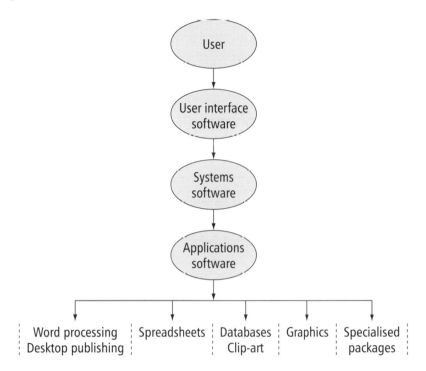

## Application packages

The third kind of software is called application software or, more often, an application package. The software flow diagram shows the most important kinds.

Word-processing and desktop publishing application packages allow anybody who can read and write to produce a clear, presentable piece of print on paper without the help of outsiders or specialists.

Desktop publishing packages were developed from word-processing software. They produce pages of text and pictures to a standard high enough for publishing or mass circulation.

Spreadsheet software is designed to produce and manipulate numbers in a table format. Spreadsheets have gradually replaced manual arithmetic and calculators in the preparation of financial and management accounts. Specialist spreadsheet packages are used throughout industry and commerce for applications like VAT, salary and payroll calculations, quantity surveying, sales forecasting and the handling of experimental results.

All organisations keep records. Until the early 1970s, these were in the form of books, folders, files, card indexes and so on. The larger and more complicated an organisation becomes, the more records it has to keep. Losing a record can have serious consequences. For physically large conventional databases, filing a record in the wrong place is equivalent to throwing it away.

Database software packages help create and manage records. They are a major improvement on physical systems. Clearly a computer database takes up far less space than hundreds of filing cabinets, but also:

- Additions, deletions, corrections and updates are easier to manage.

- Looking up a record takes seconds rather than minutes or hours.

- If a computer database is well designed it is almost impossible to lose a record, or to file it in the wrong place.

- Most importantly, computer databases can be ranked, sorted or sub-divided according to any characteristic or combination of characteristics.

Later in this chapter we will look at word processing, spreadsheet and database packages in more detail.

## Integrated packages

Integrated packages combine a number of different applications in one piece of software. Typically an integrated package is sold as a CD-ROM. Integrated software is often cheaper than individual packages and, most importantly, allows transfer of information from one application to another. The best integrated software uses the same kinds of commands and instructions for all applications.

Some software concentrates on pictures rather than words or numbers. There are application packages for operations like painting, drawing and graphics. A clip-art package stores a large number of different pictures – these can be selected and then added to documents, graphs or whatever.

Most software packages are designed to be flexible and copies are sold in their thousands or hundreds of thousands to the mass market. Software can also be specially commissioned for a particular user or a one-off application. Large production units like oil refineries and car plants are run and controlled by specialist software. Any industry involving a large complex network is almost impossible to run without specialist software. Electricity supply, air traffic, rail and road systems are good examples.

## Intellectual property

We need to close this topic with a word of warning. The law in the UK and in most other countries recognises two kinds of possessions – real property and intellectual property.

Real property is all of the physical objects and things that you own. If somebody takes your real property without your permission, they can be found guilty of theft. Similarly, nobody is allowed to borrow and then return your real property without your permission.

Intellectual property is another kind of possession – it is something valuable and unique produced by your brain and intellect. A book, a song, a painting, an invention, a trade mark and a piece of software are all examples of intellectual property. Nobody may steal or borrow them without your permission.

With today's application software, it is easy to infringe intellectual property rights by accident or through ignorance.

Somewhere on every car or can of soft drink, for example, you will find a logo or trade mark. This is the intellectual property of the manufacturer. You will not find these or any other logos or trade marks in a clip-art package. However, you could easily make an exact copy using a general purpose drawing package. If you do this you are infringing the owner's intellectual property.

As an Access student, you will use software to produce work for yourself or for limited distribution to small groups. Most but not all organisations will give permission to use their intellectual property in education – provided you acknowledge their ownership. If in doubt, ask – your lecturers are there to help.

# 2 Application packages

The point of the IT unit is to give you a basic set of computer skills that will be useful during your Access course and then later at university.

Most higher-education institutions now only accept handwritten work in exceptional circumstances and, often, routine communication is by email.

As well as understanding how a computer system works, you will need to learn some practical skills – these are straightforward.

You will spend most of your IT sessions sitting in front of a screen learning how to work with the three most commonly used application packages – word processing, spreadsheets and databases. You will be given practical help and demonstrations by lecturers and other IT specialists.

These notes give an overview of how the packages work – they are not a detailed step-by-step operating guide and they are not a substitute for practical on-the-job training.

Remember that application packages are designed to be as user friendly as possible – there are just a few things to learn and the software will navigate you through each stage with clear, easily understood instructions.

## Word-processing software

Word-processing packages are used to prepare documents that are mostly or entirely text. The usual applications are letters, memos, notes, essays and reports. The quality of the end products does not depend on your ability to type at great speed – it will just take longer. Even two-finger typing with frequent corrections is quicker than handwriting.

Most text is printed onto A4 sheets but the program will give you the option of different paper sizes. You can choose between a portrait or a landscape layout.

Layout

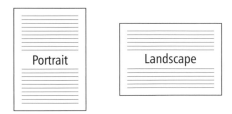

## Fonts and points

You can put together a document using a virtually endless variety of print styles and sizes. The word 'font' describes different typefaces. The size of letters and numbers is given in points. The body text in most documents is in

10, 11 or 12 point. Larger font sizes are used for sub-headings and main headings.

You also have the option of four print styles – normal, bold, italic and bold italic. Additionally, you can underline any part of the text.

Capital letters are called upper case; small letters are called lower case.

Some fonts like this are ornate. They are serif typefaces – all have a line crossing the end of each letter stroke. This shows more clearly with upper case letters and numbers – ABCD1234.

Other fonts, like this, are called sans serif. They give a cleaner and more modern-looking end product. Most students prefer sans-serif fonts.

# LARGER FONT SIZES AND UPPER CASE LETTERS ARE OFTEN USED FOR TITLES AND MAIN HEADINGS. THIS IS 18 POINT.

## Smaller fonts and a mixture of upper and lower case can be used for sub-headings. This is 14 point.

**Any text can be printed in bold.**

*Italics can add clarity and emphasis.*

***A combination of bold and italic is sometimes useful.***

Any word or <u>combination of words</u> can be underlined.

## Columns and justification

Pages can be printed as a single column like most books, or as several columns like a newspaper or magazine.

Columns

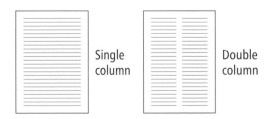

Single column

Double column

Text can be printed within columns in four different ways.

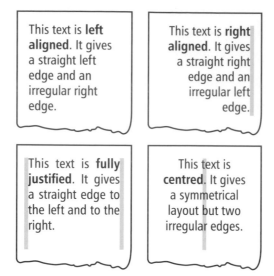

A single column of fully justified text often gives the cleanest, most attractive documents.

The software automatically allocates the right number of words line by line. The carriage return command (Enter), used in traditional typewriting at the end of each line, is used instead to create a new paragraph.

You can use page breaks, line spaces, bullet points and indents to divide text into paragraphs and to add lists and sub-headings.

Boxes and horizontal lines can be added to text pages. Date and time, headers, footers, page numbers and total number of pages can be included automatically.

All word-processing packages have a facility to insert tables of words and/or numbers into text pages.

## Spellchecking

A dictionary of all the most commonly used words is built into word-processing software. Every time you type a word, the program searches its dictionary to find a match. Unmatched words are automatically highlighted on the screen display. The usual indicator is a wavy red line shown underneath the suspect word. The computer will show a choice of alternatives and you can easily replace the suspect word with one of the program's suggestions if you wish, or add your word to the dictionary. This facility is a spellchecker – it needs to be used carefully. For instance:

**Jack and Jill whent up the hil.**

The spellchecker will underline '**whent**' and '**hil**' as mis-spellings.

However, if you type:

Jack and Jill **Blenkinsop** went up the hill.

The spellchecker will underline 'Blenkinsop' as an unknown word, even if Jack and Jill really are Mr and Ms Blenkinsop.

If you type:

Too people went up the hill.

The spellchecker will not show an error, because it finds a match for 'too', even though you should have typed 'two'.

Finally, if you enter:

Jack and **and** Jill went up the hill.

The spellchecker will highlight the second 'and' because it is probably an accidental repetition.

The differences between American English and UK English can cause spellchecker problems. Some software will show words like colour (*American – color*), harbour (*A. – harbor*) and theatre (*A. – theater*) as misspellings, suggesting the US spellings as corrections.

Some programs have an autocorrect function, which will automatically correct common misspellings.

Most word-processing packages will also spot and highlight basic grammatical errors and obvious mistakes like a new sentence beginning with a lower case letter or a wrongly placed upper-case letter.

This function needs to be used with extreme care. Grammar is complex and the program may well suggest a change that completely alters the sense of what you are trying to say.

## Edit, cut, paste and copy

Producing an A4 page of tidy word-perfect handwriting can take 30 minutes. Mistakes can be crossed through or hidden with correcting fluid but for a faultless end result you have to start all over again every time you make a mistake.

The edit, cut, paste and copy functions solve all of these problems. Taken together, they are by far the most useful features of word-processing packages. A simple mouse operation highlights words, sentences, paragraphs or whole blocks of text. This highlighted text can be corrected, deleted, copied or moved to a different part of the document using the cut and paste functions.

This kind of editing takes seconds. The user can experiment with alternative presentations without losing any of the original material.

The screen shows a continuing update of the document. At any stage you can ask the program to display a preview of how the document will look as print on paper. You tell the system to print only when you are happy with the final version. Often you will spot a mistake on the hard copy that you did not notice on the screen. Returning to the keyboard, it takes only seconds to correct the error and print a final perfect paper copy.

You will be shown how to name, save and store all of your word-processed documents. It is important to save a document at regular intervals as you put it together – if something goes wrong, you will not have to start right from the beginning again.

Remember always to make a backup floppy disk copy of anything that would be difficult or impossible to replace.

## The most common worries

It is often said that only younger people can use computers without stress and without making constant errors. This is nonsense.

In most Access classes, around half of the group use computers at home or at work. These people benefit from the IT unit because it improves their skills and understanding. Usually they are self taught or have only been told how to use a computer for a specific work-related task. The IT unit gives a wider picture and a broader range of skills.

Others, regardless of age, have an understandable fear of computers and computer systems. The most common worries can be listed:

'I am no good at maths, therefore I will never be able to use a computer.'

This fear is groundless. Only about one person in 500 who regularly uses computers is a qualified mathematician.

'I cannot type, therefore I cannot use a computer.'

This again is not true. Very few computer users could type a presentable short letter on a conventional typewriter.

'The words and the science behind computers are far too complicated – I will never understand things like hard disk drive and integrated software packages.'

You do not need to understand how a computer works – it helps, but again, very few regular computer users are electronics or software specialists. Scientists are often guilty of over-complication – they use jargon even when simple everyday words could communicate the same message. Computer scientists are among the worst offenders. Most of their specialist vocabulary is easily translated into common words that everyone can understand.

'I am frightened of doing something terribly wrong. What happens if I break the hardware or cause a major systems failure?'

Computer installations are designed to be foolproof. If you hit the wrong keys or switch on the wrong boxes, the worst that can happen is that the system will not work – nothing will explode, burst into flames or harm your fellow students.

In the same way, all software is designed to prevent disruption by new or inexperienced operators. The chances of 'crashing the system' are very low indeed. If you enter the wrong instructions, your computer may do something you had not intended, but you are very unlikely to affect other computers in the network for example.

# Databases

Database and spreadsheet packages are used to store information. Databases store information that is mostly words; spreadsheets work with numbers. Both types of package can sort the stored information, perform calculations and produce tailor-made reports.

Assembling a database is time consuming but the packages are simpler and easier to use than word-processing software.

We can show how a database works with the following example.

An engineering company has a total of 411 employees. There are two factories and a small head office, each on different sites. The personnel director uses a card index system – for each employee there is an A4 card showing personal and work-related information. These cards are stored in alphabetically indexed files. The files themselves are kept in a locked cabinet. The personnel director decides to computerise the records system. Many suitable database packages are available off the shelf.

All of the card information is entered into the computer database.

The database is named and password protected. Only directors have a password, which lets them see all of the stored information.

Each employee has an individual computer record. This corresponds to the old A4 index card.

Each record is divided into a number of fields. Each field holds a particular piece of information. This is the equivalent of a line on the index card. For instance:

| RECORD | Employee no. 0129 |
|--------|-------------------|
| *Field* | *Information* |
| 1 | Surname |
| 2 | Forenames |
| 3 | Gender |
| 4 | Address |
| 5 | Post code |
| 6 | Home telephone number |
| 7 | Date of birth |
| 8 | Date first employed |
| 9 | Work site |
| 10 | National Insurance number |
| 11 | Tax code |
| 12 | Basic salary |
| 13 | Registered disabled status |

There is no theoretical limit to the number of fields, although very large data-bases need specialist software.

The whole database could be printed. This would be a table with 5,343 pieces of information – 13 fields for each of 411 employees.

By entering an employee number or a surname, the screen will show the record for each employee. Two or more fields might be needed to distinguish between members of the same family.

The database can be sorted according to the information contained in one or more fields. In this way, any number of reports could be displayed or printed. For example:

- A list of employees sorted by length of service, or a list of those who have worked for the company for 10 years or more.

- A report showing those earning more than £20,000 per annum, working at the larger factory site.

- Using the post-code field, the personnel director could distinguish between local employees and those that have long journeys to work.

- New records for new recruits can be added to the file in minutes. Another field showing leaving date would expand the database to include existing and past employees.

Low-level passwords can be used to protect sensitive data like salaries and tax details from junior employees who do not routinely need this information.

The whole database would be backed up on CD or floppy disk. This might be kept with the company's bank or solicitor, but not at one of the firm's sites.

Two or more databases are often linked together. This personnel database could provide input for a payroll calculation program for example.

## Spreadsheets

A spreadsheet is a particular kind of database. It stores and manipulates numbers instead of words.

Displayed on a screen or printed on paper, a spreadsheet is a table. The horizontal rows are numbered and the vertical columns are marked with letters. Each box within the table is called a cell. Each cell has an 'address'.

Again, we can show how a spreadsheet works with the engineering company example.

Suppose 300 of the 411 employees are hourly paid.

There are, say, five hourly pay rates according to age, experience and length of service.

Spreadsheet cells

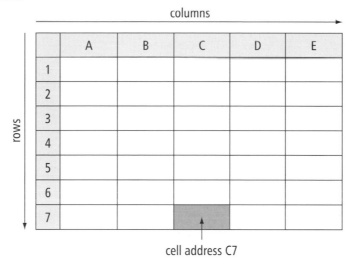

cell address C7

Weekday working hours are paid at the normal rate. Weekday hours worked before 08.30 and after 16.30 are paid at time and a half. Hours worked on Saturdays and Sundays are paid at double the normal rate.

A payroll spreadsheet would allocate one vertical column per employee. The diagram (overleaf) shows the data for one employee.

The information in the first three cells does not change from week to week unless pay rates are altered.

The information in cells A4, A5 and A6 is entered each week from time sheets, or perhaps a clock-punch system.

The spreadsheet automatically calculates the figures in cells A7 through to A14 using formulae that are entered just once by the spreadsheet user.

For instance:

| Total gross pay | = | normal pay | + | weekday overtime pay | + | weekend overtime pay |
|---|---|---|---|---|---|---|
| Number in cell A10 | = | number in cell A7 | + | number in cell A8 | + | number in cell A9 |

Spreadsheets are often linked together. In this example, tax and National Insurance paid are entered from other spreadsheets using formulae for cumulative pay, tax codes, tax allowances and percentage tax rates.

Spreadsheet data

| | A | | |
|---|---|---|---|
| 1 | JONES A.P. | Employee name | |
| 2 | 0129 | Employee number | |
| 3 | 6.20 | Standard hourly pay rate, £/hour | |
| 4 | 40 | Normal hours worked, hours | |
| 5 | 5 | Weekday overtime worked, hours | |
| 6 | 8 | Weekend hours worked, hours | |
| 7 | 248.00 | A4 × A3 | Standard pay, £ |
| 8 | 46.50 | A5 × A3 × 1.5 | Weekday overtime, £ |
| 9 | 99.20 | A6 × A3 × 2.0 | Weekend overtime, £ |
| 10 | 393.70 | A7 + A8 + A9 | Total pay for the week, £ |
| 11 | 53 | A4 + A5 + A6 | Total hours worked, hours |
| 12 | 35.43 | National Insurance paid, £ | |
| 13 | 69.70 | Tax paid, £ | |
| 14 | 288.57 | A10 − A12 − A13 | Net pay, £ |

*Input from income tax and NI spreadsheets*

# *3* Security, health and safety

Security is an essential factor in information technology. Hardware needs to be protected against loss or damage; software can be misused, as can the information stored in and produced by computer systems. The various bits of computer hardware are consumer goods that fetch reasonable second-hand prices. Normal protection against theft and burglary is important. Laptops and other portable systems are especially vulnerable. The CPU itself may not be very valuable but the information stored on the hard drive might be irreplaceable or it could be dangerous in the wrong hands.

Dust, dirt, excessive heat and high levels of humidity can cause failures in hardware and software. Physical damage to a floppy disk or CD usually means that data is lost or corrupted.

Spillage of water, drinks and food used to be the most common cause of computer failure. You will not be allowed to eat or drink in the computer room. Cigarette smoke coats the hard disk inside the CPU causing data loss and eventual failure.

The hard drive can store a great deal of information, but all of this will be lost if the hardware is stolen, damaged or destroyed by fire. All important information must be backed up or copied onto floppy disks or CDs. These backups should be stored in a different location to the computer itself – ideally at a different site altogether. Fireproof safes are available for the storage of irreplaceable disks.

It is impractical to keep copies of every document you use and produce during your Access course. However, you must keep a paper copy and a floppy disk backup of any extended or assessment material like essays, experiment reports and presentations.

Floppy disks and some CDs can be written over in exactly the same way as conventional videotapes. This means that valuable information might be accidentally erased. Floppy disks have tabs to prevent overwriting. Software is available to avoid the same problems with CDs.

The illegal copying and distribution of copyright software is a growing problem. In some countries and regions, pirate software dominates the market. Buying, using or distributing pirate software is a criminal act.

Illegal copies are often unreliable and they can disrupt systems software and/or destroy stored data.

# Viruses, passwords and encryption

Viruses are programs designed to interfere with the basic operating software of a computer system. Like the viruses that cause disease in living organisms, they have the ability to copy themselves over and over again. Most computer viruses are transmitted via email or free software, but any input or data storage device can be a virus carrier.

Anti-virus software is continuously developed and improved to identify and remove virus programs. Once installed, most anti-virus systems operate automatically at start-up.

The first viruses were designed as pranks or practical jokes, sometimes just to prove that large companies or organisations were vulnerable to the efforts of 'clever' individuals. At the other end of the scale, viruses can have the most serious consequences. The most effective anti-virus software is used to protect military and defence information systems.

Passwords are security devices. Nearly all systems can be modified to prevent access to information unless a password is entered after start-up. Many organisations use a password hierarchy. A company might store all of its financial information on one integrated system. A low-level password could let an accounts clerk into a part of the system; a director would have a different password, allowing him or her access to everything on record.

Ideally a password should be a meaningless jumble of upper case and lower case letters, numbers and symbols. Obviously, a written record of a password should not be left on or near any input device.

Encryption is the proper word for coding. Highly sensitive information is encrypted or coded before transmission and then decoded when it reaches the intended or proper user. Any outsider intercepting the transmission cannot then decode the information. In the same way, to protect against theft of sensitive material, data can be encrypted before it is stored on any kind of hardware.

# The Computer Misuse Act 1990

As the use of computer systems has grown, so have the opportunities for computer crime. In 1990 the Computer Misuse Act was introduced in the UK. It defined a number of new crimes punishable by fines and/or imprisonment.

Hacking is illegal. A hacker is a person who gains access to a computer system without authorisation. Hacking usually involves breaking or bypassing password protection.

Computer fraud, the distribution of viruses and the pirating of software are also crimes under the 1990 Act.

# The Data Protection Act 1998

The UK 1998 Data Protection Act defines particular kinds of data as personal information. For an individual this includes details of race, religion, political opinions, physical and mental health status, sexuality and sexual history.

Since 1998 individuals have had privacy rights over this personal information. Any person or organisation who stores or processes personal information has to be registered and they have obligations under the Act.

Personal information must be protected against loss or theft. It must be accurate and it must be up to date. Personal information cannot be used for illegal purposes and it must not be stored for longer than necessary

Under the Act, individuals have the right to copies of their stored personal information. Misleading or incomplete records have to be corrected and there are provisions for compensation if information is wrongly used. The police, the Inland Revenue and some other organisations are exempted from parts of the Act if they are investigating crimes or threats to national security.

# The Health and Safety at Work Act 1974

The Health and Safety at Work Act imposes duties on employers to protect their employees, neighbours and visitors against harm. Employees and others are also expected to behave and work safely.

Computer installations have to be designed to avoid eye strain, backache, repetitive strain injuries, falls and any risk of electric shock.

# *4* The internet and email

Two or more computer systems, or their hardware components, can be linked together to form a network. The simplest networks have several workstations connected to one large CPU and a single, fast, high-quality printer. The workstations are often called dumb terminals because they are just a screen, a keyboard and a mouse without a processing unit or data storage.

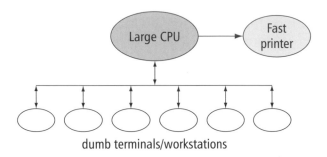

dumb terminals/workstations

Users at different terminals can communicate with each other. If the capacity of the central hardware is big enough, no one terminal has to queue for processing capacity or data storage. Network printers work on a first come, first printed basis.

In this kind of network, the interconnections are permanent physical objects, like plugs, sockets and underfloor cables. The workstations are usually concentrated on a single floor or in a single building housing one department or one organisation.

Smart terminals can be interconnected in several ways. A smart terminal has a local CPU and some storage capacity. Again, the connections are permanent cables. A large CPU can act as the centre point of the network – this is called a server or a file server. Printing may be centralised or local.

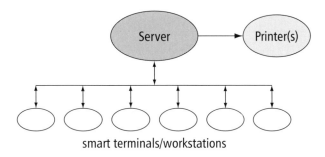

smart terminals/workstations

# The internet in theory

In theory, every computer system in the world could be interlinked into one huge network – this is the ultimate aim of the internet.

Computer systems vary from £300-worth of hardware sitting in a teenager's bedroom to the vast networks owned by governments and multinational companies. Operating systems vary and some have billions of times more capacity than others.

Physical interconnection is impossible or impractical. Most users also want the option of when to connect and when to disconnect their system from the network – they may not want a permanent connection.

There are major confidentiality issues – users will not connect if they think their security systems can be broken.

# Information transfer

Wide area networks (WANs) only became possible once specialist software had been developed to control and manage the transfer of information between different kinds of computer systems.

Specialist hardware is needed to connect systems via the telephone network. A modem can be built into an integrated package or bought as a separate box. 'Modem' is short for 'modulator-demodulator'. Computers and traditional phone systems use different technologies – a modem acts as a translator between the two.

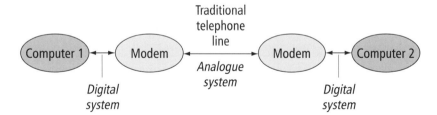

Older analogue phone networks are gradually being replaced by digital systems in exactly the same way as digital televisions are replacing traditional analogue sets. Digital technology allows more information to be transmitted across the same network. Digital TV delivers better pictures and more channels than analogue – similarly, digital phone lines carry more information. ISDN phone lines connect computer systems without the need for modems. 'ISDN' is short for 'integrated services digital network'.

ISDN lines also transmit information much more rapidly than traditional analogue phone systems.

# A global network

Essentially, the internet is a global network of hundreds of millions of computer systems connected by telephone lines. The diagram shows in general terms how it works.

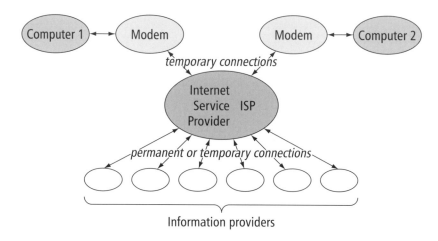

Some larger organisations have direct and permanent connections to the internet. Most users make temporary connections via a modem to the hardware owned by a commercial company – the internet service provider or ISP.

To use the net you need to pay for telephone calls in the normal way. Additionally, the internet service provider will usually charge a monthly or annual fee. Increasingly, phone companies and ISPs cooperate with each other to offer special deals. Internet users can opt for free or reduced charges in exchange for some kind of fixed-price package.

When you open an account with an ISP, you will be given a password. Your computer system will also be allocated a unique number that distinguishes it from every other system in the world.

The ISP offers a range of customer services – typically email, news reports, message boards and software.

To make a connection to the net, the modem automatically dials the ISP's telephone number, checks your password and then allows access to a massive network of interlinked computer systems – the internet itself.

When the connection is made, you are online. Sending information to the net is uploading; taking information from the net is downloading.

# The World Wide Web

Via the ISP hardware, online users have access to the World Wide Web. This is an information system divided into millions of different websites.

Websites offer goods or services for sale, or they provide information free of charge. Most websites give reliable and authoritative information. Others may just want to spread a personal view or opinion. There is no quality control.

Every website has its own address. Web browsers are specialist software systems that connect users directly to the appropriate site if you enter its address correctly. A full website address always starts with the same sequence of lower case letters and symbols:

http://www.

'http' is the abbreviation for the system used by the web browser's software. Most browsers will recognise a website address without the prefix 'http://', so website addresses are usually given as 'www.' etc.

Websites are divided into pages, each of which can be shown on a VDU screen. The home page is normally the first one you see when you are connected to the site. The home page indexes or summarises the information held on the site and gives navigation instructions so that you can easily move from one section to another. Many websites are interlinked and you can move rapidly through a series of related sites – this is commonly called surfing or surfing the net.

# Search engines

Surfing can be amusing and interesting, but it is an inefficient way of locating specific information. Search engines are massive software packages that identify potentially relevant and useful sites. The user enters a key word or a series of key words. The software then searches many websites to find a match for this word or words. A list of sites is displayed and with the click of a mouse you can call up the appropriate site.

There are dozens of search engines. Each works in a different way and may give different results.

Search engines are exceedingly efficient. They can deliver a bewildering choice of websites just seconds after you have entered the key word(s). For instance, suppose you want background information on Access education courses.

Entering *education* will produce a list of thousands of websites relating to all kinds of education throughout the world. The chances of finding what you really need are remote.

Entering *access* will produce a shorter list, but some sites will relate to access equipment – the general term describing ladders and scaffolding; others might be fan-club sites for a group of musicians calling themselves Access; yet more might describe a credit card system called Access that was introduced into the UK during the 1970s.

Entering *access to higher education* or *access education* will deliver a shortlist of relevant websites, but you might still get some sites that tell you how to work safely with ladders and scaffolding for example.

## Electronic mail

Electronic mail, or email, is a way of sending messages from one computer user to another. The diagram outlines the system.

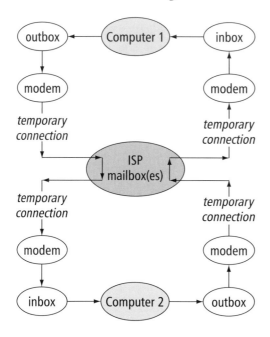

Internet service providers run the email system. When you open an account you will be given a unique email address.

Messages are usually composed off-line to save telephone charges. Any message can have an attachment – that is another computer-produced document included as part of the email. The finished message is shifted to a data store in your computer – the outbox. When you next go online – this need not be immediately – the message is sent via a modem on a phone link to the service provider. The service provider keeps many millions of email messages in a large data store, or mailbox. The recipient of the email can download your message into their inbox next time they connect to the system.

The diagram shows only one internet service provider; in reality the ISPs cooperate by passing emails between their mailboxes. The system does not restrict communications to customers of the same service provider.

Software packages usually include email support services like address books and diaries.

Messages or letters sent through the traditional postal system are sometimes called snail mail – this makes the point that email offers instant worldwide communication.

Many viruses are transmitted by email – within file attachments – and the system is sometimes used to circulate junk mail or unwanted messages –

called 'spam'. At the end of 2003 a new law was introduced in the UK to make the sending of most kinds of unsolicited emails a criminal offence.

'Intranet' is the word used to describe closed networks of computer systems, usually owned and operated by one organisation. These allow secure and confidential intercommunication, including email. A large central computer, or server, takes the place of the ISP's mailbox store.

# Chapter 8

# Application of number

National unit specification.
These are the topics you will be studying for this unit:

# Mathematics units – a special note

Numeracy requirements for Access vary according to the pathway you have chosen.

If you are not exempt because of accredited prior learning, you will have to study the Application of Number unit.

For some pathways, you will have to show that your numeracy has reached a standard similar to a GCSE maths qualification at grade C or better – this is called 'GCSE equivalence'. If GCSE equivalence is needed for your pathway, you will have to study Application of Number plus a second unit called Further Mathematics.

Your personal tutor will let you know which unit or combinations of maths units you need before you can be awarded the Access certificate for your particular pathway. Clearly it is important that you understand what is wanted as early as possible in the course so that you can plan your study time.

Whatever you need to do, it is essential that you study the maths units in the right order. You will not be able to cope with Further Mathematics until you are comfortable with Application of Number.

You might be tempted to save time by skipping between one maths unit and another. For most students this is a bad idea – you are likely to get confused.

## Calculators

For less than £10 you can now buy a machine that will instantly perform calculations that would have taken 19th-century mathematicians months to complete by hand with pencil and paper.

Calculators can be a blessing or a menace. They have to be used sensibly.

There is nothing magical or special or different about a mathematical calculator. It is just another one of the thousands of tools and machines that have been invented to make life easier, safer and more productive.

If a tool is available, it should be used properly. Nobody would consider teaching biology without a microscope or astronomy without a telescope of some kind.

No responsible professional would rely on pencil and paper or mental arithmetic to make an important calculation. Doctors, nurses, engineers, architects and airline pilots, for example, use calculators on a daily even an hourly basis. At a practical and realistic level, Access students must know how to use calculators reliably and efficiently.

Despite all this, complete dependence on calculators is exceedingly dangerous, in particular for nurses or health professionals. In any calculation, regardless of the method used, two kinds of mistakes or errors are possible.

Minor errors do not usually have serious consequences but major or gross errors can be life threatening.

If you use a calculator carelessly or without a basic understanding of mathematical operations, then you are likely to make gross errors – worse still, you will not realise that you have made major mistakes.

The commonest type of calculator gross error is where you end up with an answer that is 10, 100 or perhaps 1,000 times bigger or smaller than it ought to be.

As part of the Application of Number unit, you will be taught how to work out an approximate answer to a calculation, so you can apply a 'reality check' to the figures shown on the calculator display. This reality checking is the only sure way to avoid gross error.

# Choosing a calculator – how many buttons?

You will need to bring a calculator to every maths unit lecture, and without a calculator your private study sessions will not be productive.

Nowadays, there are hundreds of different models to choose from. Few cost more than about £10, and some cost as little as 99p. It is important to buy the right kind of calculator.

The simplest calculators have 19 buttons or keys:

| 10 | number keys | 0 to 9 |
| 1 | decimal point key | . or · |
| 5 | function keys | +, –, ×, ÷, = |
| 1 | plus/minus key | +/– |
| 1 | clear key | CE or AC |
| 1 | on/off button | |

Most simple calculators also have another five or six keys – three or four that allow numbers to be put into and taken out of a memory bank, a square root key ($\sqrt{\phantom{x}}$) and a button used to work out percentages (%).

The more complicated machines are called scientific or programmable calculators. Some also allow the user to draw graphs on a small display screen – these are called graphical calculators.

The best-selling scientific calculator has 50 keys. Because most of these can perform two different functions, this model can handle around 70 different kinds of calculations.

Calculators come in a variety of shapes and sizes. There are three main types:

- Very small machines, around the same size and shape as a credit card.

- Scientific calculators that look very much like TV or video remote controls.

- Simple desktop models, measuring about 10 cm by 15 cm (roughly 4 inches by 6 inches).

For Application of Number, the best choice by far is a simple desktop calculator. It will not have advanced function keys – which can cause confusion – and the larger buttons and number display greatly reduce the chances of number entering or misreading errors. Even if your eyesight is perfect and your fingers are delicate and dainty, you should start off with a big simple calculator.

Nearly all modern calculators are solar powered and/or work with batteries that last two or three years. Provided you press the right buttons in the right sequence, you will always get the right answer. Very few mistakes can be blamed on low-battery conditions or an unreliable power supply.

If you already have a scientific calculator, do not throw it away or lose it. You will need a more advanced machine later in the Access course and when you go to university.

The calculator function on a mobile phone is better than nothing, but not much better. The keys and the display are always too small.

# *1* The different kinds of numbers

Experiments have shown that babies are born with a basic ability to count, or at least to recognise the difference between small simple numbers. It is certain that mankind has been using numbers for tens of thousands of years, but maths really began when the ancient Babylonians and Egyptians invented symbols for writing and recording numbers. The Greeks, Romans and Chinese each developed a different set of number symbols – the system we use today was first invented by Arab mathematicians about 1,500 years ago.

Because numbers are so familiar, we usually do not recognise some very basic principles:

- We count in tens only because we are animals with ten fingers. This is called decimal notation or the decimal system. There are ten different numbers – 0 and 1 to 9. These are sometimes called digits. You will notice that this word can mean a number or a finger.

- Calculators show numbers in a standard form recognised throughout the world, but the style of hand-written numbers varies from one place to another. These variations are relatively minor and do not often cause confusion, but you should know that the French, Germans and many other Europeans write 1 as $1$ and add a horizontal bar to the number 7 – like this $7$. Many scientists and mathematicians in the UK also write 7 with a bar.

- Any number, no matter how big or small, can be written using a combination of the ten basic digits. This concept seems so obvious that we often forget it is one of the most brilliant inventions ever made. Four and nine are different numbers, but so are 4, 40 and 400 – the number 4 in a different position means a different thing.

## Positive, negative, large and small

Mathematicians group numbers together into categories – it helps to know the main kinds.

Numbers can be positive or negative. If no sign is shown in front of a number, you can assume it is positive. A minus sign is always written in front of a negative number: –4 is called 'minus four' not 'negative four'. Zero is a special number and the only one which is not positive or negative.

To make large numbers easier to read, commas are used to separate thousands. To get the comma in the right place, you start at the right and count in threes to the left like this:

1,104

12,947

6,245,998

The comma is usually hand-written, resting on the line like this: 12,947, but your calculator display might show the comma at the top of the numbers like this: 12'947. Most calculators insert the comma automatically – you never have to press a key for it. Some scientific calculators do not show the 'thousands separation' comma.

All languages have words to describe large numbers. You will almost certainly understand what one hundred and one thousand means, but you may get confused between millions and billions.

A million is '1' followed by six zeros, like this: 1,000,000. A billion is '1' followed by nine zeros, like this: 1,000,000,000. The word 'billion' is relatively new and, with this meaning, originated in the US. Economists occasionally use words like trillion and quadrillion to describe very big numbers – you do not need to remember these.

In some sciences you always work with very big or very small numbers. A medical researcher needs to describe the length of a virus and an astronomer might want to calculate the distances between stars for example. A shorthand, called scientific notation, is used to write these. This is explained later in the unit.

The idea that numbers can go on forever, getting bigger and bigger, is a difficult concept, but mathematicians call the biggest number that there is 'infinity'. Its symbol is ∞.

Maths teaching always starts with simple calculations using whole numbers. Whole numbers are often called integers. Simply enough, any number which is not an integer is called a non-integer.

## Fractions

There are two kinds of non-integers – fractional numbers and mixed numbers. Fractional numbers can be best described as those that are smaller than 1. Mixed numbers are bigger than 1, but are not whole numbers. These are ideas you use every day, even if you have never heard of the labels before:

| Whole numbers or integers | Two kinds of non-integers | |
|---|---|---|
| | Fractional numbers | Mixed numbers |
| 2 | ½ | 1½ |
| −7 | 0.25 | 12.56 |
| 1,423 | −0.736 | −5.75 |
| −6,098 | 0.004 | 1,244.784 |
| 1,245,607 | $\frac{9}{11}$ | $\frac{22}{7}$ |

From the examples you can see there are two ways of writing fractional or mixed numbers – we can use fractions or decimals. How to work with these is explained in detail later, but to start with you need to know how they are written and said.

The word 'fraction' comes from the same family of words as 'fracture' – all it means is 'take a number and break it up into, or fracture it into, smaller parts'. Most adults have problems with fractions. Many schoolchildren get as far as fractions and then give up on maths because they seem like a barrier or road-block that cannot be overcome.

Any two numbers can be turned into a fraction – you write one number on top and the other underneath, separating them with a horizontal or forward-sloping line. This line says 'take the top number and divide it by the bottom number'.

There are three ways of writing fractions:

$$2 \div 3 \qquad \frac{2}{3} \qquad 2/3$$

Modern books usually use the forward-sloping line as the symbol for fractions because the whole sum can be printed easily on a single line.

You can always tell if a fraction is bigger or smaller than 1:

$$\frac{\text{Smaller top number}}{\text{Bigger bottom number}} = \text{smaller than 1}$$

$$\frac{\text{Bigger top number}}{\text{Smaller bottom number}} = \text{bigger than 1}$$

Sometimes a calculation produces a fraction where the top and bottom numbers are the same. In this case, the value of the fraction is exactly 1.

As with the larger whole numbers, all languages have special words for the commonest fractions. You will be completely used to using words like one quarter, one half, one third, two-thirds and so on. A more complicated fraction like 51/89 might be said as 'fifty-one eighty-ninths', but it is much easier and more usual to call this kind of fraction 'fifty-one over eighty-nine'.

## Decimals

Fractions were invented before decimals. Fractions are a simple way of describing any particular number, but the addition, subtraction, multiplication or division of two or more fractions can be difficult. Decimal calculations are very much quicker and easier. All calculators use the decimal system.

The decimal point is used to separate the two parts of a mixed number. The whole numbers are written to the left of the point and the fractional part to the right.

In hand-written decimals it is usual to write the decimal point in the centre of the line, like this: 12·347. Calculators, books and computer screens usually show the decimal point at the bottom of the line, like this: 12.347.

The number 12.347 is said as 'twelve point three four seven', not as 'twelve point three hundred and forty-seven'.

Commas are not used to separate groups of three numbers to the right of the decimal point. For example, we would write 'twelve thousand four hundred and eight, point two nine eight five four' as 12,408.29854.

It is important to understand what 0 ('nought' or 'zero') placed to the right of the decimal point means; 7.02, 7.002 and 7.0002 are different numbers, but 7.02, 7.020 and 7.0200 are the same number, shown to different degrees of accuracy.

7.002 is described as 'seven point zero zero two' or 'seven point nought nought two'.

Using a calculator, every fraction can be easily converted into a decimal. Sometimes this calculation gives strange answers. Dividing 1 by 3 gives the decimal equivalent of the fraction we call 'one third'. Your calculator display will give a number like 0.333333333. If you put this same calculation into a powerful computer, this string of 3s would continue forever. A number like this is called 'zero point three recurring' – the 3 'recurs'. Some fractions produce more complicated recurring patterns when they are turned into decimals. If you divide 1 by 11, you will find that this fraction turns into a decimal where the two digits 09 recur forever:

$$1/11 = 0.09090909$$

This decimal would be described as 'zero point zero nine recurring' or 'zero point nought nine recurring'.

## Powers and roots

Other words are used to describe some kinds of multiplication and division:

$4 \times 4 = 16$ and $7 \times 7 = 49$ and $10 \times 10 = 100$. In each of these sums, you take a number and multiply it by itself. Another way of writing these calculations is:

$$4^2 = 16$$
$$7^2 = 49$$
$$10^2 = 100$$

The small number written at the top of the line, to the right of the big number, is called a power. If this power is 2, it is called a square. It is described as 'four squared equals sixteen' or 'ten squared equals one hundred'.

Powers must not be confused with simple multiplication:

$$7^2 \text{ equals } 7 \times 7 \text{ or } 49$$

$$7^2 \textit{ does not } \text{equal } 2 \times 7 \text{ or } 14.$$

The small number, properly called a superscript number, does not have to be 2. For example:

| 4 | × | 4 | × | 4 | = | $4^3$ | = | 64 |
|---|---|---|---|---|---|-------|---|----|
| 7 | × | 7 | × | 7 | = | $7^3$ | = | 343 |
| 10 | × | 10 | × | 10 | = | $10^3$ | = | 1,000 |

If the small number is 3 it is a cube and you would say 'four cubed equals sixty-four' and so on.

Again, cube powers must not be confused with simple multiplication:

$$4^3 \text{ equals } 4 \times 4 \times 4 \text{ or } 64$$

$$4^3 \textit{ does not } \text{equal } 3 \times 4 \text{ or } 12.$$

The same principle applies if the power number is bigger than 3, but slightly different words are used to describe the sum. For example:

$$10 \times 10 \times 10 \times 10 \times 10 \times 10 = 1,000,000$$

or

$$10^6 = 1,000,000$$

This is described as 'ten to the power of six equals one million'.

The system works the other way around and there are more terms used to describe particular kinds of division. The reverse of powers are called roots.

If you start with 16, divide by 4, and then divide by 4 again, you end up with 1. Put into words, this is 'the square root of 16 is 4'. You need to learn the square root symbol. We write:

$$\sqrt{16} = 4 \quad \text{or} \quad \sqrt[2]{16} = 4$$

You do not have to write the small number 2 as part of the square root symbol; the sum is assumed to be a square root if the 2 is left out.

In the same way,   $\sqrt{49} = 7$   and   $\sqrt{100} = 10$

Just as square roots are squares put into reverse, cube roots are the reverse of cubes.

343 divided by 7 is 49 and 49 divided by 7 is 7, and 7 divided by 7 is 1. This time, the division has been repeated three times rather than twice. We would say 'the cube root of 343 is seven'. We would write this as:

$$\sqrt[3]{343} = 7$$

The small number 3 must *always* be added to the cube root symbol to avoid confusion with square roots.

It is difficult to work out square roots and cube roots by hand, but most calculators have a square root button that does this instantly. Scientific calculators always have square root and cube root keys.

The squares and cubes of integers are always integers because squaring and cubing are just special kinds of multiplication. The square roots and cube roots of whole numbers are usually not integers.

1 is an unusual number because all its roots and all its powers are also 1. This has to be so, because no matter how many times you multiply 1 by 1, or divide 1 by 1, you always end up with an answer of 1.

# 2 The four rules of number

The basic arithmetic methods for addition, subtraction, multiplication and division are called the four rules of number.

Using a calculator for these four basic operations often gives an answer that fills the whole display – usually eight or ten numbers plus a decimal point. It can be difficult to know how to present the answer to a sum – different calculations require different degrees of accuracy. Put in practical terms, when your calculator shows a long string of numbers, how do you decide which are important and which can be ignored?

## Approximation and rounding

There are some rules:

- First, you have to consider why you are doing the calculation and what its answer will be used for.
  If somebody asks you how much you weigh, you might answer '10 stone' or perhaps '64 kilos'. You would not reply '10 stone, one pound and 2 ounces' or '64.2374 kilos'.
  On the other hand, an engineer designing a car gearbox might have to calculate the size of its components to fractions of a millimetre or thousandths of an inch.
  Money calculations are a good example. Your calculator might tell you that an article should cost £10.333333. The first two numbers after the decimal point have real meaning because they translate directly into 33 pence, but all the other threes can be safely ignored. The right answer here is £10.33.

- Rounding is often used to make whole numbers easier to read and understand. Say 53,739 people paid to watch a football match. This precise and accurate number will only be interesting and useful to the club accountant who has to balance the books.
  A television commentator might need to give viewers a rough idea of how many people went to the match. He or she could round the actual number to the nearest 1,000. In round thousands, 53,000 is the nearest number smaller than 53,739 and 54,000 is the nearest number bigger than 53,739. Because 53,739 is closer to 54,000 than 53,000, the number is rounded up. An attendance of 53,439 would be rounded down to 53,000.
  An attendance of 53,500 would be rounded up to 54,000. A number exactly halfway between the lower and upper brackets is always rounded up:

54,000   54,000   54,000
↑                    ↑
53,739               |
          53,500
                     53,439
                     ↓
53,000   53,000   **53,000**

Exactly the same rules apply for rounding to the nearest 100 or the nearest 10.

53,739 is closer to 53,700 than it is to 53,800, so it is rounded down to 53,700.

53,739 is closer to 53,740 than it is to 53,730, so it is rounded up to 53,740.

### Practice question

Sally wins £454,426.80 in the national lottery. How much did she win:

(i)   Rounded to the nearest pound?

(ii)  Rounded to the nearest £1,000?

(iii) Rounded to the nearest £10,000?

(iv)  Rounded to the nearest £100,000?

(v)   A newspaper reporter writes a story with the headline 'Sally wins nearly half a million pounds'. Do you think this headline is misleading?

## Correcting and decimal places

Figures that include a string of numbers after the decimal point are also frequently rounded. This is usually called 'correcting' to a certain number of decimal places. In 7.123456, 1 is in the first decimal place, 2 is in the second decimal place, 3 in the third decimal place, and so on.

If you are asked to round an answer to one decimal place, look at the first two numbers after the decimal point. If the number in the second decimal place is 5 or more, you round up. If the number is 4 or less, you round down. Decimal place can be abbreviated to d.p. For example:

| 10.65 | corrected to 1 d.p. | = | 10.7 |
|-------|---------------------|---|------|
| 10.65447 | " | " | = | 10.7 |
| 10.06 | " | " | = | 10.1 |
| 10.60 | " | " | = | 10.6 |
| 10.0739 | " | " | = | 10.1 |

In the same way, you can round, or correct, to two, three or any other number of decimal places.

To correct to two decimal places, look at the number in the third decimal place – round up if it is 5 or more, round down if it is 4 or less.

| | | | |
|---|---|---|---|
| 10.6544 | corrected to 2 d.p. | = | 10.65 |
| 10.0739 | " " | = | 10.07 |
| 10.0759 | " " | = | 10.08 |
| 10.0194 | " " | = | 10.02 |

To correct to three decimal places, look at the number in the fourth decimal place and apply the 'five up – four down' rule as before:

| | | | |
|---|---|---|---|
| 10.6544 | corrected to 3 d.p. | = | 10.654 |
| 10.0739 | " " | = | 10.074 |
| 10.0759 | " " | = | 10.076 |
| 10.00073 | " " | = | 10.001 |

Most people do not have problems with the simple addition of positive numbers, but sometimes extra care is needed. Mistakes are easily made when adding a mix of large and small numbers shown to different decimal places. For example:

$$
\begin{array}{r}
12{,}702.2 \\
6.247 \\
22.01 \\
0.0048 \\
\hline
12{,}730.4618
\end{array}
$$

It is all too easy to get the zeros after the decimal point in the wrong place. Enter the numbers carefully and repeat the calculation to double-check the first answer.

Sometimes you will need to add a long list of numbers together. In this situation, even experienced mathematicians often get the wrong answer first time around. Be careful not to miss a number and not to enter a number twice. Always repeat addition sums if you are working with more than about a dozen numbers.

## Like with like

The four rules of number only apply if you are working with the same kind of numbers or with measurements shown in the same kind of units. You can only add, subtract, multiply or divide like with like. For example:

- If you weigh eight stone and you put on two kilos in weight, you do not weigh ten stone or ten kilos. You cannot add 8 and 2 to give 10, because the units are different.

- If the temperature is 70°F at midday and increases by 4°C over the next three hours, the temperature at three o'clock in the afternoon is not 74°F or 74°C.

- If you have £25 in your purse or wallet and somebody gives you $5, you do not end up with £30 or $30.

All this seems obvious common sense, but in the same way, you cannot directly add, subtract, multiply or divide a mixture of fractions and decimals.

Using a calculator, any fraction can easily be turned into a decimal. Make sure you can do this quickly and accurately.

## Practice question

Fill in the gaps in the table:

| Fraction | Decimal equivalent corrected to 3 d.p. |
|---|---|
| $\frac{1}{2}$ | 0.500 |
| $\frac{1}{4}$ | 0.250 |
| $\frac{3}{4}$ | 0.750 |
| $\frac{1}{3}$ | 0.333 |
| $\frac{2}{3}$ | 0.667 |
| $\frac{3}{8}$ | 0.375 |
| $\frac{22}{7}$ | 3.143 |
| $\frac{2}{7}$ | |
| $\frac{3}{11}$ | |
| $\frac{9}{100}$ | |
| $\frac{101}{100}$ | |
| $\frac{35}{34}$ | |
| $\frac{2}{9}$ | |

You will see that some fractions have precise decimal equivalents, but many do not no matter how many decimal places you include in the calculation.

Converting fractions into decimals is easy, but turning a decimal back into a fraction is more difficult. You will soon remember some of the commonest equivalents, like ½ = 0.5 and ¾ = 0.75, but you do not need to know how to convert more complicated decimals into fractions.

Clearly, decimals and fractions can be added, but the calculation involves two stages. In a mixed sum, you first convert any fractions present to decimals and then add all the decimals together in the usual way. Taking a simple example:

$$\frac{1}{2} \; + \; \frac{3}{7} \; + \; 0.216 \quad = \quad ?$$

is the same as

$$0.500 \; + \; 0.429 \; + \; 0.216 \; = \; 1.145$$

The same two stages are used if you need to subtract, multiply or divide a mix of fractions and decimals.

## Practice question

Rearrange these numbers into ascending order. Ascending order means that your answer list should begin with the smallest number, followed by numbers increasing in size, ending with the biggest one. Descending order means you make the list the other way around – starting with the biggest and ending with the smallest.

Arrange into ascending order:

38/35

35/38

1.012

36/35

4/3

1.276

35/36

0.846

Different methods are used to add, subtract, multiply and divide groups of numbers where every one is a fraction. These methods are covered later in the Application of Number unit.

Again, most people can handle simple subtraction and sums involving a mixture of addition and subtraction. In addition and subtraction you get the right answer regardless of order.

We all know that $7 + 3 + 10$ is the same as $3 + 7 + 10$. Also, $7 + 10 - 3$ is the same as $10 - 3 + 7$.

## Negative numbers

Subtraction is easy, but many students have problems with negative numbers. At primary school you were taught that 'ten apples, take away two apples is eight apples' but the answer to 'two apples, take away ten apples' is 'can't do it'. At first glance, this seems obvious and logical because there is no such thing as a minus or negative apple.

The real meanings of negative numbers are easiest to explain using debt and temperature scales as examples.

### Example

Zareen has £500 in her bank account on 1 January. During January she writes cheques for a total of £595. At the end of the month she will owe the bank £95 – this is the value of her debt or overdraft. We can summarise what happened to Zareen's money during January as:

$$500 - 595 = -95$$

This negative number, –95, means something real – it is what she owes her bank.

On 1 February, Zareen pays £640 into her account. Once the cheque has cleared, her new credit balance will be £545. This is a positive number because this time the bank owes her money. The second transaction can be summarised as:

$$-95 + 640 = +545$$

You will see that we have put a plus sign in front of the 545. A number without a sign is always assumed to be positive – in this example we have included all of the signs just for clarity.

You must always use the minus sign in front of a negative number.

Zareen's bank statements for January, February and the rest of the year are no more than a series of additions and subtractions.

Sometimes the running total will be positive, meaning her account is in credit; at other times the running total will be negative, showing that Zareen has an overdraft.

A diagram called a number line makes negative numbers easier to understand. Additions are the same as moving up the line, subtractions mean you are moving down the line.

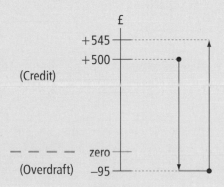

The centigrade temperature scale was invented by a Swedish scientist called Anders Celsius in 1742. Degrees Celsius is an alternative name for degrees centigrade. For convenience, Mr Celsius decided to call the freezing point of pure water 0 °C and the boiling point of pure water 100 °C. Nobody has problems with temperatures above 0 °C, because only simple addition is involved. However, negative temperatures need a bit more thought.

The zero point on the centigrade scale was chosen just to make life easy – it is not the lowest temperature possible. Temperatures of, say, –5 °C are common in British winters and a temperature of –89 °C was recorded in Antarctica in 1983. Temperatures very much lower than –89 °C can be reached in laboratories and in outer space.

A number line for temperature looks very much like an ordinary thermometer. The diagram shows the midday and midnight temperatures for a December day in London.

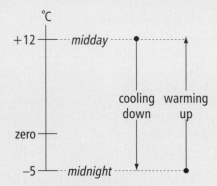

Subtraction, or cooling, means moving down the number line.

Warming is the same as addition, or moving up the line. In this example, the difference between the midnight and midday temperatures is 17 °C not 12 °C, 7 °C or 5 °C. The difference between the two numbers, whatever their sign, is called the range. We would say that the temperature range on this day was 17 °C.

## Practice question

The table shows maximum and minimum daily temperatures in eight cities. Fill in the gaps in the table.

| City | Maximum °C | Minimum °C | Range °C |
|---|---|---|---|
| Cairo | 32 | 20 | 12 |
| Nairobi | 31 | 31 | zero |
| Paris | 9 | –2 | 11 |
| Moscow | –4 | –18 | 14 |
| Chicago | –10 | –27 | |
| Edinburgh | zero | –9 | |
| Mexico City | 39 | 26 | |
| Birmingham | 9 | –4 | |

# Multiplication, division and common sense

If you multiply one number by another you expect the answer to be bigger than the numbers you started with.

Do the following sums on your calculator:

$$3 \times 4 \qquad =$$
$$7 \times 10 \qquad =$$
$$123 \times 141 \qquad =$$
$$1 \times 92 \qquad =$$
$$1.01 \times 1.01 \qquad -$$

This common-sense rule is only true if the numbers you are multiplying together are 1 or bigger.

If one or more of the numbers is less than 1, multiplication gives an answer smaller than one or more of the numbers you started with.

Do these sums on your calculator:

$$0.1 \times 1 \qquad =$$
$$0.1 \times 0.18 \qquad =$$
$$0.1 \times 0.2 \qquad =$$
$$0.3 \times 0.24 \qquad =$$
$$73 \times 0.342 \qquad =$$

Any number multiplied by zero is zero.

If you divide one number by another, you expect the answer to be smaller than the numbers you started with. Again, this common-sense rule is not always true. Remember, there are three ways of writing a division sum.

For example:

$$4 \div 5$$
$$4/5$$
$$\frac{4}{5}$$

If the top number is smaller than the bottom number and if both numbers are larger than 1, then common-sense rules apply. Do these sums on your calculator.

$$1/4 \quad =$$
$$2/8 \quad =$$
$$100.7/100.9 \quad =$$
$$1,247/4,369 \quad =$$

If the top number is larger than the bottom number, and if both numbers are larger than one, then again common sense rules apply.

$$4/1 \; =$$

$$6/2 \; =$$

$$100.9/100.7 \; =$$

$$4{,}369/1{,}247 \; =$$

However, if the top number is less than 1, or the bottom number is less than 1, or if both numbers are less than 1, then life gets more complicated.

Do these sums on your calculator:

$$0.5/1.0 \; =$$

$$0.5/0.8 \; =$$

$$0.43/0.57 \; =$$

$$0.5/0.5 \; =$$

$$0.4/0.8 \; =$$

$$0.2/0.2 \; =$$

$$0.9/0.3 \; =$$

$$0.9/0.03 \; =$$

$$0.9/0.003 \; =$$

$$0.9/0.0003 \; =$$

In division calculations, as the bottom number gets smaller, the answer gets bigger.

Any number divided by zero is infinity.

## Different signs

There is one last basic number rule that you need to learn. This concerns the multiplication or division of pairs of numbers with different signs.

Multiplying or dividing two numbers that have the same sign gives an answer that is always positive. For example:

| $4 \times 8$ | $=$ | 32 | and | $-2 \times -6$ | $=$ | 12 |
|---|---|---|---|---|---|---|
| $4/8$ | $=$ | 0.5 | and | $-8/-4$ | $=$ | 2 |

Multiplying or dividing two numbers that have different signs gives an answer that is always negative. For example:

| $4 \times -7$ | $=$ | $-28$ | $6 \times -3$ | $=$ | $-18$ |
| $8/-2$ | $=$ | $-4$ | $-10/5$ | $=$ | $-2$ |

Many students have problems at first with the multiplication or division of two negative numbers giving a positive answer.

# 3 Fractions

Because powerful calculators are now cheap, efficient and reliable, decimals have largely replaced fractions in day-to-day, business and professional life. If you can use a calculator, it is possible to get by without knowing much about how to add, subtract, multiply and divide fractions by hand. All you have to do is turn fractions into decimals and then complete the calculations in the ordinary way. For example:

$$\frac{1}{2} + \frac{1}{4} + \frac{1}{8} + \frac{3}{20} = \ ?$$

is the same as

$$0.500 + 0.250 + 0.125 + 0.150 = 1.025$$

1.025 written as a fraction is $^{41}/_{40}$ but there are not many occasions in real life when you would use or write a number like $^{41}/_{40}$ – the decimal equivalent is easier to use and easier to understand.

Your maths lecturer will decide how much time and attention you need to give to handling fractions. They may not be directly useful, but fraction calculations are excellent practice in the four rules of number and, for many students, they help build confidence and all-round numeracy. In this topic, we briefly outline the main points.

Remember what you have learned so far – a fraction is just two numbers separated by a line. The line is a symbol which means 'take the top number and divide by the bottom number'. A fraction is a division sum written in shorthand.

Fractions do not have to be smaller than 1. If the top number is bigger than the bottom number, the fraction will represent a value greater than 1.

## Simplification and cancelling

Some fractions may look different at first glance, but on further examination you find they mean the same thing. Take a very simple example of a pie that is cut into four equal slices. A single slice is one quarter, two slices are half of the pie and three slices are three-quarters of the pie. Another way of describing half of a pie is to call it two-quarters of a pie. Turning these words into numbers:

$$\frac{1}{2} = \frac{2}{4}$$

This is the easiest example of what are called equivalent fractions: ²⁄₄ is a more complicated way of describing ½, but the two fractions mean the same.

Again in this example, ½ is the fraction in its simplest form. Converting another equivalent fraction into the simplest form is called simplification or cancelling.

There is an endless list of fractions equivalent to ½. 10,058/20,116 is an equivalent, for example, because here the bottom number is exactly twice as big as the top number.

Dividing the top and bottom parts of a fraction by the same number does not change its value. This rule is the basis of cancelling. The table gives some examples.

| Equivalent fraction | Divide both top and bottom by | Simplest fraction |
| --- | --- | --- |
| 2/4 | 2 | 1/2 |
| 40/100 | 20 | 2/5 |
| 9/27 | 9 | 1/3 |
| 21/70 | 7 | 3/10 |
| 125/100 | 25 | 5/4 |
| 126/441 | 63 | 2/7 |
| 19/21 | none | 19/21 |

The final fraction shown is an example of one that cannot be simplified – there is no whole number that divides exactly into both 19 and 21.

Top-heavy fractions – where the top number is bigger than the bottom – can be shown in another way. For example:

$$5/4 = 4/4 + 1/4$$
$$4/4 = 1$$
$$\text{so} \quad 5/4 = 1\tfrac{1}{4}$$

$$22/7 = 21/7 + 1/7$$
$$21/7 = 3$$
$$\text{so} \quad 22/7 = 3\tfrac{1}{7}$$

Remember that any fraction where the top and bottom numbers are the same is equal to 1. This is a special kind of simplification or cancelling.

Numbers like 1¼ and 3¹⁄₇ are called mixed numbers because they include a mixture of whole numbers and fractions.

## Multiplying and dividing fractions

Multiplying a pair of fractions is easy. All you have to do is multiply the two top numbers together and the two bottom numbers together.

The new fraction is the answer. For example:

(i)
$$\frac{2}{3} \times \frac{6}{7} = \frac{2 \times 6}{3 \times 7} = \frac{12}{21}$$

(ii)
$$\frac{1}{4} \times \frac{3}{8} = \frac{1 \times 3}{4 \times 8} = \frac{3}{32}$$

You can often simplify the answer to a fraction multiplication sum. In the examples above, $^3/_{32}$ cannot be simplified further, but $^{12}/_{21}$ cancels to $^4/_7$ if you divide top and bottom by 3.

Multiplying a fraction by a whole number is also straightforward.

$$\frac{3}{10} \times 7 \text{ is the same as } \frac{3}{10} \times \frac{7}{1}$$

because dividing any number by one does not change its value. You now just multiply the two fractions together.

$$\frac{3}{10} \times \frac{7}{1} = \frac{3 \times 7}{10 \times 1} = \frac{21}{10}$$

Dividing one fraction by another is nearly as easy as multiplication, provided you remember a simple rule: take the second fraction, turn it upside down and then use the multiplication method. For example:

$$\frac{3}{11} \div \frac{2}{3} \text{ is the same as } \frac{3}{11} \times \frac{3}{2}$$

The second fraction has been inverted, or turned upside down, so that $^2/_3$ becomes $^3/_2$. The answer to the division is therefore:

$$\frac{3}{11} \times \frac{3}{2} = \frac{3 \times 3}{2 \times 11} = \frac{9}{22}$$

To divide fractions by whole numbers, you again have to remember that dividing any number by 1 does not alter its value. This kind of calculation has three stages:

$$\frac{4}{7} \div 11 \text{ is the same as}$$

$$\frac{4}{7} \div \frac{11}{1} \text{ which is the same as}$$

$$\frac{4}{7} \times \frac{1}{11} \text{ which is the same as}$$

$$\frac{4 \times 1}{7 \times 11} \text{ which equals } \frac{4}{77}$$

# Adding and subtracting fractions

Adding and subtracting fractions without a calculator is difficult.

Of all the basic operations, these are the ones that trouble most students. You should not get anxious if adding fractions does not make immediate sense or if you find you need lots of practice.

Previously, we have shown that the four rules of number only apply if like is added to like. Adding stones to kilos, or degrees Fahrenheit to degrees Celsius, gives nonsense answers. Adding and subtracting fractions only works if like is added to like.

Start with an addition like this:

$$\frac{3}{16} + \frac{5}{16} + \frac{7}{16} = ?$$

You can see this addition is straightforward because you are being asked to add like with like. To take a simple comparison:

3 oranges + 5 oranges + 7 oranges = 15 oranges

The fraction sum and the oranges sum are identical – in the first you are adding things called $\frac{1}{16}$ths together and in the second you are adding things called oranges together. The like for like rule applies and the calculation is straightforward. That is:

$$\frac{3}{16} + \frac{5}{16} + \frac{7}{16} = \frac{3 + 5 + 7}{16} = \frac{15}{16}$$

The method does not change if a subtraction is included. For example:

$$\frac{3}{16} + \frac{5}{16} - \frac{7}{16} = \frac{3 + 5 - 7}{16} = \frac{1}{16}$$

The bottom number shows how to add and subtract fractions – if all of the bottom numbers in the sum are the same, then the calculation is easy.

Weights shown in stones and kilos can be added together, but not in a single step. First, you have to convert stones into kilos, or kilos into stones and then you can, in a second step, add like to like. The right answer will be shown in stones or kilos but never as a mixture of both.

# Making the bottom numbers the same

If you understand this fundamental idea, adding and subtracting fractions will begin to make sense. Take another example:

$$\frac{1}{2} + \frac{3}{8} = ?$$

Put into words, this calculation says 'add one half to three eighths'. You cannot do this sum in a single step, because it breaks the like for like rule. If you add things called halves to things called eighths, the answer will be rubbish.

As the first of two steps you need to convert the two fractions into the same things – then you can add them together.

You cannot convert $^3/_8$ into a whole number of halves, but you can change ½ into a whole number of eighths. As equivalent fractions you can see that:

$$\frac{1}{2} = \frac{4}{8}$$

This is simplification in reverse – you multiply the top and bottom parts of $^1/_2$ by 4 to give $^4/_8$.

Now you can add the fractions together to get the right answer. In words, four things called eighths added to one thing called an eighth equals five eighths. We can turn all this back into numbers again:

(i) $\qquad\qquad\qquad\qquad \frac{1}{2} + \frac{3}{8} = ?$

(ii) $\qquad\qquad\qquad\qquad \frac{1}{2} = \frac{4}{8}$

(iii) $\qquad$ Therefore $\quad \frac{1}{2} + \frac{3}{8} \quad$ is the same as

(iv) $\qquad\qquad\qquad\qquad \frac{4}{8} + \frac{3}{8} = ?$

(v) Applying the like for like rule:

$$\frac{4}{8} + \frac{3}{8} = \frac{4+3}{8} = \frac{7}{8}$$

If you understand this two-stage process, then with a little practice you will be able to cope with any kind of addition or subtraction involving fractions. Once you get the principle, all the rest is detail.

At the beginning of this topic we used the following as an example of how to convert a fraction addition calculation into decimals. It was:

$$\frac{1}{2} + \frac{1}{4} + \frac{1}{8} + \frac{3}{20} = ?$$

To do this sum by hand, several steps are involved:

(i) Look at the four bottom numbers – they are all different. If you add these fractions directly, it would be the same as adding apples, oranges, pears and bananas.

(ii) As a first step, you have to find just one number that can take the place of all four bottom numbers. This is called the lowest common denominator.

(iii) In this example, the lowest common denominator is 40 because (taking the bottom number of each fraction in turn):

$$40 \div 2 = 20$$
$$40 \div 4 = 10$$
$$40 \div 8 = 5$$
$$40 \div 20 = 2$$

(iv) Using the lowest common denominator, we can convert each of the four fractions into the same 'kind of thing':

$$\frac{1}{2} = \frac{20}{40}$$
$$\frac{1}{4} = \frac{10}{40}$$
$$\frac{1}{8} = \frac{5}{40}$$
$$\frac{3}{20} = \frac{6}{40}$$

(v) We can now use the like for like rule to complete the calculation:

$$\frac{1}{2} + \frac{1}{4} + \frac{1}{8} + \frac{3}{20} = ? \quad \text{is the same as}$$

$$\frac{20}{40} + \frac{10}{40} + \frac{5}{40} + \frac{6}{40} = ? \quad \text{is the same as}$$

$$\frac{20 + 10 + 5 + 6}{40} = ? \quad \text{which is the same as}$$

$$\frac{41}{40} \quad \text{which is the same as}$$

$$1\frac{1}{40} \quad \text{which is the same as}$$

1.025 shown as a decimal.

# *4* Decimals – the theory

Modern calculators are designed to make the addition, subtraction, multiplication and division of decimals as trouble free as possible. You can be reliable and accurate without knowing what is going on inside your machine and without knowing what a decimal really is. However, you are much less likely to make gross calculator errors if you understand the basic idea behind decimals and the link between decimals and fractions.

If you use a calculator to turn the fraction $\frac{1}{8}$ into a decimal, the display will show the number 0.125.

There is a 1 in the first decimal place, a 2 in the second decimal place and a 5 in the third decimal place. There are no figures in the fourth or subsequent decimal places.

## A string of fractions

A decimal is really just a string of fractions.

The first decimal place shows the number of $\frac{1}{10}$, the second decimal place the number of $\frac{1}{100}$, the third decimal place the number of $\frac{1}{1000}$, and so on. We can turn these words back into numbers:

$$\frac{1}{8} = 0.125 = \frac{1}{10} + \frac{2}{100} + \frac{5}{1,000}$$

0.125, 0.1250 and 0.12500 and so on mean the same thing because the extra noughts tell you only that there are no $\frac{1}{10,000}$ and no $\frac{1}{100,000}$ and so on.

If you realise that decimals are strings of fractions, then the difference between numbers like 1.07 and 1.007 becomes obvious:

$$1.07 \text{ equals } 1 + \frac{7}{100}$$
$$1.007 \text{ equals } 1 + \frac{7}{1,000}$$

The commonest calculator errors happen when the zeros after the decimal point are entered in the wrong place or in the wrong order.

You do not need a calculator to multiply or divide a decimal by 10 or any multiple of 10, like 100 or 1,000.

To multiply a decimal by 10, you shift the decimal point one place to the right. Shifting the point two places to the right is the same as multiplying by 100, and so on:

# 5 Percentages

Many researchers believe that school maths teaching often fails because students cannot see how what they are taught relates to daily life. If a subject seems useless and irrelevant, you are not likely to study it with enthusiasm or interest. This criticism might be valid for some maths topics, but not for percentages. Of all the numeracy skills, an understanding of percentages is the most useful.

Every newspaper and most TV or radio news reports contain at least one reference to percentages and they are especially important in handling money. You cannot properly understand price changes, inflation, interest rates, income tax, VAT and pay rates unless you are comfortable with percentages.

This topic includes a selection of practice questions to develop and test your understanding.

'Per cent' means 'of 100'. The percentage sign has been simplified over the years, but the meaning has remained the same:

*Original meaning*    of 100
$^0/_{100}$
$^0/_{00}$
*Now shown as*    $^0/_0$

In some old maths books you might find the symbol $^0/_{00}$ – nowadays the symbol for percentage is always %.

You describe a percentage as, for example, '67.1 per cent'. You do not say '67.1 per cent out of a hundred'.

Percentages are used for two main purposes:

- To compare numbers or groups of numbers.
- To show how numbers, quantities or values have changed.

## Percentage comparisons

Two different groups of Access students take the same test. They are graded either pass or fail. The table shows what are called the raw results or raw data.

Which group had the higher pass rate?

|         | No. of students | | |
|         | Pass | Fail | Total |
|---------|------|------|-------|
| Group A | 53   | 8    | 61    |
| Group B | 74   | 13   | 87    |

You cannot tell just by looking because the groups are different sizes and 61 and 87 are both awkward numbers. This is how you do it:

$$0.03125 \times 10 = 0.3125$$
$$0.03125 \times 100 = 3.125$$
$$0.03125 \times 1{,}000 = 31.25$$

In the same way, shifting the decimal point one place to the left is the same as dividing by 10; two places is dividing by 100 and so it goes on:

$$112.75 \div 10 = 11.275$$
$$112.75 \div 100 = 1.1275$$
$$112.75 \div 1{,}000 = 0.11275$$

Previously, we have talked about decimals that include recurring numbers. $\frac{1}{3}$ turned into a decimal is 0.3 recurring. The string of threes after the decimal point would continue forever if you used a big enough calculator or computer. $\frac{1}{3}$ is an example of a fraction that cannot be exactly converted into a decimal.

Step (i)    Turn the two pass rates into fractions, that is 53/61 and 74/87.

Step (ii)   With your calculator, turn each fraction into a decimal.

Step (iii)  Multiply each decimal by 100 to give a percentage.

Step (iv)   Present the percentage figure to a sensible number of decimal places.

|         | Step One | Step Two | Step Three | Step Four |
|---------|----------|----------|------------|-----------|
| Group A | 53/61    | 0.86885  | 86.885     | 86.9      |
| Group B | 74/87    | 0.85057  | 85.057     | 85.1      |

Group A had the higher pass rate of 86.9%; group B was slightly lower at 85.1%.

Remember, to multiply any number by 100, just shift the decimal point two places to the right.

There are several ways of presenting these two percentages.

None of these comparisons are wrong, but some are more useful than others.

|                      |        | Group A   | Group B   |
|----------------------|--------|-----------|-----------|
| Corrected to         | 3 d.p. | 86.885    | 85.057    |
|                      | 2 d.p. | 86.89     | 85.06     |
|                      | 1 d.p. | 86.9      | 85.1      |
| Nearest whole number |        | 87        | 85        |
| 'Roughly'            |        | nearly 90 | nearly 90 |

### Practice question

The table shows exam results for seven groups of Access students.
Rank the seven groups in descending order of pass rate.
Which two groups have very similar pass rates?
It helps to do your calculations as a table:

| Group | No. of students — Taking the exam | Passing the exam |
|-------|------------------|------------------|
| A | 58 | 35 |
| B | 61 | 51 |
| C | 16 | 11 |
| D | 32 | 27 |
| E | 20 | 11 |
| F | 23 | 16 |
| G | 31 | 28 |

**Practice question**

Susan plants 561 seeds and 482 germinate. Calculate the germination rate as a percentage correct to two decimal places.

Bert plants 347 seeds and 108 germinate. Calculate the germination rate as a percentage correct to two decimal places.

A park gardener planted 14,729 daffodil bulbs last year. 69% of these bulbs produced flowers. How many bulbs did not produce flowers?

# Percentage increases

Increases and decreases are easier to understand and compare if they are calculated as a percentage change.

A washing machine cost £299 in January, but its price was increased to £319 in June. What percentage price increase does this represent?

Step (i)   Divide the new price by the old price to give a fraction and then a decimal – which will always be bigger than 1 if it is a percentage increase.

$$319/299 = 1.06689$$

Step (ii)   Subtract one from this decimal.

$$1.06689 - 1 = 0.06689$$

Step (iii)   Multiply this number by 100 to give the percentage increase.

$$0.06689 \times 100 = 6.689\%$$

Step (iv)   Round as needed.

$$6.689\% = 6.7\%$$

# Percentage decreases

A packet of cornflakes cost 89p in January. Its price was reduced to 79p in June. What percentage price decrease does this represent?

Step (i)   Divide the new price by the old price to give a fraction and then a decimal – which will always be smaller than 1 if it is a percentage decrease.

$$79/89 = 0.88764$$

Step (ii)   Subtract this decimal from 1.

$$1 - 0.88764 = 0.11236$$

Step (iii)   Multiply this number by 100 to give the percentage decrease.

$$0.11236 \times 100 = 11.236\%$$

Step (iv)   Round as needed.

$$11.236\% = 11.2\%$$

## Practice question

Calculate the percentage change correct to one decimal place:

|  | Before | After | % change |
|---|---|---|---|
| House | £125,000 | £158,000 | |
| Television | £199.99 | £149.99 | |
| Red dress | £34.90 | £30.00 | |
| Salary | £21,400 | £22,250 | |
| Salary | £21,400 | £30,000 | |
| Baby | 7 lb | 11 lb | |

# Value added tax (VAT)

The standard rate of VAT in the UK is currently 17.5%. You need to know how to do two kinds of VAT sums; you should be able to:

- Calculate a tax inclusive price starting with a base price that does not include VAT.

- Calculate the base and tax parts of a tax inclusive price.

Take a simple example – a portable TV with a retail price of £117.50.

| BASE PRICE £100.00 | VAT £17.50 |
|---|---|
| RETAIL PRICE £117.50 | |

Starting with the retail price, the base price is calculated as follows:

$$\text{Base price} = \frac{\text{retail price} \times 100}{117.5}$$

Starting with the retail price, the tax paid is calculated as follows:

$$\text{Tax paid} = \frac{\text{retail price} \times 17.5}{117.5}$$

Starting with the base price, the retail price is easily calculated:

$$\text{Retail price} = \frac{\text{base price} \times 117.5}{100}$$

Or more simply:

$$\text{Retail price} = \text{base price} \times 1.175$$
$$\text{because} \quad 117.5/100 = 1.175$$

---

**Practice question**

Fill in the gaps in the table; present your answers correct to 1p.

| Base price | VAT (£:p) | Retail price |
|---|---|---|
| £50.00 | | |
| | | £99.99 |
| 85p | | |
| | | £159.90 |
| | | £959 |
| | | £19,499 |
| 10p | | |
| £32 | | |

---

**Practice question**

Most EU Member States have different VAT rates. Calculate retail prices given the following base prices and tax rates:

| Base price | VAT rate | Retail price |
|---|---|---|
| €150 | 22.5% | |
| €8 | 8.0% | |
| €40 | 15.0% | |
| €95 | 18.0% | |

# Percentage change – flowchart method

Use this method if you are comfortable with negative numbers.

This diagram summarises the methods for calculating percentage change, using, as examples:

- What is the percentage change if 400 is increased to 450?

- What is the percentage change if 400 is reduced to 320?

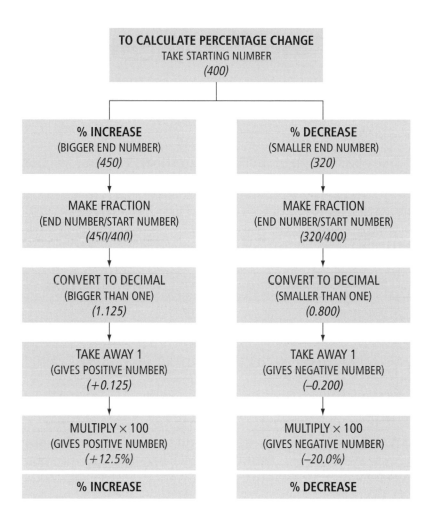

**TO CALCULATE PERCENTAGE CHANGE**
TAKE STARTING NUMBER
*(400)*

| **% INCREASE** | **% DECREASE** |
|---|---|
| (BIGGER END NUMBER) | (SMALLER END NUMBER) |
| *(450)* | *(320)* |
| **MAKE FRACTION** | **MAKE FRACTION** |
| (END NUMBER/START NUMBER) | (END NUMBER/START NUMBER) |
| *(450/400)* | *(320/400)* |
| **CONVERT TO DECIMAL** | **CONVERT TO DECIMAL** |
| (BIGGER THAN ONE) | (SMALLER THAN ONE) |
| *(1.125)* | *(0.800)* |
| **TAKE AWAY 1** | **TAKE AWAY 1** |
| (GIVES POSITIVE NUMBER) | (GIVES NEGATIVE NUMBER) |
| *(+0.125)* | *(−0.200)* |
| **MULTIPLY × 100** | **MULTIPLY × 100** |
| (GIVES POSITIVE NUMBER) | (GIVES NEGATIVE NUMBER) |
| *(+12.5%)* | *(−20.0%)* |
| **% INCREASE** | **% DECREASE** |

# 6 Units of measurement

Maths can be seen as a special type of science or as a subject that underpins all the sciences. Science is based on observation, experiment and measurement. Without accurate and consistent measuring systems, science would be impossible.

Early units of measurement were based on familiar objects. A foot was originally just that – the length of an adult man's foot. The mile was invented by the Romans and it used to be 1,000 paces – 'mille' is Latin for 1,000.

People vary in size – it follows that units like feet and paces are unreliable. As science progressed, units were standardised – today a foot is always 12 inches and a mile is always 5,280 feet, for example.

Different units were developed independently in different countries and regions. That is why there is no simple relationship between units like stones and kilos or metres and feet.

## The imperial and metric systems

Most of the world now uses the metric system, the imperial system or a mixture of both.

Throughout the world, all sciences, including all branches of medicine, work with the metric system. Most countries also use metric measurements in daily life. The US is the only large country where non-scientists always use imperial units.

Even if you currently think in units like stones, pounds, ounces, inches, feet, yards, miles, pints and gallons, you will need to get used to the metric system in preparation for your future career. It is especially important that nurses, midwives and health professionals are completely comfortable with metric units, because these, exclusively, are used in calculating drug dosages.

We will be describing the units used to measure six quantities – length, mass, capacity, temperature, time and degrees of angle.

Mass and weight are very slightly different concepts, but in all practical situations, they are identical quantities and the terms 'mass' and 'weight' can be used interchangeably.

Decimal currency was introduced in the UK on 15 February 1971. You have to be at least 40 to have much personal experience of the old money, where £1.00 was worth 20 shillings and one shilling was divided into 12 pennies. A return to the old currency will never happen because decimal money is much easier to use.

The same general principle holds true for all calculations with metric units – they are quicker, simpler and more reliable than working with the imperial system.

# Six important units

The table shows the six important metric units with some imperial measures for comparison:

| Quantity | Metric unit (symbol) | Imperial units |
|---|---|---|
| Length | metre (m) | inch, foot, yard, mile |
| Mass/weight | kilogram (kg) | ounce, pound, stone, ton |
| Capacity/volume | litre (l) | fluid ounce, pint, gallon |
| Temperature | degree Celsius °C* | degree Fahrenheit °F |
| Angle | ——————— degree ° ——————— | |
| TIme | ——————— second (sec) ——————— | |

*\* degrees Celsius are also called degrees centigrade – the abbreviation for both is °C.*

The imperial system is irregular – this means that different multiples are used to turn smaller imperial units into bigger ones. This sounds complicated but it is a familiar everyday idea. For example:

| Multiple | Smaller unit | | Bigger unit |
|---|---|---|---|
| 12 | inches | = | 1 foot |
| 3 | feet | = | 1 yard |
| 1,760 | yards | = | 1 mile |
| 16 | ounces | = | 1 pound |
| 14 | pounds | = | 1 stone |
| 8 | stones | = | 1 hundredweight |
| 20 | hundredweight | = | 1 ton |

All these different multiples have to be learned and life gets even more complicated if you need to convert between the largest and smallest units. One ton, for example, is 35,840 ounces and one mile is 63,360 inches.

The metric system is regular because it uses multiples of 10 and standardised names for bigger and smaller units. A prefix is a short word which is placed in front of a longer one. The metric system works with four main prefixes:

| Prefix | Means take the basic unit and |
|---|---|
| kilo | multiply by 1,000 |
| centi | divide by 100 |
| milli | divide by 1,000 |
| micro | divide by 1,000,000 |

The prefixes always have the same meaning. A kilometre is 1,000 metres, a kilogram is 1,000 grams and a kilowatt is 1,000 watts. In the same way, a millimetre is $1/_{1,000}$ of a metre and a milligram is $1/_{1,000}$ of a gram.

You must learn the meanings of the four main prefixes.

# Weight or mass

This table shows the common metric units for weight or mass:

| | | | | |
|---|---|---|---|---|
| 1,000 micrograms | (mcg) | = | 1 milligram | (mg |
| 1,000 milligrams | (mg) | = | 1 gram | (g) |
| 1,000 grams | (g) | = | 1 kilogram | (kg) |
| 1,000 kilograms | (kg) | = | 1 tonne | |

All of the symbols are written using small letters like mg, g and kg, not Mg, G or Kg.

There are two symbols for micrograms: mcg and $\mu$g. $\mu$ is the Greek letter mu (pronounced 'mew' not 'moo').

1,000 kilograms are equal to one metric tonne. The imperial ton, sometimes called the 'long ton', is slightly larger than the metric one.

To avoid confusion, the French spelling 'tonne' is used for the metric measurement.

# Length

This table shows the common metric units for length:

| | | | | |
|---|---|---|---|---|
| 1,000 millimetres | (mm) | = | 1 metre | (m) |
| 10 millimetres | (mm) | = | 1 centimetre | (cm) |
| 100 centimetres | (cm) | = | 1 metre | (m) |
| 1,000 metres | (m) | = | 1 kilometre | (km) |

Again, all of the symbols are written as lower case rather than capital letters.

# Volume or capacity

To measure liquid volumes, the imperial system uses pints and gallons.

The main metric volume units are the litre and the millilitre.

| | | | |
|---|---|---|---|
| 1,000 millilitres | (ml) | = | 1 litre (l) |

A cubic box with inside measurements of 10 cm by 10 cm by 10 cm holds exactly one litre of water. The volume of this box is 1,000 cubic centimetres, because:

$$10 \text{ cm} \times 10 \text{ cm} \times 10 \text{ cm} = 1,000 \text{ cubic centimetres}$$

This means that 1,000 cubic centimetres equal one litre and that one cubic centimetre and one millilitre are different ways of describing the same volume.

| 1,000 cubic centimetres | (*cc/cu.cm./cm$^3$) | = | 1 litre |
|---|---|---|---|
| 1,000 millilitres | (ml) | = | 1 litre |
| so | 1 cubic centimetre | = | 1 millilitre |

*Unfortunately there is no single abbreviation for cubic centimetres. The symbols cc, cu.cm. and cm$^3$ are used interchangeably.*

The most familiar everyday use of cubic centimetres is in describing car engine sizes. A small car might have an engine capacity of 1,000 cc, so you could also say that this is a 'one litre car'. A more powerful one might have an engine capacity of 2,500 cc, which is also called a 2½ litre engine.

# Temperature

Scientists measure temperatures in degrees centigrade or Celsius. Most people in the UK think in degrees Fahrenheit. There are six important numbers to remember:

| Reference points | °C | °F |
|---|---|---|
| Water freezes at | 0 °C | 32 °F |
| Water boils at | 100 °C | 212 °F |
| The difference between the boiling and freezing points of water is | 100 centigrade or Celsius degrees | 180 Fahrenheit degrees |

Most of us realise that the two main temperature scales use different reference points, but it may not be immediately obvious that one Celsius degree and one Fahrenheit degree are different things.

A temperature change of 10 °C = a temperature change of 18 °F.

# Time

We do not measure time in metric units. Seconds, minutes, hours, days, months and years are the most universal units of all. Scientists and non-scientists throughout the world use the same system. We can all tell the time, but it is still possible to make time calculation mistakes.

A day is 24 hours, not 12 hours. Mathematicians and scientists do not usually think in terms of 12-hour days and 12-hour nights.

When you write a clock time or use a digital watch, you end up with numbers that look just like decimals. For example:

| 00.30 | Half past midnight |
| 07.45 | Quarter to eight in the morning |
| 11.55 | Five to midday |
| 17.00 | Five o'clock in the afternoon |
| 23.30 | Half past eleven at night |

It is important to remember that, in this case, the dot is not a decimal point – it is just one of the usual ways of showing the difference between hours and minutes.

A clock time of 23.30 does not mean the same thing as a time interval of 23.3 hours because there are 60 minutes in an hour, not 100.

A time interval can be shown in hours and minutes or as decimal hours – be careful not to confuse the two.

| Time interval – hours and minutes | Convert to fraction | Time interval – decimal hours |
| --- | --- | --- |
| 15 minutes | 15/60 hour | 0.25 |
| 30 minutes | 30/60 hour | 0.5 |
| 45 minutes | 45/60 hour | 0.75 |
| 6 minutes | 6/60 hour | 0.1 |
| 20 minutes | 20/60 hour | 0.333* |
| 2 hours 40 minutes | $2^{40}/_{60}$ hours | 2.667* |
| 7 hours 19 minutes | $7^{19}/_{60}$ hours | 7.317* |

*\* corrected to three decimal places*

## Angles

There are several systems for measuring angles – you only need to understand the commonest one, which uses degrees as units.

A full circle is divided into 360 degrees (360°). A quarter turn is 90°, a half turn is 180° and a three-quarter turn is 270°. Angular measure is easy to understand using a compass diagram.

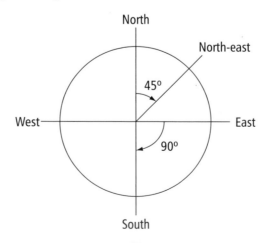

If you are walking north, and then you change direction to walk north-east, you have moved through an angle of 45°. Changing direction from east to south is the same as moving by 90°, and so on.

An angle of 90° is usually called a right angle.

Degrees of angle are most often used to label diagrams of triangles, squares, rectangles and other kinds of regular shapes. Notice that the small square symbol is used to label a right angle.

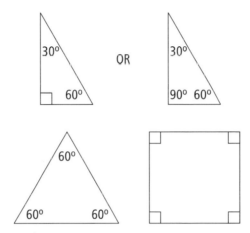

# Scientific notation

Scientific notation is a shorthand used to describe very large or very small numbers.

The total weight of the Earth is 6,000,000,000,000,000,000,000 tonnes.

This is a 6 followed by 21 zeros. Numbers like this are difficult to understand, take a long time to write down and are unreliable, because it is easy to add too many zeros or to miss some out.

Previously, we have talked about squares, cubes and higher powers. As a reminder:

$10 \times 10$             $= 10^2$ called '10 squared'

$10 \times 10 \times 10$        $= 10^3$ called '10 cubed'

$10 \times 10 \times 10 \times 10 \times 10 \times 10$   $= 10^6$ called '10 to the power of 6'

Put another way, we can say:

$10^2 = 100$

$10^3 = 1,000$

$10^6 = 1,000,000$

The power number is the same as the number of zeros following the 1.

In the same way, instead of writing a string of 21 zeros we can describe the weight of the Earth as

$$6 \times 10^{21} \text{ tonnes.}$$

Because 1,000 kilograms equals 1 tonne and 1,000 grams equals 1 kilogram, we can easily give the weight of the Earth in these smaller units.

$$6 \times 10^{21} \text{ tonnes is the same as}$$

$$6 \times 10^{24} \text{ kilograms, which is the same as}$$

$$6 \times 10^{27} \text{ grams.}$$

Most bacteria have a diameter of about one millionth of a metre. This measurement could be written as a fraction or a decimal:

$$1/1,000,000 \text{ metre}$$

$$\text{or } 0.000001 \text{ metre.}$$

Just like very big numbers, very small ones are difficult to use and understand – because there are too many zeros.

The power system works for small numbers as well as big ones. For example:

| Number | Equivalent power | |
|---|---|---|
| | 1,000,000 | $10^6$ |
| | 1,000 | $10^3$ |
| | 100 | $10^2$ |
| | 10 | $10^1$ |
| | 1 | $10^0$ |
| 0.1 | $1/10$ | $10^{-1}$ |
| 0.01 | $1/100$ | $10^{-2}$ |
| 0.001 | $1/1,000$ | $10^{-3}$ |
| 0.000001 | $1/1,000,000$ | $10^{-6}$ |

Negative powers are used as a shorthand to label numbers smaller than 1 or very much smaller than 1.

Using scientific notation, the diameter of the bacterium is

$$1 \times 10^{-6} \text{ metre.}$$

There are 1,000 millimetres in a metre, so we could also say that the diameter of the bacterium is

$$1 \times 10^{-3} \text{ millimetre.}$$

# 7 Reality checking

Whatever method is used, everybody makes silly mistakes from time to time – these are called gross errors. Gross errors are especially likely if you lack confidence in maths, if you do not use maths regularly at work or in your daily life, or if you are not completely comfortable with calculators.

Reality checking is a short topic but an important one. Under this heading we have collected together some tips and methods that will help you avoid most kinds of gross error.

Confusion between units is common and so are calculator decimal point entry errors. This kind of mistake often produces an answer that is impossibly big or ridiculously small.

Most people know that a newborn baby weighs about 7 lbs. If you remember that one kilogram is very roughly two pounds, then you will know that a newborn infant ought to weigh about 3.5 kilos. You will quickly realise that the baby cannot weigh 3.5 grams or 3.5 tonnes. This is called context checking. In the same way, a man cannot be 6 metres tall, a train would not have an average speed of 2,000 km per hour and the distance between London and Manchester cannot possibly be 3 km. If you get a silly answer, repeat the calculation.

It is easy to make mistakes when you are working with large numbers, small numbers or numbers that include many decimal places. Imagine that you need to do this multiplication and you are working to three decimal places:

$$3,104.267 \times 91.049 = ?$$

The answer is 282,640.406, but with a slip of the finger you might get 2,826,404.061 or 28,264.041. It will not be immediately obvious that your answer is 10 times bigger or 10 times smaller than it should be.

A preliminary calculation using rough-rounded numbers is a valuable reality check: 3,104.267 is about 3,100 and 91.049 is about 90.

$$3,100 \times 90 = 279,000$$

279,000 is much closer to the correct answer of 282,640.406 than it is to either of the two gross errors.

Checking calculations using rough-rounded numbers is most useful when you are manipulating small decimals.

$$0.06294 \times 0.00712 = ?$$

rounded    rounded

$$0.06 \quad \times 0.007 \quad = 0.00042$$

The check calculation answer has zeros in the first three decimal places and so does the correct accurate answer of 0.000448. Any answer with say one, two, four or five zeros immediately after the decimal point must be wrong.

Check calculations with rounded numbers work equally well with subtraction, multiplication and division sums.

## Into reverse

You can check the answer to a calculation by working backwards. This is not as difficult as it sounds, and you do not need to use rounded figures.

Previously, we have shown that:

$$3{,}104.267 \quad \times \quad 91.049 \quad = \quad 282{,}640.406$$

Division is multiplication put into reverse. If you divide the answer to a multiplication by one of the starting numbers, your calculator will show the other starting number. For example:

$$282{,}640.406 \quad \div \quad 91.049 \quad = \quad 3{,}104.267$$

or

$$282{,}640.406 \quad \div \quad 3{,}104.267 \quad = \quad 91.049$$

Your first calculation is wrong if the division sum does not give you back one of the numbers you started with.

You can check divisions in the same way, because multiplication is division in reverse.

Always repeat a calculation involving the addition of more than about a dozen numbers. First time, start at the top of the list and work downwards. Reverse the order for the double-check – start with the bottom number and work upwards.

## Inversion errors

Many calculations involve not only multiplication or division, but also the choice between the two operations. It is easy to divide when you should be multiplying or to multiply when you should be using division. Getting calculations 'upside down' (inversion) is one of the commonest gross errors. It is a particular risk in conversions between imperial and metric units, in switching between larger and smaller metric units and in currency exchange rate calculations.

Fortunately, there are two simple rules to help you avoid inversion errors and an easy way to remember these rules.

# Pounds and pence

Not all of us are good with money, but everyone understands the difference between pounds (£) and pence (p). You can do money sums if you have three pieces of linked information:

- The conversion rate, or exchange rate, between the two units is

  £1.00 = 100p.

- The thing called a pound (£) is the big unit.

- The thing called a penny (p) is the small unit.

To turn 1,023p into £, you divide by the conversion rate of 100 to give £10.23p.

To turn £10.23 into pennies, you multiply by the conversion rate of 100 to give 1,023p.

If you remember the simple £ and p money rules, you should not make too many inversion errors.

In more general terms:

To get from SMALL units to BIG units – **DIVIDE** by the conversion rate.

To get from BIG units to SMALL units – **MULTIPLY** by the conversion rate.

---

### Examples

- There are 2.41 Australian dollars to £1.00.
  The £ is the big unit, the A$ is the small unit. Therefore:

  | | | | | |
  |---|---|---|---|---|
  | £1,000 | = | 1,000 × 2.41 | = | A$2,410 |
  | A$1,000 | = | 1,000/2.41 | = | £414.94 |

- There are 2.204 lbs to 1 kilogram.
  The kilogram is the big unit, the lb is the small unit. Therefore:

  | | | | | |
  |---|---|---|---|---|
  | 65 kg | = | 65 × 2.204 | = | 143.26 lbs |
  | 65 lbs | = | 65/2.204 | = | 29.492 kg |

- There are 100,000 centimetres in a kilometre.
  The centimetre is the small unit and the kilometre is the big unit. Therefore:

  | | | | | |
  |---|---|---|---|---|
  | 1.247 km | = | 1.247 × 100,000 | = | 124,700 cm |
  | 124,700 cm | = | 124,700/100,000 | = | 1.247 km |

# The halfway mark

You are now about half way through the Application of Number unit and we have covered the fundamental techniques that underpin all mathematics at all levels. The following things should be happening:

- Your number confidence ought to be increasing.

- Although you may not be completely comfortable with all of the topics you have studied so far, ideas that seemed totally bewildering at school ought to begin to make sense.

Amongst the basic techniques, there are four common sticking points:

- The addition and subtraction of fractions.

- Calculations involving percentage reductions.

- Handling square roots and cube roots.

- VAT.

If your particular problem is on this list, you should not worry – you are not alone. By the end of this unit, however, the majority of students should be able to cope with all of the fundamental concepts.

You will be able to use a calculator accurately and reliably, but some operations will take what seems like too much time. In the beginning, accuracy is far more important than speed. Getting the right answer after three minutes' thought is much better than getting the wrong one in 30 seconds. Speed always increases with familiarity and practice.

From now on, the unit takes a different direction. You will be taught how to apply the fundamentals in a series of specialist topics like area, volume, probability and the presentation and interpretation of data.

Your lectures will be based around example and practice. Most of your private study time should also be spent on practice calculations. When you are working alone, 'little and often' is much better than a marathon. Maths is different from most other subjects – with 20 minutes' homework, four or five times a week, you will make major progress. A three-hour session, once a week, will be exhausting and counter-productive.

Topic eight will round off the first half of the unit with examples of the kind of basic calculation problems you can expect in Application of Number examinations.

# 8 Basic calculations

To be numerate, and to prove your numeracy in an exam, you will need to be able to do two things:

- Perform the basic operations accurately.

- Use these techniques to solve real-life problems. You must be able to recognise what kinds of calculations are needed and know how to present your answers sensibly. Many problems need a combination of two or more techniques.

Most Application of Number exams are multiple-choice papers. You will be given a problem and then asked to choose one of four possible answers. The last topic in this unit gives some advice on handling these kinds of assessments.

## Correction and rounding

You are unlikely to be given simple, all-decimal addition sums unless they are designed to test your ability to correct to a given number of decimal places. The numbers will be given as a potentially confusing string, not as a neat vertical table.

### Example

| | |
|---|---|
| *Question* | *Add these figures together and give your answer corrected to three decimal places:* |
| | *8.4 + 17.00043 + 0.16989 + 12,421.98327* |
| *Answer* | Your calculator will show 12,447.55359 |
| | The answer is 12,447.554 |

Questions on rounding whole numbers are not difficult – you will be given a large whole number and asked to round it for presentation to an 'audience' who do not need or want too much detail. The large whole number might relate to money, people or something like the precise results of a census or survey.

### Example

| | | | |
|---|---|---|---|
| *Question* | *At the end of its financial year, a company had 213,476 employees. The* Daily Mirror *reported this number to the nearest 10,000, the* Daily Mail *rounded it to the nearest 1,000 and* The Financial Times *ran a story giving the number of workers to the nearest 100. What three numbers were printed?* | | |
| *Answer* | *Daily Mirror* | 210,000 | – (ends with 4 zeros) |
| | *Daily Mail* | 213,000 | – (ends with 3 zeros) |
| | *The Financial Times* | 213,500 | – (ends with 2 zeros) |

# Sequence

You are certain to be asked questions involving maxima, minima, range and sequence. The maximum is the largest number or quantity and the minimum the smallest. Range is the difference between the biggest and smallest. Sequence questions ask you to put numbers or quantities in order, according to size. Always double check to make sure you have not confused ascending order and descending order.

A sequence question might be used to test your ability to turn fractions into decimals.

---

### Example

Question    *Rearrange these fractions into ascending order:*

$$\frac{1}{3}$$

$$\frac{33}{102}$$

$$\frac{15}{44}$$

$$\frac{3}{10}$$

Answer    Smallest    $\frac{3}{10}$    (0. 300 )

$\frac{33}{102}$    (0. 324 )

$\frac{1}{3}$    (0. 333 )

Biggest    $\frac{15}{44}$    (0. 341 )

---

You might need more than three decimal places to distinguish between some sets of fractions.

Some sequence questions involve mixed units.

## Example

Question   At a school fête, four friends take part in a competition to guess how full a bucket is. Arrange their estimates into descending order.

$^2/_3$

0.8

60%

$^3/_4$

Answer   Biggest      0.8      (0.80)

$^3/_4$      (0.75)

$^2/_3$      (0.67)

Smallest   60%      ($= {}^{60}/_{100} = 0.60$)

Sequence questions are often used to test your knowledge of metric units and their various multiples and sub-multiples.

**You have to remember the symbols and what the prefixes mean – you will not be given a guide as part of an exam question.**

## Example

Question   Rearrange these weights into ascending order:

0.5 g

50 mg

600,000 mcg

700 mg

10,000 mcg

Answer   (g = grams, mg = milligrams, mcg = micrograms)

| | | |
|---|---|---|
| 10,000 mcg | = | 10,000 mcg |
| 50 mg × 1,000 | = | 50,000 mcg |
| 0.5 g × 1,000,000 | = | 500,000 mcg |
| 600,000 mcg | = | 600,000 mcg |
| 700 mg × 1,000 | = | 700,000 mcg |

# Negative numbers

The correct answer to questions like the one below shows that you can handle negative numbers.

---

### Example

The table shows the temperatures in seven cities during one day in January.

| City | Max. °C | Min. °C |
|------|---------|---------|
| Cairo | 14 | 7 |
| Birmingham | 7 | 0 |
| Moscow | −9 | −15 |
| Boston | 2 | −5 |
| Stockholm | −18 | −23 |
| Brussels | 5 | −3 |
| Melbourne | 29 | 26 |

| | |
|---|---|
| Question | *Which city had the lowest temperature?* |
| Answer | There are 14 possibilities. Of these, the lowest number is −23 °C, the minimum temperature in Stockholm. |
| Question | *Which city had the greatest range of temperatures?* |
| Answer | The temperature in Brussels changed by 8 °C. The range for Cairo, Birmingham and Boston was 7 °C. It was 6 °C in Moscow, 5 °C in Stockholm and 3 °C in Melbourne. |
| Question | *What is the difference between the maximum temperature in Melbourne and the maximum temperature in Stockholm?* |
| Answer | The answer is 47 °C, because the temperature in Stockholm would have to increase by 47 °C before it equalled the temperature in Melbourne. |

---

# Applied multiplication and division

Most exam questions involve division or multiplication, but you should not expect simple or straightforward problems. The examiner will want to find out if you know when to divide or multiply, not just how to divide or multiply. Division and multiplication problems come in many different varieties.

---

### Example

| | |
|---|---|
| Question | *How many seconds are there in a 31-day month?* |
| Answer | $60 \times 60 \times 24 \times 31 = 2,678,400$ seconds. |

Question    The petrol costs of running a car are 11p per mile. How many miles were driven in a year in which £1,052 was spent on petrol?

Answer    Miles driven        =    £1,052/0.11

                               =    9,564 miles

        Remember, 11p        =    £0.11.

You could show the answer to one or two decimal places, showing 9,563.6 miles or 9,563.64 miles.

## Example

Question    There are 71 potatoes in a 10 kilo bag. What is the average weight of each potato? Express* your answer to the nearest whole number of grams.

*Express just means 'give your answer as'.

Answer    Kilo means kilograms, so

        10 kg        =    10,000 g

        10,000/71    =    140.845 g

                      =    141 g to the nearest whole number of grams.

You have to know how to do currency conversions.

## Example

On a particular day, a bank offered the following exchange rates to its customers:

                £1.00    =    €1.44 (euros)

                £1.00    =    A$2.41 (Australian dollars)

                £1.00    =    ¥186 (Japanese yen)

                £1.00    =    $1.58 (US dollars)

The £1.00, properly called the pound sterling, is the biggest major currency unit. Put another way, you would rather be given £1.00 than one euro, one Australian dollar, one yen or one US dollar. This historical accident helps in sterling currency conversion sums. If you turn sterling into another currency, you get a bigger number. If you turn a currency back into sterling, you end up with a smaller number.

Question    Convert £1,007 to yen at an exchange rate of £1.00 = ¥186.

Answer    1,007 × 186 = ¥187,302.

Question    A traditional Japanese wedding present is a ¥100,000 note. How much is this in sterling, if £1.00 = ¥184.27?

Answer    100,000/184.27 = £542.68

Note that some exchange rates vary hour by hour and day by day. Always give sterling money answers corrected to two decimal places.

The commonest multiplication and division problems are based on conversions between metric and imperial units.

---

### Example

Question   *The distance by road between London and Manchester is 203 miles. What is this in kilometres, if 1 mile = 1.609 km? Give your answer corrected to one d.p.*

Answer   $203 \times 1.609 = 326.6$ km

The mile is a bigger unit than the kilometre, so the right answer is a bigger number than the one you started with.

---

### Example

Question   *Tariq weighs 142 lbs. How much is this in kilos, if 1 kg = 2.204 lbs? Give your answer corrected to two d.p.*

Answer   $142/2.204 = 64.43$ kg

Pounds are smaller than kilos, so the answer is a smaller number than the one you started with.

---

Be extra careful if you are working with numbers shown as mixtures of larger and smaller imperial units. These problems involve several stages.

---

### Example

Question   *Maria weighs 10 stone 4 lbs. How much is this in kilos if 1 stone = 6.35 kilos and 1 stone consists of 14 lbs?*

Answer   Step one: 10 stone 4 lbs is not 10.4 stones, because there are 14 lbs in a stone, not 10. If you enter a starting number of 10.4 into your calculator you will get the wrong answer. As a first step, you have to work out 10 stone 4 lbs as a fraction – this is $10^{4}/_{14}$ stones.

Step two: Using your calculator, turn $10^{4}/_{14}$ into a decimal:

$^{4}/_{14} = 0.286$ stones,

so 10 stone 4 lbs   $=$   $10^{4}/_{14}$ stones

$=$   10.286 stones

Step three: Carry on as before:

$10.286 \times 6.35 = 65.316$ kg

---

The table gives examples of steps one and two for some common mixed imperial or non-decimal units.

| Mixed unit | Fraction bottom number | Mixed unit as a fraction | Mixed unit as a decimal |
|---|---|---|---|
| 15 stone 7 lbs | 14 | $15^{7}/_{14}$ | 15.5 stones |
| 7 stone 13 lbs | 14 | $7^{13}/_{14}$ | 7.929 stones |
| 11 stone 2 lbs | 14 | $11^{2}/_{14}$ | 11.143 stones |
| *The fraction bottom number is 14 because 1 stone = 14 lbs.* | | | |
| 7 lbs 12 ozs | 16 | $7^{12}/_{16}$ | 7.75 lbs |
| 7 lbs 15 ozs | 16 | $7^{15}/_{16}$ | 7.9375 lbs |
| 11 ozs | 16 | $^{11}/_{16}$ | 0.6875 lbs |
| *The fraction bottom number is 16 because 1 lb = 16 ounces.* | | | |
| 2 hours 45 mins | 60 | $2^{45}/_{60}$ | 2.75 hours |
| 12 hours 51 mins | 60 | $12^{51}/_{60}$ | 12.85 hours |
| 127 minutes | 60 | $^{127}/_{60}$ | 2.117 hours |
| *The fraction bottom number is 60 because 1 hour = 60 minutes.* | | | |

# Scale models

Most of us do not realise it, but we all use scale models every day. In general terms, a model is a representation of a real-life object. The model might be smaller than the real thing, or bigger. The table gives some examples.

| Real object | Scale model |
|---|---|
| The solar system | Book diagram of the solar system |
| The world | Map of the world |
| London road system | London road map |
| Jumbo jet | Model aeroplane |
| Railway station | Train set |
| House | Doll's house |
| Your mother | Photograph of your mother |
| A flea | Enlarged photograph of a flea |
| A bacterium | Enlarged photograph of a bacterium |

A scale model is always made in the same way. Every length measurement of a big object is divided by the same number and this new set of measurements is used to build the model. Models of small things are made the other way around – every real length measurement is multiplied by the same number, to give the model's dimensions. The number used as the multiplier or divisor is the scale of the model – it can be shown in one of several ways, for example:

1 to 40

1:40

1 inch = 10 miles

1 cm = 10 miles

It is difficult to get scale model questions the wrong way around, but take care with units.

---

**Example**

Question    A real Boeing 747 airliner is 71 metres long. What is the length of a 1:500 scale model of this plane expressed in centimetres?

Answer      Clearly, the model will be much smaller than the real thing, so you divide by the scale number. You are asked for an answer in cm, so turn the length of the real thing into cm before you start.

71 m = 71 × 100 = 7,100 cm

7,100/500 = 14.2 cm

---

**Example**

Question    Your road map shows the distance between two motorway junctions as 4.6 cm. If the map scale is 1 cm = 4 miles, what is the actual distance between the two junctions?

Answer      4.6 cm × 4 = 18.4 miles

---

# Percentages

Problems involving percentages can seem deeply confusing at first glance. There are two important pieces of advice:

- First, percentage is just a special kind of fraction in which the bottom number is always 100.

- Second, percentage calculations always involve several steps – take it slowly and write down the answer to each step before you move on to the next one.

---

**Example**

Question    A town has a population of 351,274. If this increases by 7%, what will the new population be?

Answer      (i)   You are being asked to work out the new total population, not the number of extra people. The right answer must be bigger than 351,274.

(ii)  The 7% increase is the same as $^7/_{100}$ extra people, because a percentage is a fraction with a bottom number of 100.

(iii) Next work out the number of new or extra people:
$^7/_{100}$ × 351,274 = 24,589
rounded to the nearest whole person.

(iv) The new population has to be the old population plus the number of new people:

351,274 + 24,589 = 375,863

This is not the quickest way of calculating percentage changes, but until your number confidence increases, it is by far the safest and most logical. With experience, you will probably start combining two or more of the four steps. You will soon realise that all four stages can be combined into one calculation. That is:

$$1.07 \times 351,274 = 375,863$$

Percentage decrease sums are calculated in exactly the same way.

### Example

Question  In 2001 a company made a profit of £1,789,551. This decreased by 13% the following year. How much profit was made in 2002?

Answer  (i)  The answer must be smaller than £1,789,551.

(ii)  $13\% = {}^{13}/_{100}$

(iii)  ${}^{13}/_{100} \times £1,789,551 = £232,642$

(iv)  $£1,789,551 - £232,642 = £1,556,909$

or in one step:

$$£1,789,551 \times 0.87 = £1,556,909$$

Working from percentages back to real numbers is easy.

### Example

Question  A hospital admitted a total of 3,921 patients for surgical procedures in the year 1999. These patients were placed into one of four categories:

|  | % |
|---|---|
| Very overweight | 12.7 |
| Overweight | 33.2 |
| Normal weight range | 46.5 |
| Underweight | 7.6 |
|  | 100.0 |

How many patients weighed more than they ought to?

Answer  | 12.7% + 33.2% | = | 45.9% |
|---|---|---|
| $45.9\% = {}^{45.9}/_{100}$ | = | 0.459 |
| $0.459 \times 3,921$ | = | 1,800 patients. |

Always read the question very carefully when you are given a percentage problem – you might use the right method, but end up with the wrong answer.

## Example

Question   There are 459 children in a primary school. 204 are boys.
           What percentage are girls?

Answer     The number of girls is
           459 − 204 = 255

The percentage of girls is calculated first as a fraction, then as a decimal and finally as a percentage.

255/459 = 0.556 to three d.p.

(This number is actually 0.5 recurring)

0.556 × 100 = 55.6%

The percentage of boys is 44.4%. This figure is correct but would not be the right answer to the question, which asked for the percentage of *girls*.

Percentages are used to calculate the calorie content of most food and drink. These problems need a bit of thought – you are much less likely to make mistakes if you lay out your workings as a rough table.

## Example

The composition of a chocolate bar is given as a series of percentages.

|              | % by weight |
| ------------ | ----------- |
| Carbohydrate | 60          |
| Fat          | 25          |
| Water        | 15          |
|              | 100         |

Question   Carbohydrates have 4 calories per gram, fats have 9 calories per gram and water has no calories. How many calories are there in a 200 gram bar of this chocolate?

Answer     Tabulate the information you have.

|              | %    | No. of grams in 100 g | No. of grams in 200 g | Calories per gram | Total calories |
| ------------ | ---- | --------------------- | --------------------- | ----------------- | -------------- |
| Carbohydrate | 60%  | 60 g                  | 120 g                 | 4                 | 480            |
| Fat          | 25%  | 25 g                  | 50 g                  | 9                 | 450            |
| Water        | 15%  | 15 g                  | 30 g                  | zero              | zero           |
| Total        | 100% | 100 g                 | 200 g                 |                   | 930            |

The answer is 930 calories.

Changes in the money you earn, the money you spend and the taxes you pay are usually shown as percentages. All of these kinds of calculations are identical in principle.

---

### Example

*Question*    *Your pay rate of £5.80 per hour is increased by 4%. What is the new rate?*

*Answer*    104/100 × £5.80 = £6.03 per hour.

---

### Example

The list price of a bathroom tile is £1.10 each. The shop offers a discount of 7.5% on orders larger than 100 tiles and a discount of 12.5% on the total price of orders larger than 500 tiles.

*Question*    *What is the purchase price of 150 tiles?*

*Answer*    The list price is £1.10 × 150 = £165

This price is reduced by 7.5%

100% – 7.5% = 92.5%, so you pay 92.5% of the list price.

92.5% = $^{92.5}/_{100}$ = 0.925

You pay 0.925 × £165

= £152.63 for 150 discounted tiles.

*Question*    *What is the purchase price of 640 tiles?*

*Answer*    The steps in the calculation are the same:

List price = 640 × £1.10 = £704

100% – 12.5% = 87.5%, so you pay 0.875 × £704

= £616 for 640 discounted tiles.

# VAT

Many people have problems with VAT calculations. These only make sense if you understand clearly what a VAT-inclusive price really means. It helps to summarise how the system works:

• Governments decide the percentage VAT rate. It varies from country to country and from one kind of product or service to another. At the moment in the UK, there are three VAT rates. Some things like children's clothes, books, medicines and basic foods carry no VAT – this is called exemption or zero rating. Some energy supplies benefit from a reduced rate of 5%. Your home electricity and gas bills are calculated using this lower rate. Most goods and services in the UK carry VAT at 17.5%.

- When you buy something that carries VAT, your money ends up in two different places. You pay a retail, or tax inclusive, price. Part of this goes to the shopkeeper or the service provider – this is called the base price. The remainder goes to the government – this is value added tax (VAT).

- The important sum is: base price + VAT = retail price.

- This is what makes VAT sums confusing at first – the retail price is 117.5% not 100%.

## Example

Imagine you buy a washing machine for £260. Using fractions, we can work out who gets your money:

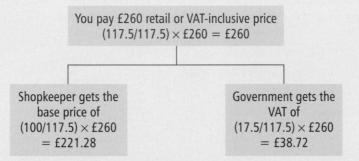

You can use a reality check for both calculations:

| 100/117.5 | + | 17.5/117.5 | = | 117.5/117.5 |
|---|---|---|---|---|
| £221.28 | + | £38.72 | = | £260.00 |

Once these principles make sense, VAT sums are easy.

The table gives some examples.

| Retail or tax inclusive price (117.5/117.5) | Base price (100/117.5) | VAT included in the retail price (17.5/117.5) |
|---|---|---|
| 99p | 84p | 15p |
| £4.99 | £4.25 | 74p |
| £19.99 | £17.01 | £2.98 |
| £49.95 | £42.51 | £7.44 |
| £499.95 | £425.49 | £74.46 |

A reality check would show that:

Retail price = base price + VAT

# How much practice do you need?

Every student is different. In this topic we have given illustrations of the kinds of problems a numerate person needs to be able to solve, but we have not shown all of the possibilities or more than a few examples of each important technique.

Some kinds of calculations will trouble you more than others. Avoid the temptation of practising the easy bits over and over again and ignoring what you do not understand.

Your maths lecturer will suggest how much overall practice you need and he or she will also be able to pinpoint your weaknesses and blind spots.

Maths private study involves sample questions, a pen, some paper and a calculator. Just reading through the theory, handouts or a textbook does not work. You need to practise *doing* the maths to master it.

# 9 Ratios

We use ratios in everyday language:

- 'Men outnumber women by twelve to one on university engineering courses.'

- 'Over the age of 90, women outnumber men by nine to one.'

- 'There were four women to every three men at the dance.'

Ratios are a rough and ready way of comparing two numbers, or two sets of numbers. They are not widely used because fractions or percentages give a more accurate picture.

Ratios are written as two whole numbers separated by a colon, or just simply in words, for example:

|       |    |        |
|-------|----|--------|
| 3:5   | or | 3 to 5 |
| 1:8   | or | 1 to 8 |
| 8:3   | or | 8 to 3 |
| 1:1   | or | 1 to 1 |
| 4:3   | or | 4 to 3 |

As an example, 36 people went to a family Christmas party:

|       |    |
|-------|----|
| Men   | 12 |
| Women | 9  |
| Boys  | 6  |
| Girls | 9  |
| Total | 36 |

Ratios for the party can be calculated as follows:

| Comparison         | Raw numbers | Ratio |
|--------------------|-------------|-------|
| Men to boys        | 12:6        | 2:1   |
| Women to girls     | 9:9         | 1:1   |
| Males to females   | 18:18       | 1:1   |
| Men to women       | 12:9        | 4:3   |
| Girls to boys      | 9:6         | 3:2   |
| Adults to children | 21:15       | 7:5   |

**Very importantly, ratios are not the same as fractions.**

For example:

- ¼ of a group of people have blue eyes and ¾ have brown eyes. The ratio of blue eyes to brown eyes is 1:3 not 1:4.

- 10% of people are vegetarians. The ratio of vegetarians to meat eaters is 1:9 not 1:10.

- 20% of viewers cannot stand televised football. The ratio of football haters to football watchers is 1:4.

## Examples

The ratios for the following groups are:

| Group | Ratio to calculate | Ratio |
|---|---|---|
| Half of people are male and half are female | Male:female | 1:1 |
| Two-thirds of adults have driving licences | Drivers:non-drivers | 2:1 |
| 10% of a school class speak French | French speakers:non-French speaker | 1:9 |

Some ratio calculations are a bit more complicated. For example:

- 45% of people wear glasses. To express this as a ratio:
  The ratio of those that wear glasses to those that do not wear glasses is 45%:55%. The ratio 45:55 can be simplified if both numbers are divided by five, giving the answer 9:11.

- 12.5% of cats are black. To show this as a ratio:
  The ratio of black cats to all other colours is 12.5%:87.5%. Again this ratio of 12.5:87.5 can be simplified if both numbers are divided by 12.5, giving the answer 1:7.

Ratios can be turned into fractions, decimals and percentages – these sums are easy, provided you remember that ratios and fractions are not the same thing.

## Example

Men outnumber women by twelve to one on university engineering courses.

Like many calculations, you are far less likely to make mistakes if you put your figures into a table.

| | Ratio | Fraction | Decimal | % |
|---|---|---|---|---|
| Male students | 12 | $^{12}/_{13}$ | 0.923 | 92.3 |
| Female students | 1 | $^{1}/_{13}$ | 0.077 | 7.7 |
| All students | 13 | $^{13}/_{13}$ | 1.000 | 100.0 |

Sometimes you will be asked to choose a ratio that best describes the relationship between two large awkward numbers.

### Example

A school has a total of 774 pupils; 344 are boys. Which of these four ratios shows the ratio of boys to girls?

(i)    2:3

(ii)   4:5

(iii)  6:7

(iv)   9:8

The raw or unsimplified ratio of boys to girls is 344:430. You cannot tell just by looking which of the four alternatives is a simplified version of these two big numbers.

However, you can compare 344:430 with each of the four possible answers if you turn all of them into decimals.

Because the pupils must be either boys or girls, you only have to convert one half of the ratio. To explain:

|         | Ratio – boys:girls | 'Boy fraction' | 'Boy decimal' |
|---------|--------------------|----------------|---------------|
|         | 344:430            | $^{344}/_{774}$ | **0.444**     |
| (i)     | 2:3                | $^2/_5$        | 0.400         |
| (ii)    | 4:5                | $^4/_9$        | **0.444**     |
| (iii)   | 6:7                | $^6/_{13}$     | 0.462         |
| (iv)    | 9:8                | $^9/_{17}$     | 0.529         |

Now you can see immediately that 344:430 can be simplified to 4:5 because the boy decimal is 0.444 in both cases.

In this example, you could have rejected 9:8 without a check calculation because this ratio would mean that the school has more boys than girls.

36157

# 10 Boundaries, perimeters, areas and volumes

A boundary or a perimeter is the total length of the continuous line surrounding a two-dimensional shape. This is a precise but complicated way of describing an idea that everyone understands.

If a garden is completely enclosed by a fence, then the total length of the fence equals the perimeter or boundary of the garden. The perimeter of a circle is called its circumference.

Perimeters are measured in simple or linear units like centimetres, metres, kilometres or inches, feet, miles, etc.

Areas are calculated by multiplying two lengths together so they are always described in square units. For example:

| Length – linear units | Area – square units | Abbreviation |
|---|---|---|
| centimetres, cm | square centimetres | sq. cm., $cm^2$ |
| metres, m | square metres | sq. m., $m^2$ |
| yards | square yards | sq. yards |

Note that the superscript power number 2 is often used to abbreviate square units.

Some imperial area units have odd names, for example, 1 acre = 4,840 square yards.

Volumes are calculated by multiplying three lengths together. For example:

| Length – linear units | Volume – cube or cubic units | Abbreviation |
|---|---|---|
| centimetres, cm | cubic centimetres | cu. cm., cc, $cm^3$ |
| metres, m | cubic metres | cu. m., $m^3$ |
| feet | cubic feet | cu. ft., $ft^3$ |

For volumes, the superscript power number is 3, because you are multiplying three numbers together, not two.

For a three-dimensional object, you can calculate a surface area as well as a volume.

A cornflakes packet could be made by gluing six pieces of card together. The total area of the six pieces of card is the total surface area of the packet.

Clearly, the surface areas of three-dimensional objects are measured in square units.

You need to know how to work out the areas and perimeters of squares, rectangles and circles.

# Squares

A square is a regular shape, where the two pairs of opposite sides are parallel, each corner is a right angle and all four sides are the same length.

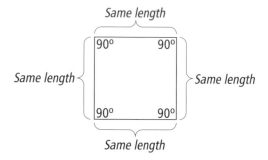

The area of a square is the length of one side multiplied by the length of another side.

Because both sides are the same length, the area is simply the length of one side squared.

$$\text{Area} = \text{length of one side} \times \text{length of one side}$$

$$\text{Area} = (\text{length of side})^2$$

$$A = s^2$$

The perimeter of a square is the total length of the outside of a square.

All four sides are the same length, therefore:

$$\text{Perimeter} = \text{length of one side} \times 4$$

$$P = 4s$$

## Practice question

How much carpet do you need to fit the following square rooms?

| Room measurement | Carpet |
|---|---|
| 4 metres × 4 metres | 16 square metres |
| 12 m × 12 m | 144 sq m |
| 3.5 m × 3.5 m | |
| 2.75 m × 2.75 m | |

How much skirting board do you need to fit the following square rooms?

| Room measurement | Skirting board |
|---|---|
| 6 m × 6 m | 24 m |
| 4.21 m × 4.21 m | |
| 7.9 m × 7.9 m | |

**Practice question**

Your back garden is in a terrible mess because you have had no free time to look after it.

The garden is a square of 24 metres by 24 metres.

There is a square pond in the garden of 3 metres by 3 metres.

How much turf do you have to buy to returf the entire garden, except the pond?

You will need to calculate the total area of the garden and subtract the total area of the pond to work out how much turf you need to buy.

What length of fence would you have to buy to enclose your garden entirely?

# Rectangles

A rectangle is a regular shape where the two pairs of opposite sides are parallel and each corner is a right angle.

Unlike a square, a rectangle has two shorter sides and two longer sides. Rectangles are sometimes called oblongs.

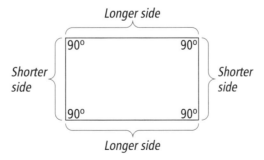

The area of a rectangle is the length of the longer side multiplied by the length of the shorter side.

Area   =   length of longer side × length of shorter side

The perimeter of a rectangle is twice the length of the shorter side, plus twice the length of the longer side.

Perimeter   =   2(length of shorter side) + 2(length of longer side)

## Practice question

Using a ruler and a calculator, calculate the area and the perimeter of this page.

## Practice question

What area of wallpaper would you need to paper the ceilings of the following rectangular rooms?

| Longer wall | Shorter wall | Wallpaper |
|---|---|---|
| 3.7 m | 3.5 m | 12.95 m² |
| 2.85 m | 4.24 m | |
| 6.22 m | 4.85 m | |

## Practice question

How much carpet do you need to fit this L-shaped room?

You will need to realise that this shape is two rectangles joined together.

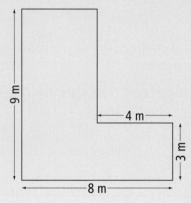

## Example

| | |
|---|---|
| Question | Your bathroom wall is 3 metres by 2 metres. |
| | You choose rectangular tiles that measure 15 cm by 10 cm. |
| | How many tiles do you need to buy to cover the bathroom wall? Assume the tiles touch each other without a space for grout, and that you do not break any. |
| Answer | First, convert the wall area into sq. cm: |
| | 3 m × 2 m = 300 cm × 200 cm = 60,000 sq. cm. |
| | Next, work out the area of one tile: |
| | 15 cm × 10 cm = 150 sq. cm. |
| | Then divide the area of the wall by the area of one tile: |
| | 60,000/150 = 400 tiles. |

## Practice question

A rectangular room is 4 metres long, 3 metres wide and 2.5 metres high from the top of the skirting board to the ceiling.

The room has one door, which is one metre wide and two metres high.

What is the total surface area of wall which you will have to paint?

If a 2.5 litre can of emulsion paint contains enough to cover 32 m² of wall, how many cans of this size will you need to buy to cover the walls with one coat of paint?

You will need to add together the area of the four walls and subtract the door area.

# Circles

Some special words are used to describe circles:

- The diameter is the length of a straight line that passes through the centre of the circle and touches both opposite perimeters of the circle.

- The radius is the distance from the centre of the circle to any point on the edge or perimeter of the circle.

- The perimeter of a circle is called its circumference.

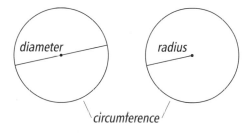

## Pi, π

For all circles, no matter how big or small, dividing the circumference by the diameter always gives the same answer.

This number is vitally important in many kinds of mathematics and is given its own special symbol, pi (pronounced 'pie' as in apple pie). Pi is a Greek letter. It is written as π.

π is a peculiar number. It cannot be calculated exactly – even with billions of decimal places, a repeating pattern has never been discovered.

| Accuracy | π |
|---|---|
| 2 d.p. | 3.14 |
| 3 d.p. | 3.142 |
| 4 d.p. | 3.1416 |
| 5 d.p. | 3.14159 |
| as a fraction | about $^{22}/_7$ |

The formula to calculate the area of a circle might be familiar:

$$A = \pi r^2 \text{ which is } \pi \times r^2$$

where A is the area

r is the radius

$\pi$ is the 'magic number'

For example, the area of a circle with a radius of 12 cm is calculated as

| | | |
|---|---|---|
| Area | = | 3.142 × 12 × 12 |
| | = | 452.448 sq cm |
| If r | = | 12, then $r^2$ = 12 × 12 = 144. |

Because $\pi$ is an awkward number, the areas of circles given as exam questions are not usually convenient, whole numbers.

## Practice question

Fill in the gaps in the table. Use a value of $\pi$ of 3.142.

| Radius | Diameter | Area |
|---|---|---|
| 6 cm | 12 cm | 113.112 sq cm |
| 9.5 m | 19 m | 283.566 sq m |
| 15 cm | | |
| | 20 m | |
| 82 cm | | |

The length of the perimeter of a circle is called its circumference.

To calculate the circumference of a circle, you multiply its diameter by $\pi$.

$$\text{Circumference} \quad = \quad \pi \times \text{diameter}$$

Because the diameter is twice the length of the radius, you can also use another way of calculating the circumference:

$$\text{Circumference} \quad = \quad \pi \times 2 \times \text{radius}.$$

## Practice question

Fill in the gaps in the table. Use a value of $\pi$ = 3.142.

| Radius | Diameter | Circumference |
|---|---|---|
| 5 cm | 10 cm | 31.42 cm |
| 40 cm | 80 cm | 251.36 cm |
| 4 metres | | |
| | 9 metres | |
| 6.2 metres | | |

# More complex shapes

If you know how to calculate the areas of squares, rectangles and circles, you can also work out the areas of some more complex shapes.

## Combinations of squares and rectangles

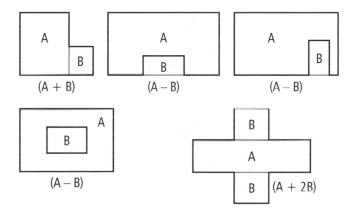

## Combinations of squares, rectangles and circles

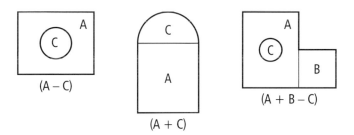

## Cubes

You need to be able to calculate the volume of three common objects: cubes, rectangular prisms and cylinders.

A cube is a very regular object – all of its edges are the same length and each of its six faces is square with the same area. A dice is the best common example of a cube.

The volume of a cube is calculated as:

$$\text{length of edge} \times \text{length of edge} \times \text{length of edge}$$

$$\text{or} \quad \text{volume} = (\text{length of edge})^3$$

$$V = e^3$$

A cube has six faces. Each face is a square. So, the surface area of a cube is calculated as:

$$6 \times \text{length of edge} \times \text{length of edge}$$

$$\text{or} \quad \text{area} = 6 \times (\text{length of edge})^2$$

$$A = 6e^2$$

## Practice question

Fill in the gaps to calculate the volumes and surface areas of the following cubes.

| Length of one edge | Volume | Surface area |
|---|---|---|
| 2 cm | 8 cm³ | 24 cm² |
| 9 cm | 729 cm³ | 486 cm² |
| 4.5 cm | | |
| 70 cm | | |
| 1 cm | | |

## Rectangular prisms

'Rectangular prism' is the proper name for a very familiar object. Bricks, corn-flake packets and most kinds of boxes are rectangular prisms.

A rectangular prism has three measurements: height, width and length. All three measurements can be different, or two can be the same and one different.

The volume of a rectangular prism is calculated by multiplying height by width by length:

$$\text{volume} = \text{length} \times \text{width} \times \text{height}$$

## Practice question

Fill in the gaps to calculate the volumes of these rectangular prisms:

| Length | Width | Height | Volume |
|---|---|---|---|
| 10 cm | 7 cm | 7 cm | 490 cm³ |
| 12 cm | 9 cm | 6 cm | 648 cm³ |
| 10.2 cm | 6.4 cm | 2.9 cm | |
| 15.25 cm | 9.28 cm | 1.07 cm | |

## Cylinders – volume

Bean cans and oil drums are good examples of cylinders. The top and bottom of a cylinder are circles with the same diameter, and the sides of a cylinder are parallel.

You can calculate the volume of a cylinder if you know the diameter of its top, or bottom, and its height. Remember that the diameter of a circle is twice the length of the radius.

The volume of a cylinder is calculated as the area of its circular top, or bottom, multiplied by its height.

$$\text{volume} = \pi \times \text{radius} \times \text{radius} \times \text{height}$$

$$V = \pi \times r' \times h$$

which is     $V = \pi r^2 h$

## Example

A 420 g can of beans has a diameter of 7.4 cm and a height of 10.8 cm.

This is how you calculate the volume of the bean can:

(Assume $\pi$ = 3.142.)

| | | |
|---|---|---|
| Diameter | = | 7.4 cm |
| *therefore* radius | = | 7.4/2 |
| | = | 3.7 cm |
| Area of circular top | = | $\pi \times 3.7 \times 3.7$ sq cm |
| | = | 43.01 cm |
| Height of cylinder | = | 10.8 cm |
| Volume of cylinder | = | $43.01 \times 10.8$ |
| Volume of cylinder | = | 464.51 cu cm |

## Practice question

Fill in the gaps in the table to calculate the volumes of the cylinders.

(Assume $\pi$ = 3.142.)

| Radius | Diameter | Height | Volume |
|---|---|---|---|
| 10 cm | 20 cm | 10 cm | 3,142 cu cm |
| 12 cm | 24 cm | 4 cm | 1,809.8 cu cm |
| | 18 cm | 20 cm | |
| 9.2 cm | | 14.7 cm | |

## Cylinders – surface area

To calculate the surface area of a cylinder, it helps to know how things like bean cans are made. A rectangular sheet of metal is rolled into a tube and the two edges joined together. Two identical circles are cut from another piece of metal – one forms the lid and the other makes the base. The tube is joined to the base – the bottom circle – and the can is filled. The top circle is used to seal the can.

To work out the total surface area of a cylinder, you need to add together the area of the two circles and the area of the rectangle used to make the tube or body of the can.

| Area | | Area calculation |
|---|---|---|
| Circular | Lid | $\pi \times$ radius $\times$ radius |
| Circular | Base | $\pi \times$ radius $\times$ radius |
| Rectangular | Body | circumference $\times$ height |
| | *or* | $2 \times \pi \times$ radius $\times$ height |

If the radius of the can is 3.7 cm, its height it 10.8 cm and $\pi = 3.142$, then the total surface area is:

| | | |
|---|---|---|
| Lid | $3.142 \times 3.7 \times 3.7$ | 43.01 |
| Base | $3.142 \times 3.7 \times 3.7$ | 43.01 |
| Body | $3.142 \times 2 \times 3.7 \times 10.8$ | 251.11 |
| Total | Total surface area | 337.13 sq cm |

# *11* Chance and probability

In day-to-day life we make continuous assessments of the chances or probabilities of things happening or not happening.

- 'There is no point in arriving at the bus stop early because the bus is nearly always late.'

- 'We do not go to Cornwall for our holidays because it often rains in the summer.'

- 'I very much doubt I could run a marathon.'

- 'Most people in the UK live to be at least 60.'

We use different words to describe different degrees of probability.

- 'I am certain that the sun will rise tomorrow morning.'

- 'July is nearly always hotter than March.'

- 'I will probably pass my driving test.'

- 'The chances of Arsenal winning the FA Cup are fifty-fifty.'

- 'I will possibly go out for dinner tonight.'

- 'Wine glasses occasionally get broken.'

- 'This horse is very unlikely to win the race.'

- 'Swimming the Atlantic Ocean is impossible.'

These statements are ranked in descending order of probability. There are two fixed points on the scale – 'certain' and 'impossible'. Every other sentence only gives a rough idea of the chances of something happening. Mathematicians use numbers instead of words to describe probabilities accurately and precisely.

Probabilities can be expressed in several ways. We will use percentage probabilities or probabilities shown as fractions where appropriate:

- A certainty has a probability of 100%.

- An impossibility has a probability of 0%.

- An evens chance has a probability of 50%.

- A one-in-three chance has a probability of 33.3%.

- A one-in-a-hundred chance has a probability of 1%, etc.

## Four assumptions

Basic probability calculations depend on four assumptions. Some of these are common sense, others seem less obvious. To explain, imagine that a £1 coin is flipped 10 times and each time the coin shows 'heads'.

Flipping the coin can be called an event, a trial or an experiment. The result of the event is called the outcome.

There are two possible outcomes: 'heads' or 'tails'. The outcomes must be equally likely – this obviously applies to simple experiments like flipping a coin or rolling a dice.

The outcomes must be mutually exclusive – again this holds true for our experiment because the outcome has to be 'heads' or 'tails'. It cannot be both and it cannot be neither.

The trials or events must be independent of each other. What happened last time must not influence what happens next time. Some people have problems with this idea. In our illustration, the probability of the eleventh flip showing a head is still 50% because each trial is an independent event. The run of 10 'heads' has not altered the eleventh flip in any way. This concept of independent events is important. Another simple experiment underlines the point.

Take 10 £1 coins, flip each one and line them up, showing the outcome of each flip. Imagine that the outcome of each has been 'heads', giving you a row of 10 coins all showing 'heads'.

Repeat the experiment with the help of a friend. This time, as you flip the coins, your friend lines them up but covers them with a cloth so you cannot see the sequence.

Because you do not know what happened before, you will correctly calculate the odds of 'heads' for the eleventh flip as 50%. The only difference between the two experiments is that you have looked at one row of coins but not at the other. You obviously cannot alter the way coins behave just by looking at them.

In any trial or experiment, the probabilities of all the possible outcomes must add up to 100%. This is common sense. In the case of the coins, there is a 50% chance of 'heads' and a 50% chance of 'tails'.

If we repeat the coin flipping a million times, long runs of heads or tails would happen, but the total number of heads would be very close to 500,000. In an infinitely long experiment, the number of heads would exactly equal the number of tails.

## Playing cards

An ordinary pack of British playing cards without jokers is made up as follows:

- There are 52 cards in all.

- There are 13 cards for each of four suits – clubs, diamonds, hearts and spades.

- Diamonds and hearts are red cards.

- Clubs and spades are black cards.

- The 13 cards of each suit are the ace, 2, 3, 4, 5, 6, 7, 8, 9, 10, Jack, Queen and King.

- The Jack, Queen and King are called face cards.

The table below shows how to calculate the probability of drawing a particular card or a particular kind of card assuming that each time a card is drawn it is examined, placed back in the pack and the pack is thoroughly shuffled.

You are calculating the probability of a single outcome, not a combination of outcomes.

| Outcome | Odds | Probability | |
|---|---|---|---|
| | | Fraction: Desired outcome/ total number of possible outcomes | % |
| Drawing a red card | 1 in 2 | 26/52 | 50 |
| Drawing a black card | 1 in 2 | 26/52 | 50 |
| Drawing a spade | 1 in 4 | 13/52 | 25 |
| Drawing a face card | 3 in 13 | 12/52 | 23.08 |
| Drawing an ace | 1 in 13 | 4/52 | 7.69 |
| Drawing a black ace | 1 in 26 | 2/52 | 3.85 |
| Drawing the ace of spades | 1 in 52 | 1/52 | 1.92 |
| Drawing an ace or a 2 | 2 in 13 | 8/52 | 15.38 |

### Practice question

What is the percentage probability of drawing a red face card?

# Combinations

Previously, we have shown that the probability of drawing an ace is 4/52 or one chance in 13, or 7.69%. If the ace is drawn from the pack but then put to one side, we can calculate the probability of drawing a second ace from a smaller pack of 51 cards. There are three aces left, so the probability of drawing another one is 3/51 or 5.88%.

Obviously, if the first four cards drawn happen to be aces and are put aside, then there is a zero probability of the fifth card being an ace because all of the aces have gone.

We all instinctively realise that the chances of a single outcome are greater than the chances of any particular combination of two or more outcomes. Large parts of the betting, gaming and gambling industries work on this principle, as do many kinds of insurance.

What are the chances of the first two cards drawn from the pack being aces? If you replace the drawn card, the chances of this combination are calculated by simple multiplication:

$$4/52 \times 4/52 \quad = \quad 16/2{,}704$$
$$= \quad 0.00592$$
$$= \quad 0.59\% \qquad \text{(about one chance in 170)}$$

If you put the first ace to one side, the chances of the first two cards being aces are obviously less:

$$4/52 \times 3/51 \quad = \quad 12/2{,}652$$
$$= \quad 0.00452$$
$$= \quad 0.45\% \qquad \text{(about one chance in 220)}$$

Logically, we know that the probability of the first four drawn cards all being aces is very small indeed, but most people do not realise just how unlikely this kind of outcome actually is. If the cards are put back into the pack each time, the probability of drawing four consecutive aces is:

$$\frac{4}{52} \times \frac{4}{52} \times \frac{4}{52} \times \frac{4}{52} = \frac{256}{7{,}311{,}616}$$

This works out as one chance in about 28,600.

If the drawn cards are put to one side, the probability of drawing four consecutive aces on the first four trials, experiments or events is even less:

$$\frac{4}{52} \times \frac{3}{51} \times \frac{2}{50} \times \frac{1}{49} = \frac{24}{6{,}497{,}400}$$

This equals about one chance in 270,000.

These simple multiplication sums explain why most regular gamblers are poor and most bookmakers and casino operators are rich. We can now put the cards away and start playing a different game.

# Playing with one dice

A dice is a cube with a different number on each face. It is easy to calculate the probability of throwing any number with a single dice.

| Outcome | Odds | Probability | |
|---|---|---|---|
| | | Fraction:<br>Desired outcome/<br>total number of<br>possible outcomes | % |
| Throwing a 1 | 1 in 6 | 1/6 | 16.67 |
| Throwing a 1 or 2 | 2 in 6 | 2/6 | 33.33 |
| Throwing a 1, 2 or 3 | 3 in 6 | 3/6 | 50.0 |
| Throwing a 1, 2, 3 or 4 | 4 in 6 | 4/6 | 66.67 |
| Throwing a 1, 2, 3, 4 or 5 | 5 in 6 | 5/6 | 83.33 |
| Throwing a 1, 2, 3, 4, 5 or 6 | 6 in 6 | 6/6 | 100.0 |
| Throwing a 1 or a 6 | 2 in 6 | 2/6 | 33.33 |

# Playing with two dice

If two dice are thrown at the same time, and the scores on the two dice are added together, then there are 11 possible scores: two is the lowest and 12 is the highest.

Common sense says that the probability of each possible score is 1 in 11, or 9.09%. However, common sense gives the wrong answer in this case and the mathematics of probability can get peculiar.

The probability of an outcome is the number of ways that the desired outcome can happen, divided by the total number of possible outcomes. The table shows how to work out the two dice probabilities. The body of the table shows the combined score.

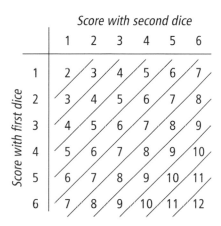

The table shows that there are 36 possible outcomes. The lowest score with two dice is two and there is only one way of scoring two, so the chances of doing this are 1 in 36.

Similarly, the highest possible score is 12 and there is only one way of doing this, so the chances of scoring 12 are 1 in 36.

All other scores can be achieved in more than one way, so the probability of scoring between 3 and 11 has to be carefully calculated.

| Two-dice score | No. of ways of achieving this score | Odds | Probability | |
|---|---|---|---|---|
| | | | Fraction | % |
| 2 | 1 | 1 in 36 | 1/36 | 2.78 |
| 3 | 2 | 2 in 36 | 1/18 | 5.55 |
| 4 | 3 | 3 in 36 | 1/12 | 8.33 |
| 5 | 4 | 4 in 36 | 1/9 | 11.11 |
| 6 | 5 | 5 in 36 | 5/36 | 13.89 |
| 7 | 6 | 6 in 36 | 1/6 | 16.68 |
| 8 | 5 | 5 in 36 | 5/36 | 13.89 |
| 9 | 4 | 4 in 36 | 1/9 | 11.11 |
| 10 | 3 | 3 in 36 | 1/12 | 8.33 |
| 11 | 2 | 2 in 36 | 1/18 | 5.55 |
| 12 | 1 | 1 in 36 | 1/36 | 2.78 |
| Total | 36 | 36 in 36 | 36/36 = 1 | 100.00 |

A combined two-dice score of seven is, for example, six times more likely than scoring 2 or 12.

# *12* Pie charts

Data presented in large numbers of rows and columns is difficult to read and understand. Nearly everyone has trouble with bus and train timetables, for example.

Different kinds of animals have evolved different kinds of eyesight. Some can see minute detail, others long distances. Colour vision varies, as does the ability to detect small movements or to see in reduced light. Humans are exceptionally good at distinguishing between very slightly different shapes, patterns and angles.

This ability means that numbers are much easier for us to understand if they can be turned into pictures of one kind or another. In this unit we will look at pie charts, bar charts and graphs – the three most common ways of simplifying and presenting data.

The following table gives the results of a survey showing how people travelled from home to work.

| Method of transport | No. of people |
|---|---|
| Private car | 237 |
| Taxi | 5 |
| Train | 54 |
| Bus | 201 |
| By foot | 81 |
| Number interviewed | 578 |

This raw data is not very helpful – you can tell more people travelled by car than any other method, but not much else.

It helps to turn the raw numbers into percentages:

| Method of transport | No. of people | Decimal | % |
|---|---|---|---|
| Private car | 237/578 | 0.410 | 41.0 |
| Taxi | 5/578 | 0.009 | 0.9 |
| Train | 54/578 | 0.093 | 9.3 |
| Bus | 201/578 | 0.348 | 34.8 |
| By foot | 81/578 | 0.140 | 14.0 |
| Total | 578/578 | 1.000 | 100.0 |

It is easier to understand the results of this survey as percentages, but you still have to look quite hard to work out what is going on.

# Circles and slices

A pie chart is tedious to construct, but once drawn it is a very effective way of communicating. A circular pie is used to represent the total number of 'things' – in this example 578 people interviewed.

The circle is divided into slices. The size of each slice is proportional, in our example, to the number of people using each kind of transport. For instance, the biggest slice would be that for private motorists and the thinnest slice for taxi users.

You will remember that angles are usually measured in degrees.

A right angle is 90 degrees. For example, if you turn left or right at a T-junction, you move through 90°. A full circle contains four right angles so there are 4 × 90, or 360° in a full circle.

$$\frac{1}{4} \text{ of a circle} \quad = \quad 90°$$

$$\frac{1}{2} \text{ of a circle} \quad = \quad 180°$$

$$\frac{3}{4} \text{ of a circle} \quad = \quad 270°$$

To construct a pie chart, the percentages are turned into angles.

| Method of transport | % | Slice angle |
|---|---|---|
| Private car | 41.0% of 360° | 148° |
| Taxi | 0.9% of 360° | 3° |
| Train | 9.3% of 360° | 33° |
| Bus | 34.8% of 360° | 125° |
| By foot | 14.0% of 360° | 51° |
| Number interviewed | 100.0% of 360° | 360° |

The slices are labelled and shaded to add clarity.

It is usual to show the first slice beginning at the '12 o'clock' position. The slices can be arranged in any order – an alternating pattern of thick and thin slices works best.

You can see that the pie chart shows the overall results of the transport survey at a single glance.

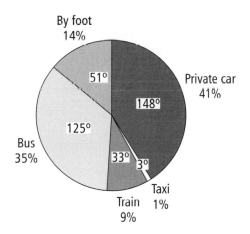

By foot
14%

Private car
41%

51°

148°

125°

Bus
35%

33° 3°

Taxi
1%

Train
9%

## Practice question

This pie chart shows the results of a survey asking a sample of readers to choose their favourite newspaper.

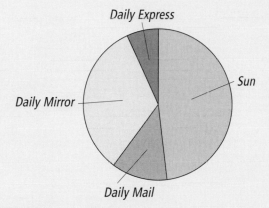

Daily Express

Sun

Daily Mirror

Daily Mail

Pick the only correct answer from the following choices.

(i)   The pie chart shows that:

    A.   Most readers prefer the *Daily Mirror*

    B.   About half of the readers prefer the *Sun*

    C.   The least popular paper is the *Daily Mirror*

    D.   The least popular paper is the *Daily Mail*

(ii)  The pie chart shows that the percentage of readers preferring the *Daily Mirror* is about:

    A.   50%

    B.   33%

    C.   85%

    D.   12%

(iii)   A total of 3,200 readers were interviewed for the survey. Of these, 224 said the *Daily Express* was their favourite. What is the approximate angle of the pie chart for this group?

A.   120°

B.   90°

C.   25°

D.   75°

# *13* Bar charts and classified information

Some experiments, surveys and observations produce hundreds, thousands or even many thousands of readings. It would be difficult and tedious to include every reading, number or observation in a description of the survey or experiment. In these cases, the information can be classified or grouped together and presented as a bar chart.

The commonest kind of bar chart is properly called a histogram.

We can show how a bar chart is put together.

## Example

Because of overfishing, the average size of plaice taken from the North Sea is reducing. The EU conducted a major experiment to find out how serious the overfishing had become.

It was decided to allow about 10,000 fish to be caught over a period of seven days. Each fish was weighed. Its weight was recorded to the nearest gram.

- 10,843 fish were caught.

- The heaviest fish weighed 2,432 grams.

- The lightest fish weighed 114 grams.

This information needs to be classified, because it would be very difficult to show 10,843 individual readings on a graph, and a table of 10,843 numbers would be virtually meaningless. So we handle the information in another way.

The total range of weights can be divided into a number of classes. There are no rules, but the clearest bar charts have between five and 12 classes.

Each class interval must be the same size. In our example, the heaviest fish was 2,432 grams, so 10 classes using 250 g intervals should produce a good bar chart.

## Classifying the raw data

| | Class<br>(weight range of fish in g) | | Number of fish<br>in this weight range |
|---|---|---|---|
| 1 | 0 | to 249 | 159 |
| 2 | 250 | to 499 | 325 |
| 3 | 500 | to 749 | 3,041 |
| 4 | 750 | to 999 | 3,238 |
| 5 | 1,000 | to 1,249 | 1,932 |
| 6 | 1,250 | to 1,499 | 1,207 |
| 7 | 1,500 | to 1,749 | 529 |
| 8 | 1,750 | to 1,999 | 264 |
| 9 | 2,000 | to 2,249 | 101 |
| 10 | 2,250 | to 2,499 | 47 |
| | Total number of fish | | 10,843 |

A bar chart can then be drawn, where the horizontal axis shows the ten classes and the height of each bar is proportional to the number of fish in each class.

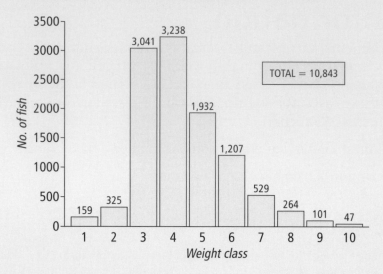

You will not be asked to construct a bar chart from a huge mass of raw data, but you do have to know how to use one. For instance:

Question     *How many fish weighed less than 1 kilogram and what percentage of the fish did this represent?*

Answer     All of the fish in the first four classes must weigh less than 1 kg (1,000 g), but all of the fish in the fifth and subsequent classes weigh 1 kg or more.

Therefore,

$$159 + 325 + 3{,}041 + 3{,}238 = 6{,}763$$

fish weighed less than 1 kg. This number can be converted into a percentage in the usual way:

$$6{,}763/10{,}843 \quad = \quad 0.6237$$

$$0.6237 \times 100 \quad = \quad 62.4\% \text{ (to 1 d.p.)}$$

Question     *How many fish weighed 2 kg or more?*

Answer     All of the fish in classes 9 and 10 must weigh more than 2 kg.

Therefore, the answer is 101 + 47 or 148 fish.

A bar chart cannot always give precise answers to some questions. For example, if a plaice has to weigh 2.1 kg or more before it can breed, how many fish in this sample are of breeding size?

All of the plaice in class 10 weigh more than 2.1 g, but using the bar chart, we cannot tell how many fish in class 9 are bigger than 2.1 kg. It could be all of them, some of them, or none of them. All we can say for sure is that at least 47 fish are heavier than 2.1 kg and no more than 101 + 47, or 148, are of breeding size. You would have to go back to the raw data to answer this question precisely.

## Practice question

You may need to use classified information that has not been converted into a bar chart.

A group of children had their height measured to the nearest 0.1 cm. The results of the height survey were classified as follows:

| Height range (cm) | Number of children |
|---|---|
| 130.0 to 139.9 | 1 |
| 140.0 to 149.9 | 7 |
| 150.0 to 159.9 | 10 |
| 160.0 to 169.9 | 12 |
| 170.0 to 179.9 | 8 |
| 180.0 to 189.9 | 2 |

(i)    How many children were measured?

(ii)   How many children are less than 160 cm tall?

(iii)  What percentage of the children are less than 150 cm tall?

(iv)  What fraction of the children are 160 cm tall or more?

# *14* Graphs

Graphs are a very common and effective way of presenting information. Like pie charts, graphs communicate visually, and complex information can be absorbed at a single glance.

There are many kinds of graph. Here we are concerned only with the most straightforward types.

We need to start with some basic definitions:

● Graphs are written or printed on a regular grid of squares. Most graph paper is metric – a pattern of larger squares divided into 10 by 10, giving 100 smaller squares.

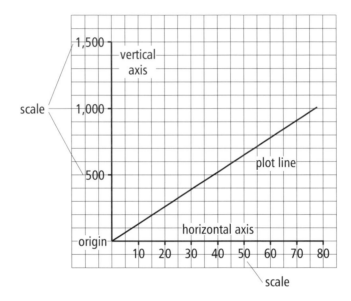

● The simplest graphs show the relationship between two variables.

● A vertical line drawn towards the left-hand side of the graph paper is called the vertical axis or the y axis – remember 'wise up'.

● A horizontal line drawn towards the bottom of the graph paper is called the horizontal axis or the x axis – remember 'x is a cross'.

● The two axes meet at the bottom left-hand corner of the graph. This meeting point is called the origin.

● Scales are drawn on each axis and the value of one variable is plotted against the value of the other variable.

## Celsius versus Fahrenheit

Take the example of a graph designed to show the relationship between the two common temperature scales.

Any temperature can be expressed as °C or °F. These are the two variables. These two variables are related. There is a formula that tells you how to calculate one if you know the other.

The table shows five Celsius temperatures and their equivalents in Fahrenheit.

| °C | | °F |
|---|---|---|
| 0 | = | 32 |
| 25 | = | 77 |
| 50 | = | 122 |
| 75 | = | 167 |
| 100 | = | 212 |

A graph can be drawn to show the relationship between the two temperature scales.

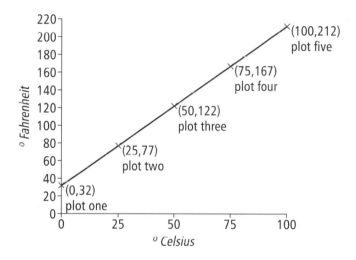

This graph is a simple straight line and therefore the relationship between the Celsius and the Fahrenheit scales is said to be linear.

A large, accurate version of this graph could be used to make rapid conversions between the two variables.

For example, if you wanted to know the Celsius equivalent of 81.1 °F, you could discover this by drawing a horizontal line connecting 81.1 °F on the vertical scale and the plot line and then a second vertical line connecting this point on the plot line to the horizontal axis. You could then 'read off' a value of 27.3 °C.

Some relationships give graphs which are smooth curves rather than straight lines – these are non-linear.

## Practice question

The following table shows the relationship between the length of the side of a square and the area of the square.

| Side of square (cm) | Area of square (sq cm) |
|---|---|
| 1 | 1 |
| 2 | 4 |
| 3 | 9 |
| 4 | 16 |
| 5 | 25 |
| 6 | 36 |

Draw a graph using these numbers to show the relationship between the length of the side of a square and its area.

# Irregular relationships

The relationship between some variables is difficult to predict. These produce irregular graphs.

## Practice question

This table shows the air temperature in Birmingham at hourly intervals on a day in November.

| Time | °C |
|---|---|
| 06.00 | 2 |
| 07.00 | 2 |
| 08.00 | 3 |
| 09.00 | 5 |
| 10.00 | 7 |
| 11.00 | 9 |
| 12.00 | 12 |
| 13.00 | 13 |
| 14.00 | 12 |
| 15.00 | 7 |
| 16.00 | 4 |
| 17.00 | 3 |
| 18.00 | 2 |
| 19.00 | 1 |

Draw a graph showing how the temperature varied across the day.

It does not usually matter which variable is shown on which axis, but time as a variable is *always* shown on the horizontal axis.

The axes of your graph for the practice question should look like this:

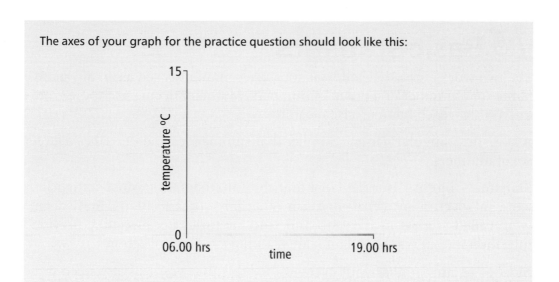

# *15* Basic statistics

The two words 'statistic' and 'statistics' are commonly used as an alternative name for a number or a group of numbers. Mathematicians use these words differently – each has a precise meaning.

A statistic – singular – is one number that summarises and describes a larger set of numbers.

Statistics – plural – is a specialist branch of mathematics. Most statisticians work in government departments or other large organisations. Statisticians were called statists in the 18th and 19th centuries because they provided information that was useful for state planning and tax collection.

Most of us are familiar with averages; for this unit you will also need to be able to use three other kinds of statistics – the median, the mode and the range. The words are confusing at first, but the calculations are simple, easy to use and easy to remember.

## The arithmetic mean or average

The words average, mean, arithmetic mean and arithmetic average are all different labels for the same thing.

The word average is the most widely used; to be completely accurate, the average should be called the arithmetic mean.

To calculate an arithmetic mean:

- Add up all the numbers in the set to give a total.

- Divide this total by the number of things in the set.

### Example

The table shows the heights of the Japanese and the Swedish national football teams:

|  | Japan (height in inches) | Sweden (height in inches) |
|---|---|---|
| 1 | 60 | 65 |
| 2 | 60 | 69 |
| 3 | 61 | 69 |
| 4 | 64 | 70 |
| 5 | 64 | 71 |
| 6 | 65 | 73 |
| 7 | 67 | 73 |
| 8 | 68 | 74 |
| 9 | 68 | 74 |
| 10 | 70 | 75 |
| 11 | 72 | 78 |
| Total height | 719 inches | 791 inches |
| Divide by | 11 footballers | 11 footballers |
| Arithmetic mean | 65.4 inches | 71.9 inches |

We can conclude that the average Swedish footballer is taller than the average Japanese footballer. We can also calculate the difference in average height.

| | |
|---|---|
| Swedish average | 71.9 inches |
| Japanese average | 65.4 inches |
| Difference in average height | 6.5 inches |

# What the average cannot show

It is vital to know what an average does not show:

- It cannot tell you the height of any individual player. Not one of the players is precisely the average height for his team. In the same way, the average UK family has 1.9 children, but nobody has 0.9 of a child.

- It does not tell you that every Swede is taller than every Japanese. In this example, five Swedes were shorter than the tallest Japanese.

- In this example, the shortest of the 22 players was Japanese, and the tallest Swedish – but this need not be so.

The average can be misleading: two obviously different sets of numbers can have identical, or very similar, averages.

### Example

The table shows the hourly pay rates for two small companies. Both have eight employees plus an owner. Both make socks.

|  |  | The Orange Sock Company £ per hour | The Pink Sock Company £ per hour |
|---|---|---|---|
| Owner |  | 16 | 62 |
| Employee | 1 | 10 | 2 |
|  | 2 | 10 | 2 |
|  | 3 | 8 | 1 |
|  | 4 | 7 | 1 |
|  | 5 | 6 | 1 |
|  | 6 | 5 | 1 |
|  | 7 | 5 | 1 |
|  | 8 | 5 | 1 |
| Total wage bill, £ per hour |  | 72 | 72 |
| Average hourly rate |  | £8.00 per hour | £8.00 per hour |

Both companies pay the same average amount per hour, but the spread or distribution of pay rates is far greater in the Pink Sock Company than in the Orange Sock Company.

The arithmetic mean, or average, does not describe or summarise the difference in pay policy between the two companies.

We need other ways to describe different kinds of spread or distribution. There are three straightforward methods of doing this – we can use the range, the median or the mode.

# Range

The range is simply the largest number in a set, minus the smallest number in the set.

For the sock companies:

This statistic shows that Pink pay rates vary more than Orange pay rates.

|  | Orange | Pink |
|---|---|---|
| Highest hourly rate | £16/hr | £62/hr |
| Lowest hourly rate | £5/hr | £1/hr |
| Range | £11/hr | £61/hr |

### Practice question

Calculate the range in heights for the Japanese and Swedish football teams shown in the previous example.

Calculate the average and the range for these eight sets of numbers:

| A | B | C | D | E | F | G | H |
|---|---|---|---|---|---|---|---|
| 10 | 10 | 10 | 10 | 9 | 4 | 1 | 1 |
| 10 | 11 | 5 | 14 | 10 | 18 | 46 | 0 |
| 10 | 10 | 10 | 10 | 8 | 20 | 1 | 48 |
| 10 | 9 | 15 | 8 | 12 | 4 | 1 | 1 |
| 10 | 10 | 10 | 8 | 11 | 4 | 1 | 0 |

# Median

Another useful statistic is called the median (not the 'medium').

In a set of numbers, the median is the middle number. Put another way: half the numbers in a set are bigger than the median – the other half are smaller.

To calculate the median, arrange the numbers in ascending or descending order. Count how many numbers you have, then count down from the top until you reach the middle number – this is the median.

**Example**

We can calculate the medians of the two football teams and the two sock companies used as previous examples.

(i)

| | Japan (height in inches) | Sweden (height in inches) |
|---|---|---|
| 1 | 60 | 65 |
| 2 | 60 | 69 |
| 3 | 61 | 69 |
| 4 | 64 | 70 |
| 5 | 64 | 71 |
| 6 | 65 | 73 |
| 7 | 67 | 73 |
| 8 | 68 | 74 |
| 9 | 68 | 74 |
| 10 | 70 | 75 |
| 11 | 72 | 78 |

There are 11 players in each team; therefore the middle player in height is footballer number 6 because five of his team are smaller and five are bigger.

|  | Japan | Sweden |
|---|---|---|
| Median height | 65 inches | 73 inches |

(ii)

|  |  | The Orange Sock Company £ per hour | The Pink Sock Company £ per hour |
|---|---|---|---|
| Owner |  | 16 | 62 |
| Employee | 1 | 10 | 2 |
|  | 2 | 10 | 2 |
|  | 3 | 8 | 1 |
|  | 4 | 7 | 1 |
|  | 5 | 6 | 1 |
|  | 6 | 5 | 1 |
|  | 7 | 5 | 1 |
|  | 8 | 5 | 1 |

There are nine people working for each company.

|  | Orange | Pink |
|---|---|---|
| Median wage | £7/hr | £1/hr* |

**\*The median is still the middle number even though some lower numbers are the same as the median.**

The middle number is easily identified if there are 11 footballers or nine sock-makers. But how is the median calculated for an even number of things?

### Example

Imagine that the referee sent Japanese player number 11 off the field. How do we then find the middle-height player from the 10 remaining?

With 11 Japanese footballers, player number 6 is the middle-height player, therefore the median is 65 inches.

With 10 Japanese footballers, because player number 11 is absent, the two middle players are then number 5 and number 6, and the median is the average of their two heights.

| Player number 5 | 64 inches |
|---|---|
| Player number 6 | 65 inches |
| Median for 10 players | 64½ inches |

# Mode

In a set of numbers, the mode is simply the commonest number – the one there is most of.

All sets of numbers have one arithmetic average and one median, but some groups of numbers do not have a mode, or they can have more than one mode.

In our previous examples, the mode pay rate for the Orange Sock Company was £5/hour and for the Pink Sock Company £1/hour.

---

### Practice questions: Mean, range, median and mode

The table shows the midday temperature at a Spanish holiday resort for the first 15 days of August.

| Day | °C | Day | °C |
|-----|----|-----|----|
| 1 | 29 | 9 | 20 |
| 2 | 30 | 10 | 19 |
| 3 | 30 | 11 | 30 |
| 4 | 30 | 12 | 31 |
| 5 | 31 | 13 | 32 |
| 6 | 34 | 14 | 30 |
| 7 | 24 | 15 | 35 |
| 8 | 23 | | |

(i) What is the temperature range, mean temperature, median temperature and mode temperature for these 15 days?

(ii) What are the range, mean, median and mode temperatures for the first 10 days of August?

You will be adding 15 numbers together – always double check your addition.

A restaurant owner buys 21 organic chickens from a local farmer. She weighs the chickens and makes a table of their weights (opposite).

Answer the following multiple-choice questions.

(i) The percentage of chickens weighing less than 1,300 g is about:

    A.   81%

    B.   33%

    C.   24%

    D.   19%

| Chicken no. | Weight (grams) | Chicken no. | Weight (grams) |
|---|---|---|---|
| 1 | 940 | 11 | 1,400 |
| 2 | 1,000 | 12 | 1,400 |
| 3 | 1,150 | 13 | 1,450 |
| 4 | 1,200 | 14 | 1,450 |
| 5 | 1,300 | 15 | 1,600 |
| 6 | 1,300 | 16 | 1,650 |
| 7 | 1,300 | 17 | 1,650 |
| 8 | 1,400 | 18 | 1,850 |
| 9 | 1,400 | 19 | 1,900 |
| 10 | 1,400 | 20 | 1,910 |
| | | 21 | 1,930 |

(ii)   The average chicken weighs:

A.   1,390 grams

B.   1,409 grams

C.   1,456 grams

D.   1,529 grams

(iii)   The range of weights for the chickens is:

A.   1,409 grams

B.   1,400 grams

C.   990 grams

D.   930 grams

(iv)   The median chicken weighs:

A.   1,450 g

B.   1,409 g

C.   1,400 g

D.   1,300 g

(v)   The mode of the chickens' weights is:

A.   1,450 g

B.   1,409 g

C.   1,400 g

D.   1,300 g

# *16* Simple formulae

The plural of formula is formulae – pronounced 'form-you-lee'.

The word 'formula' is used differently in different circumstances, but in all of its meanings it is a set of instructions written in shorthand.

A chemical formula shows the composition of a substance in a shorthand that all scientists around the world use and understand. Water is made by joining two atoms of hydrogen to one atom of oxygen. The chemical formula for water, $H_2O$, summarises this information: H is the symbol for hydrogen, O stands for oxygen and the small subscript 2, written after the H, shows that there are two hydrogen atoms for each atom of oxygen.

The kinds of formulae we are describing in this topic are properly called general mathematical formulae. They are sets of instructions showing how to perform a particular kind of calculation. Mathematical formulae always give the right answers if you use them properly.

Mathematical formulae are written as equations. In every equation:

$$\text{the left-hand side} \quad = \quad \text{the right-hand side}$$

The shorthand used in mathematical formulae is best explained using a series of examples.

The area of a rectangle is calculated by multiplying its length by its width. In words:

$$\text{Area of a rectangle} \quad = \quad \text{length multiplied by width.}$$

We can use the letter A to stand for the area of any rectangle and the letters l and w to stand for its length and width. We can then abbreviate the word equation shown above to:

$$A \quad = \quad l \times w$$

In maths formulae, the multiplication sign is left out, and the two letters are written side by side, so:

$$A \quad = \quad lw$$

is the general formula used to calculate the area of any rectangle. Because it does not matter which way around you multiply numbers together, $A = wl$ is equally valid.

Any combination of letters can be used. Most people use capital letters for the left-hand side of the equation and lower-case (or small) letters for the right-hand side, but this is not compulsory or essential.

It is vital to include a key with the formula, showing what each letter represents.

The general formula for calculating the volume of a box is

$$V \quad = \quad abc$$

where V = volume; a = length; b = width; and c = height.

A general formula works for all units, but you must use the same type of unit throughout. As in other calculations, mixing units would give a nonsense answer. For example:

V = 4 inches by 6 inches by 12 inches  =  288 cubic inches

V = 4 metres by 6 metres by 12 metres  =  288 cubic metres

## Formulae with powers

Squares and cubes are used as part of the formula shorthand. A square is a rectangle where all four sides are the same length. A cube is a box where all three edges are the same length. Therefore:

For a square   A  =  $s^2$

where A = area; and s = length of one side.

For a cube   V  =  $e^3$

where V = volume; and e = length of one edge.

Because a cube has six identical square faces

A  =  $6e^2$

where A = total surface area of the cube; and e = length of one edge.

The formula for the area of a circle is

A  =  $\pi r^2$

where A = the area of the circle; r = the radius of the circle; and $\pi$ (pi) = 3.142, correct to 3 d.p.

## Brackets

Some badly written equations can be confusing. Another shorthand method is used to make the formula instructions completely clear. Using ordinary numbers, we can write a simple equation like:

$$20 - 2 \times 4 \ = \ ?$$

The answer to this sum could be 72, or it might be 12, because it does not tell you what to do first – the subtraction or the multiplication.

Formulae use brackets to give sequence instructions – they tell you to 'do this part of the calculation first'.

$$20 - (2 \times 4) \ = \ 12$$

but

$$(20 - 2) \times 4 \ = 72$$

The multiplication sign is left out of a mathematical formula, but the horizontal or forward-sloping line to indicate division is included in the usual way:

$$(20/2) + 4 \ = \ 14$$

# Letters and numbers

Even if you have never seen a formula before, you can use it to give a completely accurate and reliable answer.

This formula shows how to calculate the volume of a ball or sphere:

$$V = \frac{4\pi r^3}{3}$$

where V — volume; r = radius; $\pi$ = 3.142.

---

### *Example*

Using this formula, calculate the volume of a sphere with a radius of 12 cm.

(i)     In the normal way, the horizontal line shows that this is a division sum.

(ii)    The top part of the fraction says you multiply three numbers together: 4, $\pi$ and $r^3$.

(iii)   $r^3$ is shorthand for $r \times r \times r$.

(iv)   Calculate the top part of the fraction first. This is:

$$4 \times 3.142 \times 12 \times 12 \times 12 = 21,717.5$$

(v)    Next work out the fraction:

$$V = \frac{21,717.5}{3} = 7,239.2$$

(vi)   Because the radius was measured in centimetres, this means that you have just worked out that:

Volume of sphere with a radius of 12 cm = 7,239.2 cu cm

---

The area of a regular hexagon, a shape with six sides all of the same length, is given by the formula

$$A \ = \ 2.598s^2$$

Where A = area; s = length of one side.

> ### Example
>
> To calculate the area of a regular hexagon with a side measurement of 7 inches, proceed exactly as before, but this time plug the new numbers into the new formula:
>
> $$A = 2.598 \times 7 \times 7 = 127.3$$
> $$A = 127.3 \text{ square inches,}$$
>
> because s was given in simple or linear inches.

# Body mass index, BMI

The medical profession uses a number called the body mass index, abbreviated to BMI, as a diagnostic tool. A BMI of between 20 and 25 is normal for an adult, but patients with a BMI of greater than 25 are usually advised to lose weight to protect their health.

The formula used to calculate BMI is

$$BMI = \frac{w}{h^2}$$

In this case, w = weight in kg; and h = height in metres.

> ### Example
>
> Calculate the BMI of a patient who weighs 78 kg and is 182 cm tall.
>
> The index works with metres, not centimetres, so first work out that
>
> $$182 \text{ cm} = 1.82 \text{ m}$$
>
> The formula tells you how to do the calculation:
>
> $$BMI = \frac{78}{1.82 \times 1.82} = \frac{78}{3.31} = 23.6$$
>
> This patient is comfortably inside the normal healthy weight range.

You can also use formulae to help with many everyday calculations.

## Example and practice question

Sean works out that the fixed costs of owning his car are £1,400 a year. This is the total of road tax, insurance and loan repayments – all of which he has to pay regardless of how much or how little he uses the car. He also works out that the variable costs are 12p per mile. This is mostly petrol, but also includes an allowance for maintenance and repair. The more miles Sean drives, the higher his variable costs.

The formula to calculate the total costs of owning and running the car is

$$C = f + 0.12m$$

In this case, C = the total car cost in £ p.a.; f = fixed costs in £ p.a.; m = number of miles driven in a year.

The formula uses a figure of 0.12, not 12, because we are working with £ as units, and 12p = £0.12.

(i)   What are Sean's total costs for the following mileages driven in one year? Fill in the gaps in the table.

| Mileage | Total cost (£) |
| --- | --- |
| 10,000 | 2,600.00 |
| 5,732 | 2,087.84 |
| 114 | |
| 23,451 | |
| 12,147 | |

(ii)  Sean buys a newer, bigger car. This time its fixed costs are £1,950 per year and the variable costs are 14.5p per mile. Recalculate the total costs for the five different annual mileages shown above.

# *17* Maths exams

You are very unusual if you do not get anxious and nervous before an exam. A certain level of tension is positive and productive – exams are designed to be demanding. Most mature students have unpleasant memories of exams in general and maths exams in particular.

You will be asked to give the answers to a relatively large number of comparatively simple calculations. You will not be asked descriptive questions like 'What are the differences between the mean and the median?'.

Aim high, but remain realistic. You probably are not the best mathematician in the world, but then you do not have to be exceptional or brilliant to be highly numerate.

Most Application of Number exams contain about 40 multiple-choice questions. However, multiple-choice exams are not an easy option. You will not be asked to choose between one right answer and three or four silly ones – answers making all of the most common errors will be included as alternatives on the paper.

More than in any other subject, it is absolutely vital that you spend the first five or ten minutes of a maths exam reading through the paper with your pen put to one side.

The questions might be numbered 1 to 40, but this does not mean that you have to start at the beginning and work steadily forward. Identify and then answer your 'banker' questions – the ones you find easiest – first, and then go back to the more difficult ones. Whatever you do, avoid spending too much time on any particular question.

In multiple-choice exams, do not leave blanks. Give it your best shot. You will not lose marks for an incorrect answer. In multiple choice, never tick more than one box. The examiner cannot give you a mark even if one of your two ticks is the right answer. Do reality checks as you go along, and try to save five minutes for a last look before the end of the exam.

In any exam, you are very unlikely to know all of the answers, but the psychology of multiple-choice assessments has been well researched. If you are asked to tick one or four boxes, you will usually be able to reject one or two of the alternatives as obviously wrong. Your first guess between the remaining two or three boxes is usually the right one. Do not be tempted to change your mind. If you do alter an answer, make sure the alteration is clear and cannot be misunderstood by the examiner.

The layout and the style of the exam paper should not come as a surprise. Make sure you have rehearsed with at least two or three past papers before you sit the real test. Your maths lecturer is there to help.

Developing a good exam technique is not underhand or sneaky or cheating in any way. Good technique just makes it more likely that you can prove to the examiner how much work you have put in and how much your knowledge has grown and improved.

# Chapter 9

# Further mathematics

## National unit specification.
## These are the topics you will be studying for this unit:

You should be comfortable with all the major topics included in the Application of Number unit before you begin to study Further Mathematics.

# 1 What is algebra?

Even the word 'algebra' unsettles some students. Like many terms used in maths and science, algebra is an Arabic expression. 'Al' just means 'the' in Arabic, 'jabr' means 'bringing together of broken parts'. This gives a clue to what algebra is all about – it is a way of manipulating or rearranging numbers to give the answers to a huge range of practical problems.

Most people are astonished to discover how straightforward algebra becomes once a short list of simple rules has been properly explained and understood. You may not realise it, but you almost certainly use algebra every day. For example:

*'I left home this morning with three £10 notes. This evening I have £7.36 left – how much have I spent during the day?'*

Turned into algebra, this calculation is:

$$\text{How much have I spent} = x$$
$$x = (3 \times 10) - 7.36$$
$$x = 30 - 7.36$$
$$x = 22.64$$

You are working with units of £, therefore you have spent £22.64.

The thing you do not know to begin with is called an 'unknown', for obvious reasons. When you do this kind of sum in your head, with pen and paper, or with a calculator, you are writing and then solving an algebraic equation.

Algebra is not a secret code where every letter represents a particular fixed number. The 'how much have I spent' equation works equally well with any kind of letter. It might be a capital or lower-case letter. Mathematicians often use the Greek alphabet as well as the English. All of these equations are identical, perfectly accurate and valid:

$$x = (3 \times 10) - 7.36$$
$$A = (3 \times 10) - 7.36$$
$$a = (3 \times 10) - 7.36$$
$$\alpha = (3 \times 10) - 7.36$$
$$\Delta = (3 \times 10) - 7.36$$

$\alpha$ = alpha, the Greek letter a; $\Delta$ = delta, the Greek letter D.

You always use different letters for different unknowns.

> ### Example
>
> Jenny has twin girls and a son. What formula tells you how to calculate their combined ages?
>
> $$A = 2a + b$$
>
> where A = the children's combined age; $a$ = the age of one of the girls; and $b$ − the boy's age.
>
> Notice that A and $a$ mean different things and that $2a$ is shorthand for $2 \times a$.

Although you can use any combinations of letters to stand for the unknowns, mathematicians have conventions or agreements where some letters are usually used for certain kinds of unknowns.

The formula $A = \pi r^2$ tells you how to calculate the area of a circle.

r stands for radius – this is a convention. $\pi$ usually means pi, the number approximately equal to 3.142.

You need to grasp one more essential idea before we move on to the detail. You may have noticed the brackets in the 'how much have I spent' equation. We wrote:

$$x = (3 \times 10) - 7.36$$
$$\text{and} \quad x = 22.64$$

Here, the brackets are a sequence instruction – they tell you to do the multiplication sum in the brackets before you subtract 7.36.

The equation below is completely different from the one above:

$$x = 3 \times (10 - 7.36)$$
$$x = 3 \times 2.64$$
$$x = 7.92$$

This second equation does not describe what actually happened, so it gives a nonsense answer – £7.92 is nothing like £22.64.

If you perform a multi-stage calculation in the wrong order, you will nearly always get the wrong answer. You will be taught a simple set of rules and symbols that tell you precisely what to do first, second, third and so on.

# 2 Algebra and the four rules of number

The four rules of number are universal. They apply to algebra in exactly the same way as they apply to pure numbers. In this topic we use simple comparisons to show how to add, subtract, multiply and divide algebraic expressions.

Numbers can be added together in any order. Scrambling does not alter the answer.

$$10 + 7 + 3 = 7 + 10 + 3$$

$$a + b + c = b + a + c$$

Algebraic terms can be collected or grouped together, provided like is added to like.

$$4 \text{ oranges} + 3 \text{ oranges} = 7 \text{ oranges}$$

$$4a + 3a = 7a$$

$$7 \text{ apples} + 12 \text{ apples} + 2 \text{ pears} = 19 \text{ apples} + 2 \text{ pears}$$

$$7a + 12a + 2b = 19a + 2b$$

The same addition rules hold for decimals and fractions:

$$0.736 + 1.012 = 1.748$$

$$0.736a + 1.012a = 1.748a$$

$$0.736a + 2.052b + 1.012a + b = 1.748a + 3.052b$$

As long as you are adding like to like, the four rules of number always work. The expression '$ab$' says 'multiply $a$ and $b$ together', so:

$$3ab + 7ab = 10ab$$

$$3ab + 7ab + 6b + 2b = 10ab + 8b$$

The expression $a^2$ says 'multiply $a$ by itself'; the expression $a^3$ says 'multiply $a$ by itself three times'.

If $a = 3$ then $a^2 = 9$ and $a^3 = 27$.

You can add power numbers together only if the powers are the same:

$$4a^2 + a^2 = 5a^2$$

$$5a^3 + b^2 + a^3 + 2a^2 = 6a^3 + 2a^2 + b^2$$

Expressions like $7a^3 + a^2 + a$ cannot be simplified further because you would not be adding like to like.

# Signs and sequence

Sequence makes no difference in subtraction sums or mixtures of additions and subtractions – however, this may not be immediately obvious. These two equations look the same and seem to prove that order does make a difference in subtraction:

$$10 - 2 = 8$$

$$2 - 10 = -8$$

When you look more closely, you can see these are different subtractions, the signs have been switched: in the second equation 10 becomes $-10$ and $-2$ becomes $+2$.

If you repeat the exercise, taking care not to switch signs, the true picture emerges:

$$+10 - 2 = 8$$

$$-2 + 10 = 8$$

Therefore, when subtracting algebraic expressions:

$$4a - 3a = a$$

$$0.736a - 1.012a = -0.276a$$

$$a - \frac{a}{4} = \frac{3a}{4}; \text{because } a = \frac{4a}{4}$$

$$7ab - 2ab = 5ab$$

$$5a^3 - 2a^3 = 3a^3$$

and so on.

# Reality checking

You can reality check nearly any simple algebraic calculation by substituting a three or a higher whole number into the equation. For example:

(i)   $4a^2 + 3a^2 = 7a^2$

if $a = 3$, then $a^2 = 9$, so

$36 + 27 = 63$

shows this equation is right.

(ii)  Perhaps    $4a^2 + 3a = 7a^2$

$36 + 9 \neq 63$

shows this equation is wrong.

The symbol $\neq$ means 'does not equal'.

Do not use 1 or 2 for reality checks because these will not pick up many common errors:

If $a = 1$, then $a^2$, $a^3$ and all higher powers also equal 1.

If $a = 2$, then $2a = a^2$, so using two as a reality check will not highlight most confusions between simple multiplication by two and squaring a number.

# Multiplication

Multiplying algebraic expressions is straightforward if you remember that multiplication signs are left out and you understand power notation:

$$a \times a = a^2$$

$$a \times b = ab = ba$$

$$a \times b \times c = abc = bac = cba$$

Sequence does not matter in multiplication. In all future examples we will show only one of the many ways of writing an algebraic multiplication.

$12 \times a = 12a$

$a \times b = ab$

$a \times a \times b = a^2 \times b = a^2b$

$a \times a \times b \times b = a^2 \times b^2 = a^2b^2$

$7a^2 \times b = 7a^2b$

It may not be immediately obvious that

$$9a \quad \times \quad 9a \quad = \quad 81a^2$$

$$\text{or that} \quad 1.7a \quad \times \quad 11.3a \quad = \quad 19.21a^2$$

However, remember that the left-hand side of each of these equations is four numbers all multiplied together, not three.

From the previous examples you might see that multiplication of power numbers is the same as adding the power numbers together. To explain:

$$a^2 \quad \times \quad a^3 \quad = \quad a^{(2+3)} \quad = \quad a^5$$

$$a^4 \quad \times \quad a^2 \quad = \quad a^{(4+2)} \quad = \quad a^6$$

$$a \quad \times \quad a^2 \quad = \quad a^{(1+2)} \quad = \quad a^3 \text{ (because } a = a^1\text{)}$$

$$\text{Also} \quad a^3b \quad \times \quad ba^2 \quad \times \quad b \quad = \quad a^5b^3$$

$$4a^3b \quad \times \quad 3ba^2 \quad \times \quad b \quad = \quad 12a^5b^3$$

Algebra is a very efficient shorthand; $12a^5b^3$ stands for a string of nine numbers multiplied together.

# Multiplication using brackets

You will often need to multiply expressions which include brackets. Again, the rule is straightforward – multiply everything inside the brackets by everything outside the brackets.

$$4\,(a + b) = 4a + 4b$$

$$4a\,(2a + 3b) = 8a^2 + 12ab$$

It gets a bit more complicated if you are multiplying two bracketed expressions together.

$$(2x + 3)\,(5x + 10) = 10x^2 + 15x + 20x + 30$$

$$= 10x^2 + 35x + 30$$

If this looks odd, do a reality check using $x = 3$:

$$(6 + 3)\,(15 + 10) = 90 + 45 + 60 + 30$$

$$9 \times 25 = 225$$

Notice that the expression

$$10x^2 + 15x + 20x + 30 = 10x^2 + 35x + 30$$

but it cannot be simplified further.

Square roots are squared numbers in reverse. Therefore:

$$\sqrt{x} \times \sqrt{x} = x$$

As a reality check, insert $x = 49$

$$\sqrt{49} \times \sqrt{49} = 49$$

$$7 \times 7 = 49$$

# Division

For clarity, algebraic divisions are usually written using a horizontal line as the division symbol rather than a forward-sloping line.

Be careful when you are hand-writing fractions – make sure you extend the horizontal line sufficiently to the right.

$$\frac{4 + 6}{8} \neq \frac{4}{8} + 6$$

The division horizontal line, like brackets, is another kind of sequence instruction. It tells you to work out the top number first, then work out the bottom number, and finally complete the division sum.

Using brackets *and* the division line is not wrong. Complicated formulae often include both, just to make the mathematical instructions completely clear. Always include brackets if you use the forward-sloping line for the division symbol.

$$\frac{4+6}{8} = \frac{(4+6)}{8} = (4+6)/8$$

In the same way, $\quad \dfrac{a+b}{c} = \dfrac{(a+b)}{c} = (a+b)/c$

Getting division sums upside down is a gross error:

$$\frac{10}{5} \neq \frac{5}{10} \quad \text{and} \quad \frac{(a+b)}{c} \neq \frac{c}{(a+b)}$$

# Fractions

Some algebraic divisions are potentially confusing if you are not confident working with pure number fractions. The rules are best explained using pure number calculations to start with:

(i)  $\quad \dfrac{(20+7)}{(7+2)} = \dfrac{27}{9} = 3$

Once again, the brackets and the division line are sequence instructions – they tell you to add the two top numbers together, then add the two bottom numbers together, then divide the top number by the bottom number. Obviously, the answer to this division sum is 3. Divisions like this can be simplified, or broken down, but only one method is correct. We can test the other possibilities using this pure number division. If the answer is three, then the method is correct. Any different result shows an incorrect method that breaks the rules of number.

(ii)  We could split the fraction into two, breaking both the top and bottom brackets, but this method is *wrong*.

$$\boxed{\text{WRONG!}} \qquad \frac{(20+7)}{(7+2)} \rightarrow \frac{20}{7} + \frac{7}{2} \qquad \boxed{\text{WRONG!}}$$

$$\rightarrow 2\frac{6}{7} + 3\frac{1}{2}$$

$$\rightarrow 6.357 \text{ to 3 d.p.}$$

(iii) We might split the fraction by breaking the bottom bracket and leaving the top bracket untouched. This method is also clearly *wrong*.

$$\begin{array}{c} \textbf{W} \\ \textbf{R} \\ \textbf{O} \\ \textbf{N} \\ \textbf{G} \\ \textbf{!} \end{array}$$

$$\frac{(20+7)}{(7+2)} \quad \rightarrow \quad \frac{(20+7)}{7} \quad + \quad \frac{(20+7)}{2}$$

$$\rightarrow \quad 3\frac{6}{7} \quad + \quad 13\frac{1}{2}$$

$$\rightarrow \quad 17.357 \text{ to 3 d.p.}$$

$$\begin{array}{c} \textbf{W} \\ \textbf{R} \\ \textbf{O} \\ \textbf{N} \\ \textbf{G} \\ \textbf{!} \end{array}$$

(iv) A third possibility is to break the top bracket and leave the bottom one alone. This is the only one that gives the right answer.

$$\begin{array}{c} \textbf{R} \\ \textbf{I} \\ \textbf{G} \\ \textbf{H} \\ \textbf{T} \\ \textbf{!} \end{array}$$

$$\frac{(20+7)}{(7+2)} \quad \rightarrow \quad \frac{20}{(7+2)} \quad + \quad \frac{7}{(7+2)}$$

$$\rightarrow \quad 2\frac{2}{9} \quad + \quad \frac{7}{9}$$

$$\rightarrow \quad 3$$

$$\begin{array}{c} \textbf{R} \\ \textbf{I} \\ \textbf{G} \\ \textbf{H} \\ \textbf{T} \\ \textbf{!} \end{array}$$

In division sums, you can split the top bracket but not the bottom one. Breaking the bottom bracket gives a false equation where you are not adding like to like.

The top bracket may include subtractions – again, you get the right answer as long as you leave the bottom half of the fraction alone. For example:

$$\frac{(a+b)}{(c+d)} = \frac{a}{(c+d)} + \frac{b}{(c+d)}$$

$$\frac{(a-b)}{(c+d)} = \frac{a}{(c+d)} - \frac{b}{(c+d)}$$

If algebra is new to you, simple checks with pure numbers can be a very effective way of learning and remembering the basic rules.

# Cancelling

Division sums can often be simplified or cancelled. You will remember how to do this with pure number fractions. If you multiply or divide the top and bottom of a fraction by the same number, its value does not change. For example:

$$\frac{6}{10} = \frac{3}{5}$$

because $\dfrac{(2 \times 3)}{(2 \times 5)} = \dfrac{6}{10}$

In exactly the same way, you can cancel algebraic fractions:

$$\frac{4x}{2x} = \frac{4}{2} = 2 \quad \text{(cancelling } x \text{ and then 2)}$$

$$\frac{4ab}{a} = 4b \quad \text{(cancelling } a\text{)}$$

$$\frac{12abc}{6a} = 2bc \quad \text{(cancelling } 6a\text{)}$$

$$\frac{(x+1)(y+2)(p+3)}{(y+2)} = (x+1)(p+3)$$

In this last example, you are dividing top and bottom by $(y + 2)$. The brackets 'give you permission' to treat it like a single letter or number.

## Cancelling powers

Dividing power numbers is straightforward:

$$\frac{a}{a^2} = \frac{1}{a}$$

$$\frac{a^4}{a^2} = a^{(4-2)} = a^2$$

$$\frac{a^2 b}{a} = ab$$

$$\frac{p^3 q}{qp} = p^2$$

$$\frac{10a^5 x^3}{5a^3 x} = 2a^2 x^2$$

This last simplification is much easier if you break it down into stages, for example:

(i) $\dfrac{10a^5 x^3}{5a^3 x} = \dfrac{2a^5 x^3}{a^3 x}$ (cancelling 5)

(ii) $\dfrac{2a^5 x^3}{a^3 x} = \dfrac{2a^2 x^3}{x}$ (cancelling $a^3$)

(iii) $\dfrac{2a^2 x^3}{x} = 2a^2 x^2$ (cancelling $x$)

You can sometimes simplify expressions involving square roots:

$$\frac{x}{\sqrt{x}} = \sqrt{x}$$

because

$$x = \sqrt{x} \times \sqrt{x}$$

Similarly, and for the same reason:

$$\frac{\sqrt{x}}{x} = \frac{1}{\sqrt{x}}$$

Many fractions cannot be simplified. This holds true for pure number and algebraic fractions. For example:

$$\frac{2}{7}, \ \frac{9}{11}, \ \frac{ab}{d}, \ \frac{(a+b)}{c}, \ \frac{4a^2}{x}$$

## More sequence instructions

So far we have only considered two kinds of sequence instructions – brackets and division lines. For most of the algebraic expressions you are likely to use, you will not make sequence errors provided you remember that these two symbols mean 'do this first'. For example, this formula tells you how to calculate the total surface area of a cylinder:

$$A \qquad = \qquad 2\pi r \, (r + h)$$

where A = surface area; r = the radius of one end of the cylinder; h = the height of the cylinder.

---

### Example

If r = 9 cm and h = 30 cm, and using a value of $\pi$ = 3.142, calculate the surface area of the cylinder.

(i)      Work out the bracket first:

        (r + h) = (9 + 30) = 39

(ii)     Next, work out $2\pi r$. This is just three numbers multiplied together:

        $2\pi r$ = 2 × 3.142 × 9 = 56.556

(iii)    Finally, you multiply the two numbers together:

        39 × 56.556 = 2,205.684

(iv)    You started off with centimetre measurements and you are calculating an area, so your answer must be in square centimetres:

        A = 2,205.684 sq cm or cm²

Taking a second example, this formula gives the volume of a sphere:

$$V = \frac{4\pi r^3}{3}$$

---

### Example

If r = 11 cm, and using a value of $\pi$ = 3.142, calculate the volume of the sphere. You would probably do this calculation in four stages:

(i)    $r^3 = 11^3 = 1{,}331$

(ii)   $4\pi = 4 \times 3.142 = 12.568$

(iii)  $4\pi r^3 = 1{,}331 \times 12.568 = 16{,}728$

(iv)   $V = 16{,}728/3 = 5{,}576$ cu cm, or cm³

Note that volumes are always shown in cubic units.

# BODMAS

A mnemonic is a nonsense word or rhyme that helps you remember sequences and order. Some people find them very useful, others think they are irritating.

The mnemonic BODMAS gives complete sequence instructions for all types of calculations, no matter how complicated:

**B**rackets
p**O**wers
**D**ivide
**M**ultiply
**A**dd
**S**ubtract

Sequence in which these actions should be performed

The mnemonic is not quite perfect – you have to remember that the division line should be treated like a bracket and that square roots and cube roots are special kinds of powers.

### Example

Calculate the value of *x* if

$$x = \frac{(b^2 - 4ac) + 2a}{4a + 7c}$$

and *a* = 1, *b* = 10 and *c* = 3.

(i)    Brackets come first and the division line acts as another kind of bracket. Do the top of the fraction first and start with the bracket.

(ii)   Inside the bracket there is a power sum, a multiplication and a subtraction, therefore:

$$b^2 = 100 \qquad \text{(pOwer)}$$
$$4ac = 12 \qquad \text{(M)}$$
$$b^2 - 4ac = 88 \qquad \text{(S)}$$

(iii)  Now you have got rid of the bracket, you can work out the rest of the top half of the fraction:

$$2a = 2 \qquad \text{(M)}$$
$$88 + 2 = 90 \qquad \text{(A)}$$

so, the top half of the fraction = 90.

(iv)   Now you work on the bottom half of the fraction:

$$4a = 4 \qquad \text{(M)}$$

$$7c = 21 \qquad \text{(M)}$$

$$21 + 4 = 25 \qquad \text{(A)}$$

so, the bottom half of the fraction = 25.

(v)    Finally, you finish off with the fraction calculation:

$$x = 90/25$$

$$x = 3.6$$

# 3 Rearrangement and transposition

Every equation has a left-hand side, an equals sign and a right-hand side. The simplest equations of all have a single term on each side of the sign, for example:

$$x = 3$$

Apart from turning it around so that $3 = x$, there is no way of rearranging or transposing this kind of equation.

Most equations have two or more terms on one or both sides of the equals sign. For example:

(i)   $7 + x = 10$

(ii)  $6 + y = 5 + x$

(iii) $V = \dfrac{4\pi r^3}{3}$

(iv)  $A = 2\pi r \, (r + h)$

(v)   $\dfrac{6 + x^2}{y} = \dfrac{1}{2p}$

The two sides of the equation can include any combination of powers, roots, addition, subtraction, multiplication or division.

Rearrangement and/or transposition are the words used to describe the manipulation of an equation or any operation that moves a term across the equals sign. Rearrangement and transposition are most often used to alter the subject of an equation.

Equations like this:

$$\frac{x^2}{y} = \frac{1}{2p}$$

do not have a subject, but you could rearrange this starting equation to give three different variations, one with $x$ as its subject, another with $y$ as its subject and a third with $p$ as the subject. All of these rearrangements would have the single term $x$, $y$ or $p$ on the left-hand side.

As with everything mathematical, there are rules for rearrangement and transposition. If you follow these, you always get the right answer. If you break them, you get nonsense. Again, we will start with pure number rearrangements and then move on to their algebraic equivalents.

# The sign change rule

If the equation includes additions, subtractions or a mixture of both, the sign change rule applies. For example:

$$10 + 7 + 6 - 27 - 4$$

You can move any combination of these numbers from the left-hand to the right-hand side, but you must change the sign as you pass over the equals symbol.

By convention, to save time, the first figure in an addition string like this does not show the plus sign, but you should not forget that it exists.

For clarity, you could include all of the signs in the starting equation:

$$+10 +7 +6 = +27 -4$$

This equation can be rearranged in several different ways:

(i) $7 + 6 = 27 - 4 - 10$

(ii) $7 = 27 - 4 - 10 - 6$

(iii) $10 + 7 + 6 - 27 = -4$

(iv) $10 + 7 + 6 - 27 + 4 = 0$

By convention, in this last kind of rearrangement you put the zero on the right-hand side; however, writing the equation the other way around is still mathematically correct.

The same sign change rule applies equally for algebraic expressions:

(i) $x + 7 = 10$

$x = 10 - 7$

$x = 3$

(ii) $a + b + 7 = 100$

$a = 93 - b$

Here you have made $a$ the subject of the equation.

(iii) $a + b + 7 = 100$

$b = 93 - a$

Here you have made $b$ the subject of the equation.

If you want to rearrange addition and/or subtraction sums that include multiplication, division or power terms, the sign change rules still hold. However, you have to be a bit more careful.

Start with this pure number equation:

$$6 + 7 = 9 + 4$$

(i)  Each of these four numbers could be replaced with an equivalent multiplication or division term to give an identical pure number equation. For example:

$$2 \times 3 + \frac{49}{7} = \frac{81}{9} + 2 \times 2$$

This equation is a mess. However, we can tidy it up by adding an extra set of instructions:

(ii)

$$(2 \times 3) + (\frac{49}{7}) = (\frac{81}{9}) + (2 \times 2)$$

Think of the brackets as parcels – you can move the parcels across the equals sign but you must not unwrap them. So:

$$(2 \times 3) = (\frac{81}{9}) + (2 \times 2) - (\frac{49}{7})$$

is the same as:

$$6 = 9 + 4 - 7$$

or
$$6 = 6$$

And so on – you get the right answer, as long as you do not start moving one of the numbers inside the bracket without the others – do not unwrap the parcels!

The same rules apply to the addition and/or subtraction of algebraic terms that include multiplications, divisions or powers. Do not forget that an expression like *ab* or 7*a* includes an unwritten multiplication sign.

There are very many examples of these kinds of algebraic rearrangement:

(i)
$$x^2 + 6x + 9 = 0$$
$$x^2 + 6x = -9$$
$$6x = -9 - x^2$$

(ii)
$$A = 2\pi r^2 + 2\pi rh$$
$$2\pi r^2 = A - 2\pi rh$$

(iii)
$$P = \frac{x^2}{2} - \frac{4}{x}$$
$$\frac{x^2}{2} = P + \frac{4}{x}$$

(iv)
$$\frac{4\pi}{3} - \frac{1}{\sqrt{x}} = 27$$

$$\frac{4\pi}{3} = 27 + \frac{1}{\sqrt{x}}$$

You do not need to write in the brackets to do these rearrangements, but often it helps.

# Cross multiplication

Now we have covered the sign change rule, we can move on to cross multiplication.

We all know these two fractions are equivalent:

$$\frac{10}{5} = \frac{6}{3}$$

Delete the equals sign and replace it with a large cross made from two double-headed arrows:

$$\frac{10}{5} \quad \frac{6}{3}$$

The arrows show how to cross multiply:

(i)   You can move numbers up the arrows or down the arrows.

(ii)  Moving upwards changes a division to a multiplication.

(iii) Moving downwards changes a multiplication to a division.

(iv)  You can move up or down either arrow or both arrows

(v)  **All of these rearrangements shift numbers across the equals symbol, but with cross multiplication you do not change the sign.**

You should not worry if this sounds complicated. Cross multiplication is difficult to describe but very easy to do. If we go back to the pure number equation, the rules become clear. The table overleaf shows some, but not all, of the possible rearrangements of

$$\frac{10}{5} = \frac{6}{3}$$

| Rearrangement | Reality check |
|---|---|
| $10 \times 3 = 5 \times 6$ | $30 = 30$ |
| $10 = \dfrac{5 \times 6}{3}$ | $10 = 10$ |
| $6 = \dfrac{10 \times 3}{5}$ | $6 = 6$ |
| $5 = \dfrac{10 \times 3}{6}$ | $5 = 5$ |
| $3 = \dfrac{6 \times 5}{10}$ | $3 = 3$ |

You will most often use cross multiplication to change the subject of an equation.

(i)
$$\frac{C}{2r} = \pi$$

where C = the circumference of the circle; and r = its radius.

Rearranging by cross multiplication:  $C = 2\pi r$

(ii)
$$A = \pi r^2$$

where A = the area of a circle; and r = its radius.

Rearranging by cross multiplication:

$$r^2 = \frac{A}{\pi}$$

and then taking the square root of each side of the equation:

$$r = \sqrt{\left(\frac{A}{\pi}\right)}$$

Remember that brackets are a sequence instruction. For example: what is the radius of a circle with an area of 1,000 sq cm?

Assume $\pi = 3.142$.

(a)  $(A/\pi) = r^2$

Do the bracket first: $1{,}000/3.142 = 318.27$

(b)  $r = \sqrt{318.27}$

(c)  Using a calculator:  $\sqrt{318.27} = 17.84$

(d)  The radius of the circle = 17.84 cm

(iii) The volume of a box is calculated by multiplying its length by its width by its height. Any letters could be used to write this calculation as an algebraic equation, but for simplicity we would probably use something like:

$$V = l\,w\,h$$

Here V is the subject of the equation.

Suppose we know the volume of the box and the area of its lid and we want to calculate its height.

Start by rearranging the first formula:

$$\frac{V}{l\,w} = h$$

$l\,w$ — the area of the box lid; $V$ = the volume of the box; $h$ — the height of the box.

Because $l\,w$ = the area of the lid and $A = l\,w$, you could write a second equivalent equation:

$$\frac{V}{A} = h$$

## Celsius and Fahrenheit

We can illustrate many of the main ideas in this topic by using the Celsius and Fahrenheit temperature scales:

(i)   The two common scales use different reference points.

|  | °C | °F |
|---|---|---|
| Boiling point of pure water | 100 | 212 |
| Freezing point of pure water | 0 | 32 |

(ii)  You can also see that the difference between the two reference points is divided into different numbers of units.

Boiling point minus freezing point   =   100 Celsius degrees

=   180 Fahrenheit degrees

(iii) This formula tells you how to turn a Celsius temperature into Fahrenheit. Fahrenheit is the subject of the formula:

$$F = \frac{180C}{100} + 32$$

This formula can be simplified by cancelling the fraction:

$$F = \frac{9C}{5} + 32$$

We could also turn the fraction into a decimal:

$$F = 1.8C + 32$$

All three are valid formulae for turning °C into °F.

(iv) We will use the simplified fraction formula because it best illustrates the sign change and cross multiplication rules – not because it is any more or less valid than the other variants.

(v) Convert 21 °C into Fahrenheit:

$$F = \frac{9C}{5} + 32 \qquad \textit{starting formula}$$

$$9C = 9 \times 21 = 189 \qquad \textit{work out fraction top number}$$

$$\frac{9C}{5} = \frac{189}{5} = 37.8 \qquad \textit{work out value of the fraction}$$

$$F = 37.8 + 32 \qquad \textit{complete the addition}$$

$$F = 69.8° \qquad \textit{answer}$$

(vi) Convert 0 °C into Fahrenheit:

$$F = \frac{9C}{5} + 32$$

$$9C = 0 \times 9 = 0 \qquad \left.\begin{array}{l} \\ \\ \end{array}\right\} \text{Any number multiplied}$$

$$\frac{9C}{5} = \frac{0}{5} = 0 \qquad \text{by zero is zero}$$

$$F = 0 + 32$$

$$F = 32°$$

(vii) Convert 100 °C into Fahrenheit:

$$F = \frac{9C}{5} + 32$$

$$\frac{9C}{5} = \frac{9 \times 100}{5} = \frac{900}{5} = 180$$

$$F = 180 + 32$$

$$F = 212°$$

If we want to convert Fahrenheit temperatures into Celsius, the first equation has to be rearranged so that C becomes its subject. We can do this in several stages – each involving the sign change rule or cross multiplication.

(i) $$F = \frac{9C}{5} + 32 \qquad \textit{starting formula}$$

(ii) $$F - 32 = \frac{9C}{5} \qquad \textit{sign change}$$

(iii) $$\frac{9C}{5} = F - 32 \qquad \textit{switch}$$

(iv) $$9C = 5(F - 32) \qquad \textit{cross multiplication and adding brackets for clarity}$$

(v) $$C = \frac{5(F - 32)}{9} \qquad \textit{cross multiplication}$$

Step (iii) is a simple switch. By convention the subject of the equation is shown on the left-hand side.

The rearranged equation is used in exactly the same way as the original. For example, converting 85 °F into Celsius:

$$C = \frac{5(F - 32)}{9}$$

$$(F - 32) = 85 - 32 = 53$$

$$C = \frac{5 \times 53}{9} = 29.44$$

$$C = 29.44°$$

## Practice and private study

A page or whiteboard covered in algebra seems complicated and daunting. Just the 'look of the thing' is intimidating. However, Access students nearly always find that once the rules are explained, their fears and doubts evaporate. The rules never vary and there are only about half a dozen of them to learn.

In the beginning, the most common problems are manipulating brackets and some kinds of cross multiplication. Your maths lecturer will provide practice questions in class and for private study. As we have said previously, 20 minutes' practice five or six times a week is much more productive than infrequent two- or three-hour sessions. If a particular technique troubles you, use an equivalent simple pure number calculation as a reality check – this is an especially valuable way of learning how to rearrange by cross multiplication.

# 4 Linear equations and inequalities

Some equations are more complicated than others. These four examples are called linear equations and they describe simple relationships between $x$ and $y$.

(i)     $y = 9x$

(ii)     $y = 5x + 9$

(iii)     $y = 7x - 10$

(iv)     $y = 34 - 4x$

More generally, a linear equation can be written as $y = ax + b$, where $x$ and $y$ are variables and $a$ and $b$ are constant pure numbers. In the above examples:

| Linear equations | $a$ | $b$ |
|---|---|---|
| $y = 9x$ | +9 | 0 |
| $y = 5x + 9$ | +5 | +9 |
| $y = 7x - 10$ | +7 | -10 |
| $y = 34 - 4x$ | -4 | +34 |

Non-linear equations describe more complex relationships. Some non-linear equations include squares, cubes or higher powers. For example:

$y = x^3 + 7$

$y = 2x^2 + 3x$

$y = 4x^2 - 7x + 9$

Other non-linear equations involve square roots, for example:

$y = 7\sqrt{x} + 9$

$y = 2x + \sqrt{x} - 5$

A third kind of non-linear equation contain what are called reciprocals. These have a variable as part of the bottom half of a fraction. For example:

$$y = \frac{1}{x}$$

$$y = \frac{7}{x^2} + 9$$

$$y = \frac{1}{x} + \frac{9}{x^2} + 4$$

$$y = \frac{1}{\sqrt{x}} - 3$$

# Straight-line graphs

Any equation with two variables like x and y can be plotted as a graph.

Linear equations are called this because they always give a straight line on a graph.

Take this linear equation:

$$y = 2x + 5$$

Then for any value of $x$, we can calculate a corresponding value of $y$:

| x | y |
|------|----|
| zero | 5 |
| 1 | 7 |
| 2 | 9 |
| 3 | 11 |
| and so on | |

By convention, the vertical axis on a graph is called the $y$ axis, and the horizontal axis is called the $x$ axis. Remember 'wise up' and 'x is a cross'.

The graph of $y = 2x + 5$ looks like this:

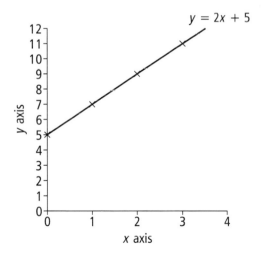

All of the possible combinations of $y$ and $x$ produced by the linear equation $y = 2x + 5$ could be plotted on this same straight line.

We have just plotted a graph where, in the general equation, $a = 2$ and $b = 5$. Other kinds of linear equations produce different sorts of straight lines.

A graph of $y = 2x$ would have the same slope as the graph of $y = 2x + 5$ but the line would be shifted downwards on the vertical scale.

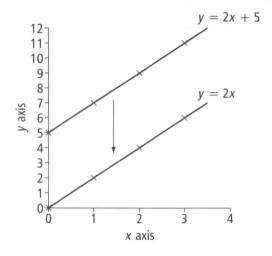

Looking again at the general linear equation $y = ax + b$

The value of $a$ determines the slope or gradient of the graph's straight line.

| Value of $a$ | Slope or gradient |
| --- | --- |
| $a$ = larger positive number | 'steeply uphill' |
| $a$ = smaller positive number | 'moderately uphill' |
| $a$ = zero | 'flat ground' |
| $a$ = smaller negative number | 'moderately downhill' |
| $a$ = larger negative number | 'steeply downhill' |

The graph below shows plot lines for five linear equations:

| | |
| --- | --- |
| $y = 2x + 20$ | $a = +2$ |
| $y = x + 20$ | $a = +1$ |
| $y = 20$ | $a = $ zero |
| $y = 20 - x$ | $a = -1$ |
| $y = 20 - 2x$ | $a = -2$ |

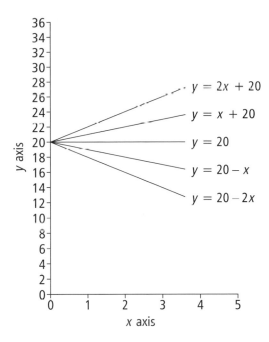

Non-linear equations give smooth curves rather than straight lines. For example:

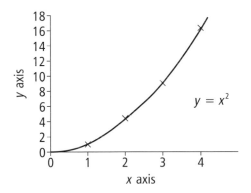

# Solving linear equations

Very many real-life situations can be described using linear equations. Solving a linear equation just means 'find the value of $y$ if you are given values for $a$, $b$ and $x$'. These calculations are straightforward.

## Example

You hire a carpet cleaner. The hire company charges a fixed £12 to cover its administration costs and then £3.00 per day for each day you keep the cleaner. What does it cost to keep the cleaner for 15 days?

$$y = ax + b$$
$$y = \text{total hire cost in £}$$
$$a = \text{£3.00 per day}$$
$$b = \text{£12.00 fixed charge}$$
$$x = \text{number of days you keep the cleaner}$$

therefore
$$y = 3x + 12$$
$$y = (\text{£3} \times 15) + \text{£12}$$
$$y = \text{£57}$$

You will need to rearrange a linear equation to solve problems put the other way around.

## Example

You cannot afford to spend more than £33 to clean your carpets. For how many days can you hire the cleaner from this company?

As above,
$$y = \text{total hire cost in £}$$
$$a = \text{£3.00 per day}$$
$$b = \text{£12.00 fixed charge}$$
$$x = \text{number of days you keep the cleaner}$$
$$y = 3x + 12$$
$$y - 12 = 3x$$
$$3x = y - 12$$
$$x = \frac{(y - 12)}{3}$$
$$y = 33$$

therefore
$$x = \frac{(33 - 12)}{3} = \frac{21}{3}$$
$$x = 7 \text{ days}$$

Previously we have considered Fahrenheit/Celsius conversions as examples of formula rearrangement. These formulae are also good examples of linear equations.

$$F = \frac{9C}{5} + 32$$

If $y = $ Fahrenheit temperature
$$a = \frac{9}{5} = 1.8$$
$$b = 32$$
$$x = \text{Celsius temperature}$$

We could rewrite this as the linear equation

$$y = 1.8x + 32$$

# Simultaneous linear equations

The solution of simultaneous linear equations sounds difficult. This is not so – the idea is straightforward.

We can draw a graph of any linear equation. On one piece of graph paper we could also draw the graphs of two or more linear equations. If the slopes – the gradients – of each equation are the same, then we end up with a family of parallel lines.

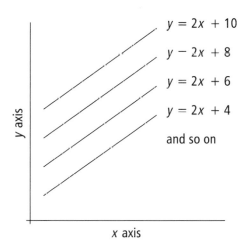

$y = 2x + 10$

$y - 2x + 8$

$y = 2x + 6$

$y = 2x + 4$

and so on

These plot lines never cross each other, because each has the same gradient.

However, if two equations with different slopes are plotted on the same piece of paper, there must be a single point where the lines cross. The following diagrams show the general idea:

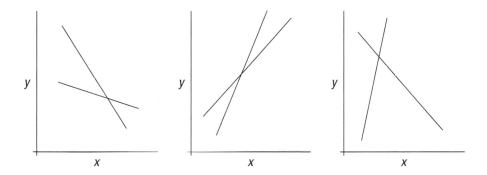

At this crossover point, there is a pair of values (one for $y$ and one for $x$) that satisfy or fit both linear equations. This crossover point is the solution to the two simultaneous equations.

We could draw graphs to solve simultaneous equations but algebraic methods are quicker.

## Example

Let us return to the carpet-cleaner problem. This time, the customer has a choice between two companies with different price structures:

(i)     The Eastern Hire Company's price terms are

£12.00 standing charge + £3.00 per day.

(ii)    The Western Hire Company's price terms are

£4.50 per day but with no standing charge.

(iii)   These price arrangements can be written as two linear equations:

| Eastern | C | = | 3d + 12 |
|---------|---|---|---------|
| Western | C | = | 4.5d |
| Where | C | = | total hire cost and d = the number of hire days. |

(iv)    The crossover can be worked out without drawing two graphs because at this point the total price charged by the Eastern Company will be the same as the total price charged by the Western Company. We can turn these words into an equation:

$$C \quad = \quad 3d + 12 \quad = \quad 4.5d$$
$$12 \quad = \quad 4.5d - 3d$$
$$12 \quad = \quad 1.5d$$
$$\frac{12}{1.5} \quad = \quad d$$
$$d \quad = \quad 8 \text{ days}$$

(v)     This value of eight days can be plugged back into both equations to check that each charges £36 to hire the carpet cleaner for eight days:

| Eastern | C | = | 3d + 12 | = | (3 × 8) + 12 | = | 36 |
|---------|---|---|---------|---|--------------|---|----|
| Western | C | = | 4.5d | = | 4.5 × 8 | = | 36 |

(vi)    The solution to this pair of simultaneous linear equations is C = 36; d = 8.

There is only one solution to simultaneous linear equations because the two straight plot lines can only cross each other at one place on the graph.

## Practice question

Which hire company do you choose if you want to hire a cleaner for 14 days?

# Substitution

The quickest way of solving most simultaneous linear equations is by direct substitution.

### Example

Look at the following equations:

$$A: \quad y - 1 \quad = \quad 2x$$
$$B: \quad 3y - 4x \quad = \quad 13$$

(i)  Work out the simplest rearrangement that gives $x$ or $y$ as the subject of a new formula. Here there are four choices:

$$y = 2x + 1$$
$$y = \frac{(13 + 4x)}{3}$$
$$x - \frac{(y - 1)}{2}$$
$$x = \frac{(3y - 13)}{4}$$

(ii)  Clearly, the simplest rearrangement is the first one from equation A, where $y = 2x + 1$.

(iii)  Substitute this rearranged formula into equation B to give another equation. To explain:

$$B: \quad 3y - 4x \quad = \quad 13$$
$$\text{and} \quad y \quad = \quad 2x + 1$$

Substituting:

$$3(2x + 1) - 4x = 13$$

Removing brackets:

$$6x + 3 - 4x = 13$$
$$6x - 4x = 13 - 3$$
$$2x = 10$$
$$x = 5$$

(iv)  Substitute this value of $x = 5$ back into the two original equations:

$y = 2x + 1$         $3y - 4x = 13$

$y = 11$; if $x = 5$      $y = 11$; if $x = 5$

(v)  The solution to this pair of simultaneous equations is

$y = 11$ and $x = 5$.

# Elimination

Another way of solving simultaneous linear equations is often obvious.

> **Example**
>
> $$\text{A:} \quad y \quad = \quad 3x + 4$$
> $$\text{B:} \quad y \quad = \quad 7x - 4$$
>
> Clearly, we can immediately eliminate $y$ by writing a third equation:
>
> $$3x + 4 \quad = \quad 7x - 4$$
> $$4 + 4 \quad = \quad 7x - 3x$$
> $$8 \quad = \quad 4x$$
> $$x \quad = \quad 2$$
>
> The value of $x = 2$ can be substituted back into the starting equations to find a value for $y$:
>
> | A: | B: |
> |---|---|
> | $y = 3x + 4$ | $y = 7x - 4$ |
> | $x = 2$ | $x = 2$ |
> | $y = 6 + 4$ | $y = 14 - 4$ |
> | $y = 10$ | $y = 10$ |
>
> The solution is therefore $x = 2$; $y = 10$.

# Addition and subtraction

Sometimes, simultaneous linear equations can be solved by addition or subtraction.

> **Example**
>
> $$\text{A:} \quad 3y - 2x \quad = \quad 17$$
> $$\text{B:} \quad y + 2x \quad = \quad 19$$
>
> You can see that the first equation includes the term $-2x$, and the second equation includes the term $+2x$. $x$ can be eliminated if the two equations are added together.
>
> Adding two equations feels wrong but it does not break any of the rules. A reality check with pure numbers confirms this:
>
> | | | | |
> |---|---|---|---|
> | A: | $10 + 7$ | $=$ | $15 + 2$ |
> | B: | $12 - 7$ | $=$ | $1 + 4$ |
> | A + B: $10 + 7 + 12 - 7$ | | $=$ | $15 + 2 + 1 + 4$ |
> | $22$ | | $=$ | $22$ |

Going back to the algebraic equations:

| A: | $3y - 2x$ | $=$ | 17 |
|---|---|---|---|
| B: | $y + 2x$ | $=$ | 19 |
| A + B: | $3y - 2x + y + 2x$ | $=$ | $17 + 19$ |

$-2x$ and $+2x$ cancel each other out, allowing $x$ to be eliminated, so

$$4y = 36$$
$$y = 9$$

As a final step, we once again substitute the value of $y = 9$ back into the starting equations to find and then check the value of $x$:

| | |
|---|---|
| $3y - 2x = 17$ | $y + 2x = 19$ |
| $y = 9$ | $y = 9$ |
| $27 - 2x = 17$ | $9 + 2x = 19$ |
| $27 - 17 = 2x$ | $2x = 19 - 9$ |
| $10 = 2x$ | $2x = 10$ |
| $5 = x$ | $x = 5$ |

The solution is $y = 9$; $x = 5$.

# Inequalities

Equations always include an equals sign, but there are other symbols used to indicate that the left- and right-hand sides of an expression are not equal. These are called inequalities, not equations.

Inequalities are not widely used, but you need to understand the basic ideas and the inequality symbols. The following table explains.

| Symbol | Meaning | Example |
|---|---|---|
| $=$ | LHS equals RHS | $x = 3$ |
| $\neq$ | LHS does not equal RHS | $4 \neq 7$ |
| $\sim$ | LHS roughly equals RHS | $3.12 \sim 3$ |
| $>$ | LHS is bigger than RHS | $7 > 6$ |
| $<$ | LHS is smaller than RHS | $10 < 21$ |
| $\geq$ | LHS is bigger than or equal to RHS | $x \geq 3$ |
| $\leq$ | LHS is smaller than or equal to RHS | $a \leq b$ |

Most people do not have problems with inequalities, but you have to think carefully about the real meaning of negative numbers. For example:

$x > 0$ means that $x$ is a positive number.

$x < 0$ means that $x$ is a negative number.

−15 is a smaller number than −5, because it is further away from zero. Therefore,

$$-15 < -5$$

The symbols > and ≥ have slightly different meanings:

$x > 10$ says that $x$ can have any value larger than 10, but $x$ cannot equal 10.

$x \geq 10$ means that $x$ can equal 10 or any other number larger than 10.

Inequalities involving additions and/or subtractions can be rearranged in exactly the same way as equations. For example:

$$6x - 9 \quad > \quad 3x$$
$$6x - 3x \quad > \quad 9$$
$$3x \quad\quad > \quad 9$$
$$x \quad\quad > \quad 3.$$

# 5 Space and shape

The unit specification for this topic says 'students should show an understanding of space and shape'. In practical terms, this means you must be comfortable with the three basic ideas of area, volume and angle.

We assume that you already know how to calculate the area of a square, a rectangle and a circle, and how to work out the volume and total surface areas of a cube, a box and a cylinder.

Angles are easiest to explain using the properties of triangles as a starting point. The next topic covers angles and triangles in detail. Here we briefly summarise the concepts of dimension and introduce some more unusual shapes and objects.

Any two points on a flat surface can be joined by a straight line. This line has one dimension – its length – measured in simple or linear units like cm, metres, km, or miles. A flat surface is properly called a plane.

A two-dimensional shape has area. An area is calculated by multiplying two lengths together – so areas are measured in square units like sq cm, sq m or sq miles.

A three-dimensional object encloses an amount of space – it has volume. Volumes are calculated by multiplying three lengths together and are measured in cubic or cubed units like cu cm, cu m or cubic inches.

We have different names for different kinds of two-dimensional shapes. Some are in common use, others are specialist or jargon words. A distinction is made between irregular and regular. A circle, for example, is a regular shape, but an outline of your left hand drawn on this piece of flat paper is an irregular shape. For this topic we will only be concerned with regular shapes and objects.

The circle is the most regular of all two-dimensional shapes – its perimeter or circumference is a smooth continuous curve. An ellipse is a circle that has been pushed or squeezed so that it has a longer radius and a shorter radius. This is another regular object bounded by a smooth continuous curve. 'Oval' is another word for ellipse.

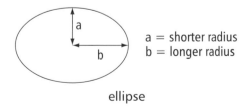

a = shorter radius
b = longer radius

ellipse

# Polygons

A two-dimensional shape bounded by three or more straight lines is called a polygon. The name of a polygon depends on its number of sides. For example:

| Name of polygon | Number of sides |
|---|---|
| Triangle | 3 |
| Quadrilateral | 4 |
| Pentagon | 5 |
| Hexagon | 6 |
| Heptagon | 7 |
| Octagon | 8 |

The prefixes penta-, hexa-, hepta- and octa- are taken from Greek and there are names for all possible polygons, but most of these are very obscure.

A regular pentagon, hexagon or octagon, for example, has respectively five, six or eight sides, all of the same length:

pentagon          hexagon          octagon

Triangles and quadrilaterals are the commonest polygons and we have more specialist names for their different types.

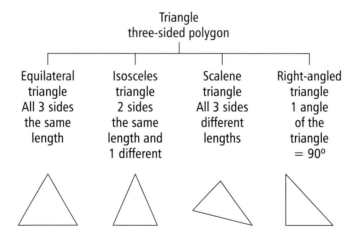

Triangle
three-sided polygon

| Equilateral triangle | Isosceles triangle | Scalene triangle | Right-angled triangle |
|---|---|---|---|
| All 3 sides the same length | 2 sides the same length and 1 different | All 3 sides different lengths | 1 angle of the triangle = 90º |

You will need to remember the terms equilateral, isosceles and right-angled triangle. Scalene is rarely used.

# Quadrilaterals

There are five common kinds of regular quadrilateral.

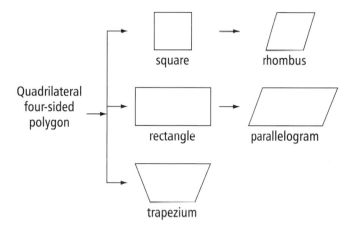

Some quadrilaterals are more regular than others:

- A square has four equal sides and four 90° angles. This also means that the two pairs of opposite sides are parallel.

- A rhombus is like a square that has been 'leaned on'. It still has four equal sides and two pairs of parallel opposite sides, but none of its four angles are 90°.

- A rectangle has two longer sides and two shorter sides. Opposite sides are parallel and of the same length and all of its angles are 90°.

- A parallelogram is again like a rectangle that has been 'leaned on' or 'pushed sideways'. It has two longer and two shorter sides. Opposite sides are the same length and parallel, but none of its four angles are 90°.

- A trapezium has one pair of opposite parallel sides – two sides of the same length and two of different lengths.

# Volumes

The most regular three-dimensional object is a sphere. All lines drawn from the centre of a sphere to any point on its surface are the same length – this is the radius of the sphere. The formula for the volume of a sphere illustrates an essential feature of three-dimensional objects

$$V = \frac{4\pi r^3}{3}$$

$\frac{4\pi}{3}$ is a number approximately equal to 4.19 and this number is the same for spheres of all sizes. So approximately

$$V = 4.19r^3$$

This is clearly a volume formula because it includes a cubed term – that is, the radius multiplied by itself three times.

There are many other regular three-dimensional objects. You need a basic understanding of how they differ but you do not need to remember formulae for calculating the surface areas or volumes of the less common ones.

A cube has six square faces. It follows that each face has the same surface area and the length of all 12 edges is the same.

# Prisms

A prism is the proper term describing a three-dimensional object with the same cross-section all along its length. Many real-life objects are prisms of one kind or another – the building and construction industry, for example, depends on prisms. If you cut a prism at any point along its length, at right-angles to its length, the exposed cross-section is always the same two-dimensional shape.

- A piece of timber measuring 4 cm by 4 cm by 2 metres is a square prism – its cross-section is a square with a surface area of 16 sq cm.

- A box measuring 12 cm by 10 cm by 50 cm is a rectangular prism.

- A cylinder or a metal rod is a circular prism.

- A steel girder is a prism, usually with a cross-section in the shape of an I or a T. Skirting boards are prisms, so are hollow tubes.

The volume of all prisms can be calculated using the same formula

$$V = Al$$

where A is the area of the cross-section and l is the length of the prism.

# Cones and pyramids

Things like cones and pyramids belong to another family of three-dimensional objects.

The most familiar kind of pyramid has a square base and it tapers to a point, or apex, directly above the centre of the base. Each of its four sides is then an identical triangle. Horizontal cross-sections of a square pyramid are all squares but they get progressively smaller as you move upwards from the base to the apex.

Regular pyramids need not have square bases – they can be triangular, rectangular or any kind of regular polygon. A pyramid with a triangular base is called a tetrahedron.

A cone is a special kind of pyramid with a circular base.

The volumes of regular pyramids or cones are given by the same general formula

$$V = \frac{Ah}{3}$$

where A = the area of the base; and h = the vertical height.

# 6 Angles and triangles

Angles are measured in degrees. There are 360° in a full circle and 90° in a right-angle. An angle between 0° and 90° is called an acute angle.

There are two common ways of labelling angles:

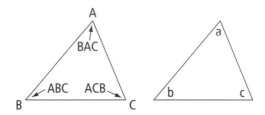

Using these diagrams     BAC = a

ABC = b

ACB = c

We will use the simpler labelling system, with single small letters to indicate angles.

Angles on a straight line add up to 180°.

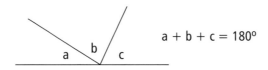

$a + b + c = 180°$

The inside or interior angles of a triangle also add up to 180°.

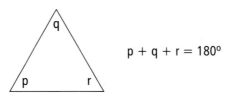

$p + q + r = 180°$

A polygon can be divided up into a number of triangles:

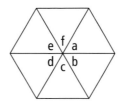

The angles around a point add up to 360°:

$$a + b + c + d + e + f = 360°$$

The interior angles of all quadrilaterals also add up to 360°:

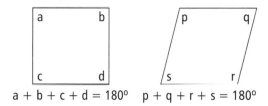

$a + b + c + d = 180°$    $p + q + r + s = 180°$

# Triangles and trigonometry

Trigonometry is a specialist branch of mathematics. The word means 'triangle measuring'. There are relationships between the angles of a triangle, the length of its sides and its area – this is what trigonometry is all about.

In the previous topic, we looked at four kinds of triangles. We know that the interior angles of all triangles must add up to 180°.

All three angles of an equilateral triangle must be the same.

It follows that each angle must be 60° because $\dfrac{180°}{3} = 60°$.

An isosceles triangle has two sides of equal length and a third which may be longer or shorter. The two base angles of an isosceles triangle are equal:

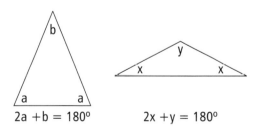

$2a + b = 180°$       $2x + y = 180°$

If you know one angle of an isosceles triangle, you can work out the other two:

If a = 74° then b = 32°

because (2 × 74) + 32 = 180°

If y = 156° then x = 12°

because (2 × 12) + 156 = 180°

A right-angled triangle can have three different angles or it can be isosceles; it cannot be equilateral. Note the small square symbol for a right-angle.

An isosceles right-angled triangle must have two angles of 45° and one of 90°

$$45 + 45 + 90 = 180°$$

In this kind of right-angled triangle, $a + b = 90°$

$$a + b + 90 = 180°$$

# Areas of triangles

A rectangle can be turned into two right-angled triangles using a diagonal line.

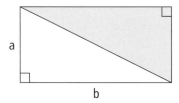

If a = the length of the shorter side of the rectangle and b = the length of the longer side, we know that

$$\text{Area, rectangle} = ab$$

The two right-angled triangles have the same area. Therefore

$$\text{Area, triangle} = \frac{ab}{2}$$

This general formula can be shown to apply to all triangles:

$$\text{Area} = \frac{\text{length of base} \times \text{vertical height}}{2}$$

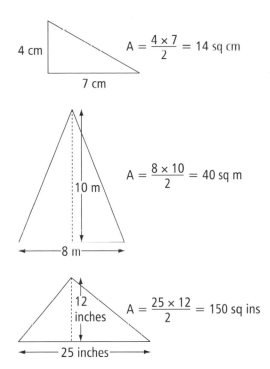

$$A = \frac{4 \times 7}{2} = 14 \text{ sq cm}$$

$$A = \frac{8 \times 10}{2} = 40 \text{ sq m}$$

$$A = \frac{25 \times 12}{2} = 150 \text{ sq ins}$$

# Right-angled triangles

The rules of trigonometry can be extended to all kinds of triangles and then to most two- and three-dimensional shapes and objects. However, the theories were developed using right-angled triangles as a starting point. This is how to label the three sides of a right-angled triangle:

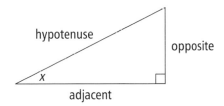

The side of the triangle that faces the right-angle must always be the longest. This is called the hypotenuse.

For angle $x$, the two other sides are called the adjacent side and the opposite side.

# Pythagoras

There is a relationship between the lengths of the three sides of a right-angled triangle. This was first discovered by the Greek mathematician Pythagoras 2,550 years ago. This relationship is called Pythagoras' Theorem.

In this right-angled triangle, the length of the hypotenuse is a, the length of one of the two shorter sides is b and the length of the other one is c.

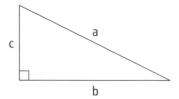

Pythagoras found that

$$a^2 = b^2 + c^2$$

The theorem is often quoted using words that some people find old fashioned and confusing:

'The square on the hypotenuse is equal to the sum of the squares on the other two sides.'

Pythagoras works for all right-angled triangles. It helps to start with a simple example:

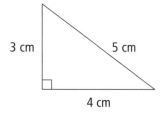

$$5^2 = 3^2 + 4^2$$

$$25 = 9 + 16$$

If you know the length of two sides of a right-angled triangle, you can calculate the length of the third.

You need to handle square and square-root calculations in the right order. Imagine you are given the lengths of the two shorter sides and asked to calculate the length of the hypotenuse.

$$a^2 = 3^2 + 4^2$$
$$a^2 = 25$$
$$a = \sqrt{25}$$
$$a = 5$$

Pythogoras' formula can be rearranged. Say you are given the length of the hypotenuse and one of the other two sides, then:

$$a^2 = b^2 + c^2$$
$$5^2 = 4^2 + c^2$$
$$25 = 16 + c^2$$
$$9 = c^2$$
$$\sqrt{9} = 3$$
$$c = 3 = \text{the length of the third side.}$$

These first examples are based on 3-4-5 right-angled triangles. Few calculations using Pythagoras produce neat whole numbers; the 3-4-5 triangle is an oddity. You will usually get answers that need to be corrected to a certain number of decimal places. You will need a calculator with a square-root key.

---

### *Example*

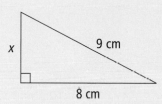

Calculate the length of side **x**.

From Pythagoras we know that

$$9^2 = x^2 + 8^2$$

Remember the hypotenuse is always the longest side.

$$81 = x^2 + 64$$
$$x^2 = 81 - 64$$
$$x^2 = 17$$
$$x = \sqrt{17}$$
$$x = 4.12 \text{ cm, corrected to 2 d.p.}$$

---

A diagram helps, but you do not need one to use Pythagoras' Theorem.

---

### *Example*

The two shorter sides of a right-angled triangle are equal and measure 13 cm. What is the length of the hypotenuse?

Call the length of the hypotenuse $x$ cm.

$$x^2 = 13^2 + 13^2$$
$$x^2 = 338$$
$$x = \sqrt{338}$$
$$x = 18.385 \text{ cm, corrected to 3 d.p.}$$

---

# Applying Pythagoras

Mathematicians are fascinated by triangles and in the exam you are almost certain to get a Pythagoras question. This is the kind of calculation you should expect:

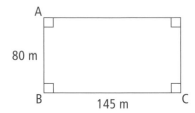

This is a plan of a rectangular field. There is an existing path around the edge of the field following the route ABC. The farmer decides to build a new path connecting A and C directly in a straight line. What is the difference in length between the old path and the new one?

Give your answer corrected to 1 d.p.

(i)  The new path is a diagonal line, AC, which is the hypotenuse of a right-angled triangle. Call the length of the new path $x$.

(ii)  $x^2 = 80^2 + 145^2$

$x^2 = 6{,}400 + 21{,}025$

$x^2 = 27{,}425$

$x = \sqrt{27{,}425}$

$x = 165.6\,\text{m}$

(iii) ABC $-$ AC $= (80 + 145) - 165.6$

Difference in length $= 59.4\,\text{metres}$

# 7 Tangents, sines and cosines

Maths is about numbers, but obviously you need words to teach maths – and to learn it. Some words are very familiar and not therefore intimidating – for example add, multiply, equals, square, circle and so on. Others are used less often in daily life but these do not stop most students in their tracks – radius, circumference, isosceles and hypotenuse are good examples. Tangents, sines and cosines, like algebra, sound difficult and at school you may not have understood them.

These ideas are easy, provided, as always, you understand a small set of straightforward rules. You will need a calculator which shows tangents, sines and cosines.

The collective name for tangents, sines and cosines is trigonometrical ratios.

These three right-angled triangles are scale models of each other:

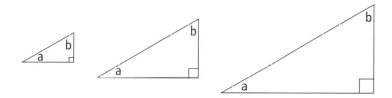

They vary in size, but in each case their angles are the same. This is called a set of similar triangles.

The actual lengths of the sides of each similar triangle differ, but the ratio between these lengths   taken two at a time – is always the same, regardless of the size of the triangle. We will start with tangents.

## Tangents

Here, we are looking just at angle a – forget the other angle at the top of the triangle.

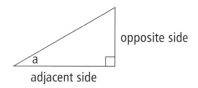

The number produced by dividing the length of the opposite side by the length of the adjacent side is called the tangent of angle a. It is the same for all similar triangles:

$$\text{tangent of angle a (or tan a)} = \frac{\text{opposite}}{\text{adjacent}}$$

In the range between 0° and 90°, every angle has a different value for its tangent. A very small angle has a very small tangent – a small angle is produced when the opposite side is much shorter than the adjacent side. As angle a increases, the opposite side gets relatively longer and the adjacent side relatively shorter – so the value of the tangent increases. Check these figures using your calculator.

| Angle ° | Tangent (tan) |
|---|---|
| 0° | 0 |
| 10° | 0.176 |
| 30° | 0.577 |
| 45° | 1.000 |
| 60° | 1.732 |
| 75° | 3.732 |
| 85° | 11.430 |
| 89° | 57.290 |
| 89.95° | 1,145.915 |

**Practice questions**

(i)  Why is the tangent of 45° exactly 1?

(ii)  Why does your calculator give an error message if you ask it to work out the tangent of 90°?

## Tangent calculations

If you know the length of one side of a right-angled triangle and one of its angles, you can calculate the length of all three sides. For example:

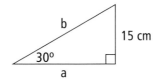

By definition

$$\tan 30° = \frac{\text{opposite}}{\text{adjacent}} = \frac{15}{a}$$

$$\tan 30° = 0.577 \text{ from your calculator}$$

$$0.577 = \frac{15}{a}$$

$$a = \frac{15}{0.577} = 25.997 \text{ cm}$$

# Sines and cosines

A triangle has three sides, so the tangent is just one of the ratios that can be chosen. Sines and cosines are the two other important ratios. The diagrams explain – again we are working with angle a.

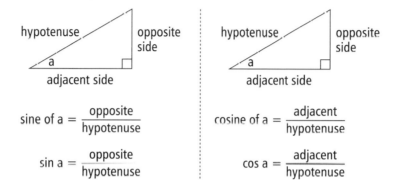

sine of a = $\dfrac{\text{opposite}}{\text{hypotenuse}}$    cosine of a = $\dfrac{\text{adjacent}}{\text{hypotenuse}}$

sin a = $\dfrac{\text{opposite}}{\text{hypotenuse}}$    cos a = $\dfrac{\text{adjacent}}{\text{hypotenuse}}$

The abbreviation for sine is sin, but sine and sin are both always pronounced like 'sign', never 'sin'. Cos is pronounced 'coz'.

Check these sine and cosine values using your calculator:

| Angle° | Sine (sin) | Cosine (cos) |
|--------|------------|--------------|
| 0°     | 0          | 1.000        |
| 10°    | 0.174      | 0.985        |
| 30°    | 0.500      | 0.866        |
| 45°    | 0.707      | 0.707        |
| 60°    | 0.866      | 0.500        |
| 75°    | 0.966      | 0.259        |
| 88°    | 0.999      | 0.035        |
| 90°    | 1.000      | 0            |

# Sine and cosine calculations

Sines and cosines are used to solve triangle problems in exactly the same way as tangents. For example:

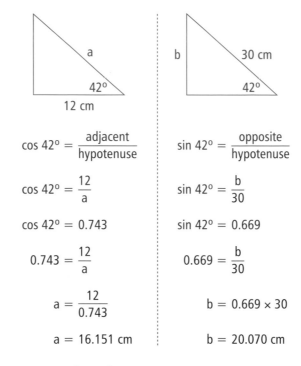

$$\cos 42° = \frac{\text{adjacent}}{\text{hypotenuse}}$$

$$\cos 42° = \frac{12}{a}$$

$$\cos 42° = 0.743$$

$$0.743 = \frac{12}{a}$$

$$a = \frac{12}{0.743}$$

$$a = 16.151 \text{ cm}$$

$$\sin 42° = \frac{\text{opposite}}{\text{hypotenuse}}$$

$$\sin 42° = \frac{b}{30}$$

$$\sin 42° = 0.669$$

$$0.669 = \frac{b}{30}$$

$$b = 0.669 \times 30$$

$$b = 20.070 \text{ cm}$$

# Rules for remembering

In the beginning, everybody gets the tangent, sine and cosine ratios confused. There are two ways of remembering what goes where. Use the first method if triangles and trigonometry are beginning to make sense; use the second if you are struggling.

## First method

Remember these values

| | | |
|---|---|---|
| *reverse* | tan 90° = | a very big number |
| *alphabetical* | sin 90° = | exactly 1 |
| *order* | cos 90° = | 0 |

Tangent must be **opposite/adjacent** because as the angle increases the adjacent side becomes smaller and smaller.

Sine must be **opposite/hypotenuse** because as the angle increases the opposite side gets nearer and nearer to the length of the hypotenuse. At 90°, these lengths become equal, so sin 90° = exactly 1.

Cosine must be **adjacent/hypotenuse** because as the angle gets bigger, the adjacent side gets smaller – until at 90°, the adjacent side has zero length and cos 90° = 0.

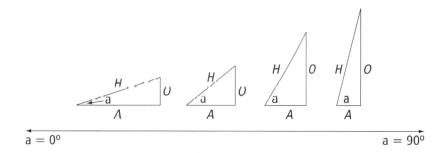

a = 0°                                    a = 90°

## Second method

If you like mnemonics, this might help:

| | |
|---|---|
| **CAN** | **C**osine is |
| **A** | **A**djacent over |
| **HORSE** | **H**ypotenuse |
| **TAKE** | **T**angent is |
| **OATS** | **O**pposite over |
| **AND** | **A**djacent |
| **SLIP** | **S**ine is |
| **OFF** | **O**pposite over |
| **HOME** | **H**ypotenuse |

# Triangle problems

Using formulae for area, Pythagoras and the tangent, sine and cosine ratios there are an endless number of problems that could be set to test your knowledge of this topic and the previous one. You will not be asked complicated questions involving many different stages, but you do need to understand the basic ideas of angle and how to solve simple triangle problems.

Your maths lecturer will suggest practice questions with the right mix of techniques and the appropriate level of difficulty. Trigonometry looks complicated at first; however, nearly all students improve rapidly and dramatically with just a few hours' teaching and private study.

# Calculators

You will need a scientific calculator for tangents, sines and cosines. Nearly all models now use a logical key sequence, for example:

| sin | 4 | 5 | = | 0.707106781 |

*(display)*

For                     sine of 45°    =    0.707106781

Trigonometrical ratios are very rarely nice round numbers. You can usually correct to three or four decimal places as you go along.

$$\sin 45° = 0.707 \text{ or}$$

$$\sin 45° = 0.7071$$

Nearly all scientific calculators have at least six trigonometrical keys:

| sin | cos | tan |

| $\sin^{-1}$ | $\cos^{-1}$ | $\tan^{-1}$ |

Often you will need to press a shift key to use the $\sin^{-1}$, $\cos^{-1}$ or $\tan^{-1}$ functions.

$\sin^{-1}$ is an odd-looking shorthand for a sine calculation put into reverse. For example:

$$\sin 45° = 0.7071$$

$$\sin^{-1} 0.7071 = 45°$$

The second expression means 'the angle whose sine is 0.7071 is 45°'.

A typical key sequence for this sum is:

| shift | $\sin^{-1}$ | 0 | . | 7 | 0 | 7 | 1 | = | 45 |

*(display\*)*

\*The calculator display will probably show a number very slightly less than 45, like 44.99945053

Not many calculators show the degree symbol '°'.

You must know how your particular calculator works. There are no general rules for key sequence. Never take an unfamiliar or a borrowed scientific calculator into an exam.

# *8* Circles

We need to start with a list of definitions. Some ought to be familiar, others will be new.

The circumference of a circle is the length of its perimeter or boundary.

The diameter of a circle is the length of a straight line connecting two opposite points on the circumference and passing through the centre of the circle.

The radius of a circle is the length of a straight line joining the centre of a circle to any point on its circumference. The radius is half the length of the diameter.

The area of a circle is given by the formula

$$A = \pi r^2$$

Concentric circles have the same centre but different radii. (Radii (pronounced 'ray-dee-eye') is the plural of radius.)

Concentric circles

A chord is any straight line connecting two points on the circumference that does not pass through the centre of a circle. The length of a chord has to be less than the diameter.

A chord

An arc is any part of the circumference of a circle.

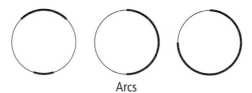

Arcs

A sector of a circle is a shape bounded by two radii and an arc – just like a slice taken from a pie.

A sector

The word 'segment' is very commonly used interchangeably with the word 'sector'. To be mathematically correct, a segment is the part of a circle bounded by a chord and an arc.

A segment

Quadrant is the name given to a sector that occupies a quarter of the area of a circle.

A quadrant

# Pi, π

π appears in all of the formulae associated with circles, spheres and curved shapes in general. It is a bizarre number, since it can be defined precisely, but as yet has never been calculated with complete accuracy.

If you divide the circumference of a circle by its diameter, you get the number π – it does not matter how big or small the circle is.

$$\frac{C}{d} = \pi$$

where C = circumference; d = diameter.

Because the radius is half the length of the diameter, this formula can be rewritten and rearranged into something more familiar:

$$\frac{C}{2r} = \pi$$

$$C = 2\pi r$$

where C = circumference; r = radius.

Early mathematicians used a figure of 3 for $\pi$. It was then discovered that the real value was a bit bigger. Some fractions give close approximations, for example:

$$\frac{22}{7} \quad \text{and} \quad \frac{355}{113}$$

No fraction yet discovered gives a precise value for $\pi$.

A scientific calculator will display $\pi$ to nine or 10 decimal places:

$$\pi = 3.141592654$$

There are formulae that can work out $\pi$ to any number of decimal places. If these are programmed into very large computers, the calculation never ends. $\pi$ has been calculated to more than 50 billion decimal places and no pattern or sequence has ever been found. $\pi$ is a non-recurring non-terminating decimal – it just goes on forever.

A value of $\pi = 3.142$ is close enough for most practical calculations.

You need to be comfortable with the formulae used to calculate the circumference and the area of a circle.

$$\mathbf{C = \pi d} \qquad \mathbf{C = 2\pi r} \qquad \mathbf{A = \pi r^2}$$

$$\frac{C}{d} = \pi \qquad \frac{C}{2r} = \pi \qquad r^2 = \frac{A}{\pi}$$

$$\frac{C}{\pi} = d \qquad \frac{C}{2\pi} = r \qquad r = \sqrt{\left(\frac{A}{\pi}\right)}$$

A = area; C = circumference; d = diameter; r = radius.

Memorise just the three formulae shown in bold, and rearrange them as you go along if a calculation needs to be worked backwards.

### Example

What is the radius of a circle with an area of 1,240 sq cm?

Assume $\pi = 3.142$.

$$A = \pi r^2$$

$$1{,}240 = \pi r^2$$

$$\frac{1{,}240}{3.142} = r^2$$

$$r^2 = 394.653$$

$$r = \sqrt{394.653}$$

$$r = 19.866 \text{ cm}$$

As a reality check, you might put your calculated radius back into the starting formula:

$$A = \pi r^2$$

$$A = 3.142 \times 19.866 \times 19.866$$

$$A = 1{,}240.015 \text{ sq cm}$$

Because of rounding, the reality check answer will usually be very slightly different from the starting number.

# Circle calculations

In Further Mathematics exams, you may get some slightly more complicated circle-related questions. These are not difficult, provided you work methodically – always number the stages in your calculation.

### Example

The diagram shows two circles. The smaller has a diameter of 8 cm and the larger has a diameter of 9 cm.

Question    *Calculate the shaded area.* $\pi = 3.142$.

Answer    (i)    The shaded area is the area of the larger circle minus the area of the smaller one.

(ii)    You are given diameters; the area formula works with radii. Therefore:

| | Larger circle | | | Smaller circle | | |
|---|---|---|---|---|---|---|
| (iii) | d | = | 9 cm | d | = | 8 cm |
| (iv) | r | = | 4.5 cm | r | = | 4 cm |
| (v) | A | = | $\pi r^2$ | A | = | $\pi r^2$ |
| (vi) | A | = | $20.25\pi$ | A | = | $16\pi$ |
| (vii) | A | = | 63.626 | A | = | 50.272 |
| (viii) | Shaded area | = | 63.626 – 50.272 | | | |
| | | = | 13.354 sq cm | | | |

## *Example*

*Question*   Calculate the area of the shaded sector of the circle.
$\pi = 3.142$. Given that angle a is 61° and the radius of the circle is 30 cm, give your answer to the nearest square centimetre.

*Answer*   (i)   The total area of the circle is

$$A = \pi r^2$$
$$A = 900\pi$$
$$A = 2{,}827.8 \text{ sq cm}$$

(ii)   There are 360° in a full circle. If the sector angle is 61°, then the sector must be $\frac{61}{360}$ th of the total area of the circle.

$$\frac{61}{360} = 0.1694$$

(iii)   The area of the sector is

$$0.1694 \times 2{,}827.8 = 479 \text{ sq cm.}$$

# References

Maslow, A (1970). *Motivation and Personality*. New York, Harper and Row.

Honey, P, and Mumford, A (1986). *Learning and Teaching Styles*. Maidenhead, Peter Honey.

Rogers, C (1974). *On Becoming A Person*. London, Constable & Robinson.

# Bibliography

Baly, M (1994). *Nursing and Social Change*. London, Routledge.

Baxter, R (1995). *Study Successfully*. Ray Baxter and Aldrough St. John Publications.

Bell, J (1999). *Doing Your Research Project: A Guide for First Time Researchers in Education and Social Science*, 2nd edition. Buckingham, Open University Press.

Berry, R (1995). *The Research Project*. London, Routledge.

Bourner, T, and Race, P (1995). *How to Win as a Part-Time Student: A Study Skills Guide*. Kogan Page.

Britton, A, and Cousins, A (1998). *Study Skills: A Guide for Lifelong Learners*. South Bank University, Distance Learning Centre.

Buzan, T (2000). *Use Your Head*. BBC Consumer Publishing.

Chambers, E, and Northedge, A (1997). *The Good Study Guide*. Open University Press.

Cormac, D Ed. (2000). *The Research Process in Nursing*. Oxford, Blackwell Science.

Cotterell, S (1999). *The Study Skills Handbook (Macmillan Study Guides)*. Palgrave Macmillian.

Donleavy, P (1999). *University Study Skills*. Macmillian.

Ellis, R et al. (1995). *Interpersonal Communication in Nursing Theory and Practice*. Edinburgh, Churchill Livingstone.

Erikson, B, and Nosanchul, T (1992). *Understanding Data*. Oxford, Oxford University Press.

Goodman, N (1992). *Introduction to Sociology*. Harper Perennial.

Haralambos, M et al. (1995). *Sociology: Themes and Perspectives*. Collins Educational.

Hockey, L (1985). *Nursing Research: Mistakes and Misconceptions*. Edinburgh, Churchill Livingstone.

Homan, R (1992). *The Ethics of Social Research*. Longman.

Hugman, R, and Smith, D Eds. (1995). *Ethical Issues in Social Work*. Routledge.

Morse, J and Field, P (1995). *Nursing Research: The Application of Qualitive Approaches*. London, Chapman & Hall.

Morton, A (1997). *A Guide Through the Theory of Knowledge*. Blackwell.

O'Connor, J, and Seymour, J (1993). *Introducing NLP Neuro-Linguistic Programming*. HarperCollins.

Ogier. M (1989). *Reading Research*. London, Scutari Press.

Owen, D, and Davis, M (1991) *Help with Your Project*. London, Hodder Arnold.

Peake, J, and Coyle, M (1999). *The Learners Guide to Writing*. Macmillian.

Roper, N et al. (1996). *The Elements of Nursing: a Model for Nursing Based on a Model of Living*. Edinburgh, Churchill Livingstone.

Seedhouse, D (1998). *Ethics: the Heart of Health Care*. John Wiley and Sons Ltd.

Smith, P (1997). *Research Mindedness for Practice*. Edinburgh, Churchill Livingstone.

Smith, P Ed. (1998). *Nursing Research: Setting New Agendas*. London, Hodder Arnold.

Stein-Parbury, J (1993). *Patient and Person: Developing Interpersonal Skills in Nursing*. Edinburgh, Churchill Livingstone.

Walsh, M (2001). *Research Made Real*. Cheltenham, Nelson Thornes Ltd.

# Index

36157